MODERN CHINESE

现代中文 SECOND EDITION

TEXTBOOK 1A
SIMPLIFIED CHARACTERS

BetterChinese

BetterChinese

MODERN CHINESE 现代中文

Textbook Volume 1A

Second Edition

Project Director:	James P. Lin
Editorial Consultant:	Li-Hsiang Yu Shen
Project Manager:	Angel Yeh
Assistant Editors:	Sue-Ann Ma and Christopher Peacock
Curriculum Advisors:	Norman Masuda and Rebecca Starr
Executive Publisher:	Chi-Kuo Shen
Illustrations:	Better World Ltd

© 2013 BETTER CHINESE LLC (a Better World LTD company)

Library of Congress Cataloging-in-Publication Data: To be Assigned

ISBN: 978-1-60603-571-9

3 4 5 XLA 22 21 20

For more information about our products, contact us at:

United States
640 Waverley Street
Palo Alto, CA 94301
Tel: 888-384-0902
Fax: 888-384-0901
Email: usa@betterchinese.com

Contents 目录

We are so grateful for the warm reception *Modern Chinese* received in its first year. It confirmed our belief that there is a real need for a refreshing and relevant beginner-level college program that is engaging, encouraging, and intuitive, and that includes empowering technology.

We were encouraged by the professors' positive feedback and university adoptions. This Second Edition incorporates many suggestions based on classroom experiences. We are especially grateful to Professor Hong Jiang of Northwestern University and Professor Hong Zeng of Stanford University. They have helped to make this Second Edition more engaging and relevant to students through their detailed feedback. We also took this opportunity to strike a better balance between delivering authentic text and achieving learning goals.

The creation of *Modern Chinese* incorporates all of the pedagogical experiences that have made us the leading Chinese curriculum publisher in the world. We researched what teachers liked about our existing K-12 programs and what they looked for in a college program: the result was *Modern Chinese*.

The program is revolutionary in many ways. The lessons appear in a complete story-based format that scaffolds vocabulary and grammar patterns from prior lessons to instill confidence in new learners. We take a new approach to the presentation of grammar, focusing on simple explanations and offering practical examples. In addition, we include enriching cultural spotlights to cultivate cultural awareness as well as a variety of exercises to encourage real-life communication. An accompanying website also offers supplemental learning tools such as lesson animations, audio recordings, and online practices.

We are thankful to all those who have helped us with the creation of *Modern Chinese*. Special thanks go to our Executive Publisher, Chi-Kuo Shen, for supporting this project; Chief Educator, Li-Hsiang Shen, for sharing her love of education and inspiration; Norman Masuda for sharing his years of classroom teaching experience and expertise in the area of language acquisition; Professor Rebecca Starr for her invaluable insights as a linguist and providing a non-native learner's perspective; and some of the early team members who contributed to the research and pilot of the program, including Stephanie Puk, Sandra Tung, Chung Trung, and Hope Tammany. We would like to express our gratitude to the professors who provided feedback through numerous rounds of reviews: Wenhui Chen of Washing University in St. Louis; Hong Li of Emory University; Xianmin Liu of Vanderbilt University; Xuehong Lu of State University of New York at Buffalo; Christopher Lupke of Washing State University; Michelle DiBello, Youping Zhang, and Chao Fen Sun of Stanford University. We also wish to thank our advisory board professors for their insightful and constructive feedback: Yujie Ge of Santa Clara University; Li Ma of Florida International University; Hong Jiang of Northwestern University; Cynthia Hsien Shen of University of Florida. Most importantly, Better Chinese would like to recognize the core *Modern Chinese* team: Project Manager, Angel Yeh, for her creative story-telling abilities and critical eye in overseeing every detail of the *Modern Chinese* project; Cheuk-Yue Fung, Sue-Ann Ma, Christopher Peacock, Tiantian Gao, Lauren Chen, and Bin Yan for their relentless pursuit of editorial perfection; and Roger Hsieh for his technical support.

Finally, on a personal note, I would like to thank my wife, Clarissa Shen, for her support and my wonderful children, Maia and Lucas, for inspiring me to make this world a better place. I hope that by making *Modern Chinese* engaging, relevant, and effective, we will encourage more students to continue their studies of Chinese language and culture, empowering them to bring the world a little closer together.

James P. Lin
Project Director
July 2013

MODERN CHINESE 现代中文
Scope and Sequence

Units	Communication Goals	Structure Notes	Language Notes & Cultural Spotlights
中文 **Prelude:** **The Chinese** **Language**	• Learn the pinyin romanization system • Speak Chinese characters with standard tones and sentence inflection • Understand Chinese tonal changes (tone sandhi)	1. *Understand the 4 Chinese tones* 2. *Learn the Chinese phonetic system, pinyin* 3. *Understand the rules of Chinese stroke order*	• Understand the history of the Chinese language • Identify where the Chinese language is spoken today • Learn about the development of written Chinese, including simplified and traditional Chinese characters
我 **UNIT 1** **Me**	• Greet and say goodbye to people • Introduce yourself and exchange names with others • Ask and answer questions pertaining to age and nationality • Count from 1 to 99	1. *Use an adjective phrase to describe a subject* 2. *Use 们 to convert a pronoun or noun (people only) to its plural form* 3. *Use 也 to express "also"* 4. *Use 吗 to turn a statement into a question* 5. *Use 呢 to ask "What about . . .?"* 6. *Use 叫 to state one's name* 7. *Use 什么 to ask "what?" questions* 8. *Use 多大 to ask about somone's age* 9. *Add 岁 after a number to state one's age* 10. *Use 是 to indicate equivalency* 11. *Use 哪国人 to ask about nationality and country + 人 to state nationality* 12. *Use 不 to negate a verb* 13. *Use Verb + 不 + Verb to form affirmative-negative questions* 14. *Use Verb or 不 + Verb to answer affirmative-negative questions*	• Understand how Chinese greet and address one another • Learn the structure of Chinese names • Learn about the Chinese diaspora • Learn how to ask for someone's age politely • Learn how to count the numbers from 11 to 99 • Understand the rationale behind Chinese names for countries • Learn Chinese hand gestures for numbers 1 to 10 • Learn the connotations of the numbers 4 and 8 in Chinese culture • Learn about the Chinese Zodiac
家 **UNIT 2** **Family**	• Identify family members and ask others about their families • Ask whether someone has pets • Ask and answer questions regarding quantity • Inquire about someone's occupation • Ask and answer questions about what languages one can speak	1. *Use 有 to express possession* 2. *Use 没有 to express "not have"* 3. *Use 有没有 to form a "have or not have" question* 4. *Use 有什么 to ask what one has* 5. *Use 的 to indicate possession* 6. *Use number + measure word to quantify a noun* 7. *Use 几 + measure word to ask how many and number + measure word to answer* 8. *Use 这 or 那 to express "this" or "that"* 9. *Use 谁 to ask "who?"* 10. *Use 还 to express "also"* 11. *Use 会 to state what one knows how to do* 12. *Use 会不会 to ask whether or not one knows how to do something* 13. *Use 只 to express "only"*	• Learn how to address different family members in Chinese • Understand the evolution of the traditional Chinese family • Learn how people regard pets in China • Learn about the giant pandas in China • Understand the difference between 语 and 文 • Understand the global response to studying Chinese as a world language • Learn about other varieties of spoken Chinese • Learn about the traditional professions of China

Units	Communication Goals	Structure Notes	Language Notes & Cultural Spotlights
时 **UNIT 3** **Time**	• State and ask the time • Talk about future events • Make appointments • Apologize for tardiness • Ask and answer questions about days of the week and months • State and ask for the date • Wish someone "happy birthday" and offer gifts	1. Use 会 to indicate the possibility of an action taking place in the future 2. Use 什么时候 to ask "when" 3. Use 星期几 to ask "what day of the week" and 星期 + number to state the day of the week 4. Use 几点 to discuss time 5. Use 差不多 to express "almost" 6. Use 还没(有) to express "not yet" or "still have not" 7. Use 吧 to make a suggestion 8. Use 几 to ask "what month" and "what day" 9. Use 都 to mean "both" or "all" 10. Use 了 to indicate a change of state or situation 11. Use the verb 送 in the context of gift giving 12. Use 的 to modify nouns	• Learn how to say the different days of the week in Chinese • Learn about how to tell time in Chinese • Compare the differences between the lunar and Western calendars • Learn about auspicious dates in the Chinese calendar • Learn how to read a Chinese calendar • Learn how to use a timeframe to indicate tense in Chinese • Look at the ways in which birthdays are celebrated in China • Understand the symbolism of certain gifts in China
食 **UNIT 4** **Food**	• Inquire and express preferences for food and drink • Express hunger • Order food and drinks at a restaurant • Discuss various dishes and their flavors • Offer to pay for a meal	1. Use 想 to indicate a desired action 2. Use 给 to mean "to give" 3. Use 喜欢 to express liking something or someone 4. Use Verb + 不 + Verb with two-character verbs to form affirmative-negtaive questions 5. Use 那(么) to mean "Well then" or "In that case" 6. Use 好 + Verb to form a compound adjective 7. Use 怎么样 to ask for an opinion of something 8. Use 太……了 to describe an exaggerated attribute 9. Use 要 to indicate desire 10. Use 为什么 and 因为 to ask questions and give explanations respectively 11. Use 一下 to express the brevity of an action	• Look at special pronouns in Mandarin Chinese and when to omit them • Learn about regional Chinese cuisines • Learn about symbolism in Chinese cuisine • Learn about Chinese uses of onomatopoeia • Learn about the Chinese equivalents of foreign names and locations • Learn about Chinese dining etiquette • Discover the art of tea
住 **UNIT 5** **Daily Lives**	• Make simple introductions of others • Be able to state where you or others live • Name buildings and facilities on campus • Be able to describe relative locations • Name furniture and rooms in a house	1. Use 在 to indicate location 2. Use 在 as a verb complement 3. Use 哪儿/哪里 to ask "where" 4. Use 要 to talk about future events 5. Use 跟……一起 to express doing things together 6. Use 可以 to express permission 7. Use 在 with an action verb to indicate the location of an activity 8. Use 到 as a resultative complement to indicate completion of an action 9. Use 得 or 不 and a resultative complement to indicate whether it is possible or not possible to reach a result	• Learn about introductions in Chinese • Know about verb-object compounds • Learn about traditional Chinese architecture (Si He Yuan) • Discover some of the universities with study abroad opportunities in China • Learn about telephone greetings in Chinese

Units	Communication Goals	Structure Notes	Language Notes & Cultural Spotlights
	• Use the appropriate expressions on the telephone • Ask and answer questions about relative locations	10. Use 可能 to express likelihood 11. Use completion 了 to describe completed actions 12. Use 就 to indicate "right" or "precisely"	• Review some spatial location words used in Chinese • Learn some of the contemporary slang used for texting • Learn about the art of Feng Shui and its modern applications
买 **UNIT 6** **Shopping**	• Ask about the availability and cost of different items or products in a store • Understand and use different denominations and amounts of money • Negotiate prices • Indicate that you wish to pay for an item with either cash or credit card • Use the correct expressions when paying with cash and receiving change	1. Use 有 to express existence rather than possession 2. Use 得 to express "must" 3. Use 给 as the preposition "to" 4. Use 多少 to ask "how many" or "how much" 5. Use Adjectives with (一)点(儿) to express "a little more" 6. Use 还是……吧 to express a suggested alternative 7. Use 再 to indicate a repeating action 8. Use 因为…所以… to express causal relationships 9. Use 不用 to say "need not" 10. Use 这么 or 那么 to intensify adjectives 11. Use Verb + 了 to describe specific completed actions 12. Use 已经 to express "already" 13. Use 要是…(的话)…就 to say "if… then…" 14. Use (是)…还是…to express either-or questions	• Learn about Chinese currency • Learn about counting from 100 and above • Know about the Silk Street • Learn how to bargain in Chinese markets • Learn about words used in financial transactions • Learn about the currencies of different countries • Learn about trade along the Silk Road • Learn about how Western chains have impacted China
行 **UNIT 7** **Travel &** **Navigation**	• Ask and answer questions about vacation plans • Give information about one's hometown and family background • Describe the attractions of China's capital • Express the distance between two places • Give and receive directions • Describe different modes of transportation	1. Use 的时候 to create "when" expressions 2. Use 才 to indicate an action occurring later than anticipated 3. Use 从 with a place word to indicate origin 4. Use 是……的 to emphasize the time, locale, or manner of a completed action 5. Use 送……去 to mean "take" 6. Use 离 to express location relative to a reference point 7. Use 到 with place words to indicate destination 8. Use 怎么 to ask how something is done 9. Use 往 to indicate directional movement 10. Use 先…, 再…, 然后… to indicate a sequence of events	• Learn the meaning of hometown in Chinese • Discover the relationship between seasons and how it classifies vacations • Learn about various modes of transportation in China • Discover activities done during China's "Golden Weeks" • Learn common direction expressions • Discover some of Beijing's historical hotspots

Units	Communication Goals	Structure Notes	Language Notes & Cultural Spotlights
学 **UNIT 8** **Academics**	• Discuss classes and school subjects • Express interest in something • Indicate levels of difficulty • Discuss exams, homework, and classroom situations • Ask to borrow something • Express subjective opinions	1. Use 懂 as a resultative complement to indicate ability to understand 2. Use 多 or 少 to express doing an activity more or less often 3. Use 只好 to indicate the best course of action among limited options 4. Use Verb + 完 to describe completed actions 5. Use 以后 to express "after doing something" 6. Use Verb + 了 to describe a sequence of events 7. Use 把 to indicate an action performed on a specific object 8. Use 怎么 to ask "how come" questions 9. Use 怎么这么/那么 to express incredulity or amazement regarding a situation 10. Use 一…就… to express "as soon as A, B" 11. Use 觉得 to express subjective opinions 12. Use 还是 with adjectives to compare qualities 13. Use 第 to express ordinal numbers 14. Use (正)……在(呢) to indicate ongoing actions	• Review previously learned radicals and phono-semantic compounds • Learn about China's Four Great Inventions • Learn about homographs in the Chinese language • Review the use of interjections in Chinese • Learn about examinations in China • Learn about the Four Treasures of the Study
衣 **UNIT 9** **Fashion**	• Name different articles of clothing • Discuss and find appropriate sizes • Make comparisons and express sameness • List and express preferences for different colors • Make use of some basic loan words • Express superlatives	1. Use 或者 to express choices and options 2. Use 看/听 +起来 to express a subjective impression 3. Use 比 to make comparisons 4. Use 更 to say "even more" 5. Use (一)点(儿) to describe small differences 6. Use 又…又… to express "both … and …" 7. Use …跟…一样 (Adjective) to express sameness 8. Use Verb 一 Verb to describe casual or brief activities 9. Use 最 to express superlatives 10. Use reduplication to intensify adjectives or adverbs 11. Use Verb reduplication to describe casual or brief activities 12. Use 看 to mean "and see" 13. Use 有(一)点(儿) to express "somewhat" 14. Use 好 as an intensifier	• Review use of adjectives • Learn about color symbolism in Chinese • Learn about clothing terms • Explore Chinese fashion trends • Learn the history of foot-binding

Units	Communication Goals	Structure Notes	Language Notes & Cultural Spotlights
娱 **UNIT 10** **Hobbies & Activities**	• Inquire about what people like to do in their free time • Discuss sports and leisure activities • Express how often you like to do something • Discuss musical performances and instruments • Describe how well somebody does something • Indicate time periods and duration	1. Use 一边…一边… *to describe simultaneous actions* 2. Use 什么 *to mean "any"* 3. *Use topic-comment sentences* 4. Use 有的 *to mean "some"* 5. Use 对……有兴趣 *to express interest in something* 6. Use 常(常)*to express "often"* 7. Use 能 *to describe ability* 8. Use name + 他们 *to refer to a group of people* 9. Use 得 *to describe the manner of actions* 10. Use 每…都… *to express "every"* 11. *Use time periods to indicate duration* 12. *Use multiple numbers to estimate amounts* 13. Use 不是……吗? *to ask a rhetorical question* 14. Use 对 *as the preposition "to, towards"*	• Learn about pictographs and ideographs in the evolution of Chinese characters • Learn about the culture of Karaoke or Chinese KTV • Learn about Mahjong • Learn about Chinese Martial Arts
情 **UNIT 11** **Relationships & People**	• Arrange to go on a date with someone • Describe a person's qualities and attributes • Discuss relationships, marriage, and break-ups • Describe your emotions • Refer to something using the passive voice • Talk about past experiences	1. Use 得 *to indicate degree or result* 2. Use 次 *to express number of times* 3. Use 让 *to express to "let" or "make" someone do something* 4. Use 记住 *to describe keeping something in mind* 5. Use 被 *to form the passive voice* 6. Use 一直 *to express "constantly"* 7. Use Verb + 过 *to express a past experience*	• Review loan words and associative compounds • Learn about Chinese Valentine's Day and the story of Qixi • Learn about China's Tallest Couple • Discuss relationship terms • Examine Chinese punctuation • Observe Chinese wedding traditions
医 **UNIT 12** **Medicine**	• Inquire after a person's health • Describe the symptoms of an illness • Talk about the weather and the seasons • Name illness and afflictions • Refer to different parts of the body • Describe some of the differences between Chinese and Western medicine	1. Use 最好 *to make suggestions* 2. Use 带 *to express bringing objects or people* 3. *Use noun or measure word reduplication to express "every"* 4. Use name/pronoun + 那儿 *to talk about someone's location or home* 5. Use 地 *to express the manner in which an action is performed* 6. Use 帮 *to mean "for"* 7. Use 好 *as a resultative complement to describe a properly completed action* 8. Use 又……了 *to say "again"*	• Review intensifiers used in the Chinese language • Learn about expressions used to discuss the weather • Learn about massages and Chinese Morning Exercises • Identify body parts in Chinese • Understand the difference between 等一会儿 and 一下 • Review different ways to talk about weeks • Learn about Western versus Eastern medicinal differences • Understand the importance of hot and cold foods in Chinese medical tradition

Units	Communication Goals	Structure Notes	Language Notes & Cultural Spotlights
商 **UNIT 13** **Business**	• Talk about your full- or part-time job • Offer words of encouragement • Indicate that something is unexpected • Discuss internships and working in China • Talk about your employment experience and resume • Discuss your post-graduation plans • Learn about the importance of *guanxi* or "connections"	1. Use 没想到 *to introduce an unexpected event* 2. Use 难怪 *to express "no wonder"* 3. Use 什么样的 *to ask "what kind?"* 4. Use 不但… 而且… *to express "not only...but also..."* 5. Use 虽然… 但是… *to express "although . . . however . . ."* 6. Use 从…到… *to express length of time* 7. Use 想要 *to express a desire* 8. Use 极了 *as an intensifier* 9. Use 跟……有关 *to express relevance to a subject* 10. Use Noun + 这样/那样 *to say "this/ that type of . . ."*	• Identify different work titles • Learn about the concept of *guanxi*, or business relationships/networking in China • Review different professions • Examine basic characteristics of a Chinese resume • Learn about China's Special Economic Zones and state-owned enterprises in China
节 **UNIT 14** **Festivals**	• Talk about the customs and traditions of Chinese New Year • Use the appropriate expressions to convey New Year's greetings and wishes • Compare and contrast various Chinese and Western holidays • Discuss the different foods that are eaten during Chinese holidays • Expand on a topic by providing examples	1. Use 用…来… *to describe the means of doing something* 2. Use 着 *to indicate an ongoing action* 3. Use 快要……了 *to say "be about to"* 4. Use 到时候 *to express "when the time comes"* 5. Use 像 *to express "resemble" or "is like"* 6. Use 越来越 *to mean "increasingly"* 7. Use 比方说 *to say "for example"* 8. Use 连……都 *to say "even . . ."*	• Observe greetings performed during Spring Festival • Learn about the use of idioms in the Chinese language • Learn about customs related to Tomb Sweeing Festival, the Dragon Boat Festival, and the Mid-Autumn Festival • Identify important foods related to Chinese holidays • Learn about the development of writing horizontal and vertical text in Chinese • Understand customs used during Chinese New Year and the Lantern Festival

Units	Communication Goals	Structure Notes	Language Notes & Cultural Spotlights
礼 **UNIT 15** **Chinese Ways**	• Politely ask someone to do something • Understand and follow Chinese social conventions • Use correct etiquette towards one's elders • Name some features of traditional Chinese culture • Express that one has "just" done something • Make basic comparisons between ancient and modern Chinese culture • Indicate that something is an ongoing process	1. Use 麻烦 *to make requests* 2. Use 来 *before verbs to express commencing an activity* 3. Use 要不然 *to say "or else" or "otherwise"* 4. Use 正好 *to express "as it happens"; "happen to . . ."* 5. Use 刚 *or* 刚刚 *to express "just now"* 6. Use nouns with 化 *to form "-ize" verbs or "-ized" adjectives* 7. Use 比如(说) *to say "for instance" and give examples* 8. Use double-了 *to describe an action continuing up to the present*	• Understand the Chinese concept of "face" • Compare the difference between 客气 and 礼貌 • Learn about Confucius and his teachings • Learn about the difference between classical and modern Chinese language usage • Learn about Daoism • Understand the meaning of resilience found in Confucian philosophy and Daoist beliefs
@ **UNIT 16** **Technology &** **Modern China**	• Use expressions related to computers and the internet • Discuss city lifestyles • Understand and use the "besides" construction • Express that you will miss someone • Use terms for posting letters and packages as well as sending emails • Wish someone a safe trip	1. Use 除了……以外 *to say "besides…"* 2. Use question words with 都 *to express "any" or "every"* 3. Use 自己 *to refer to oneself or another* 4. Use 等 *to express "at the point when/by the time"* 5. Use Verb Phrase 给 Someone 看/听 *to express doing something to show someone else* 6. Use 陪 *to express keeping someone company* 7. Use 会…的 *to stress that something will be the case* 8. Use 死 *to mean "extremely" or "to death"*	• Learn about internet cafes • Review learned measure words • Explore modern Beijing architecture • Learn about internet use in China • Review sentence-final particles • Learn about cell phone use in China • Learn more about the Maglev Train and China's high-speed rail

中文

The Chinese Language

Communication Goals

- Learn the pinyin romanization system
- Speak Chinese characters with standard tones and sentence inflection
- Understand Chinese tonal changes (tone sandhi)

前言
Prelude

Mandarin Chinese

Mandarin Chinese is the most widely spoken variety of Chinese. Mandarin is an official language of Mainland China, Taiwan, and Singapore, and is spoken natively by approximately 900 million people, making it the language with the most native speakers worldwide.

This textbook covers Standard Mandarin, called Putonghua in Mainland China, Guoyu in Taiwan, and Huayu in Singapore. While there are small differences in those three modern standards, the core of Standard Mandarin was established in China in the early 20th century, and its pronunciation was drawn from the Mandarin spoken in Beijing at the time. As a result, many people speak Mandarin with regional accents that are not considered standard (just as there are regional accents in English). It is also quite common for people to speak Mandarin as a second language, in addition to their native variety of Chinese.

Different dialects of Chinese can be as distinct from one another as French is from Italian, but they are not usually referred to as separate languages due to political and historical factors. Besides Mandarin, some of the major dialects are Cantonese, Taiwanese, and Shanghainese. Because different varieties of Chinese share a common writing system (for the most part), the term "Chinese" is often used to refer to the written language, while "Mandarin" is used to refer to spoken Mandarin.

Chinese Characters

The basic unit of Chinese writing is called the character (字 zì). Chinese characters have evolved over thousands of years. The earliest examples of identifiable Chinese characters have been found on oracle bones used for divination, dating back to about 1200 BC.

Each Chinese character has a meaning, and a pronunciation consisting of a single syllable. In modern Chinese, most words are made up of one or two characters.

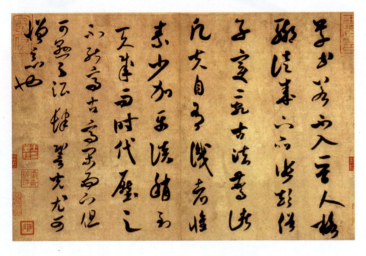

Chinese can be written in two forms: simplified characters (简体字 jiǎntǐzì) and traditional characters (繁体字 fántǐzì). Simplified characters were developed in the 1950s, and are used today in Mainland China and Singapore. Traditional characters are used in Taiwan, Hong Kong, and in many overseas Chinese communities. The two character sets contain some forms that have remained the same (你, 你), and others that look very different (让, 讓). This textbook will use simplified characters, but the traditional character forms will be displayed alongside the simplified forms in the vocabulary sections.

While there are over 80,000 Chinese characters, most of them are rarely used. Knowledge of only 3,000 characters is all that is required for daily life, and the average well-educated Chinese person knows approximately 6,000 characters.

Learning to Write Characters

Memorizing how to write characters is often identified as the most intimidating part of studying Chinese. Fortunately, learning a bit about their structure makes the process much simpler.

Every character has a radical, which is a section of the character that hints at its meaning and can be used to index it in a dictionary. For example, all characters with the 口 (kǒu) radical will be arranged together in the dictionary. 口 means "mouth," and characters with this radical generally have something to do with the mouth, such as 咬 (yǎo "to bite"), 叫 (jiào "to call"), and 吃 (chī "to eat").

Every character is written as if it were in a grid: each character should take up approximately the same amount of space, and there should be no spaces between words as there are in English.

Most characters can be broken down into smaller components, which may be organized according to the following common structures:

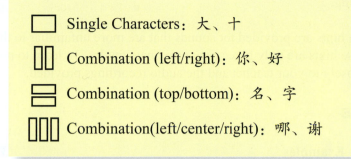

Single Characters：大、十

Combination (left/right)：你、好

Combination (top/bottom)：名、字

Combination(left/center/right)：哪、谢

Strokes

Although in modern times characters are generally written with pens and pencils (and indeed computers), calligraphy using a brush still forms the basis of how characters are understood. This is why the lines that make up characters are called strokes. It is important to know how many strokes a character has, because this is how characters are arranged in Chinese dictionaries. Typically, the strokes comprising a character are written sequentially from top to bottom and left to right. In this book, each character that you are required to write will be accompanied by a diagram demonstrating the correct stroke order.

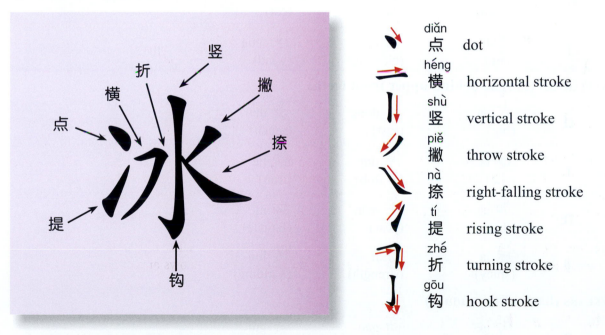

diǎn 点 dot

héng 横 horizontal stroke

shù 竖 vertical stroke

piě 撇 throw stroke

nà 捺 right-falling stroke

tí 提 rising stroke

zhé 折 turning stroke

gōu 钩 hook stroke

Writing in Chinese on an Electronic Device

To type Chinese characters on a computer or mobile device, switch the language input method to Chinese (pinyin) then simply spell out the words in pinyin (see the following section) and select the apporiate character from the list that appears. Note that the pinyin letter 'ü' is typed using the 'v' key.

Many dictionary applications and online dictionaries also allow you to write out the characters you want to look up. These programs use stroke order to determine what character your are writing, which is another reason that learning correct stroke order is very important when studying Chinese.

Pronunciation

Because Chinese characters do not contain detailed pronunciation information, various Chinese-speaking regions have developed different methods of representing the sounds of Mandarin. This textbook will use pinyin, the Mainland Chinese Mandarin romanization system, meaning a way of representing Mandarin pronunciation using the Roman alphabet.

Syllables in Chinese are traditionally divided into initials (the first consonant) and finals (the rest). The initials and finals of pinyin are presented below. You should use the following section in combination with the online audio recording.

Some pronunciation hints are provided for sounds that are more unfamiliar to the native English speaker. Please note that these hints are only given as approximate guides. To learn to pronounce Mandarin sounds accurately, listen closely to your teacher and the audio recordings provided.

🎧 Initials

Initial	Examples			Pronunciation Notes
LABIALS (using lips)				
b	爸 bà (dad)	杯 bēi (cup)	比 bǐ (to compare)	
p	怕 pà (to fear)	破 pò (broken)	票 piào (ticket)	
m	妈 mā (mom)	名 míng (name)	猫 māo (cat)	
f	法 fǎ (law)	福 fú (blessing)	风 fēng (wind)	
ALVEOLARS (tongue behind upper front teeth)				
d	大 dà (big)	东 dōng (east)	多 duō (much)	
t	她 tā (she)	停 tíng (to stop)	铁 tiě (iron)	
n	那 nà (that)	年 nián (year)	女 nǚ (female)	
l	辣 là (spicy)	力 lì (strength)	楼 lóu (building)	
VELARS (back of the mouth)				
g	哥 gē (older brother)	高 gāo (tall)	贵 guì (expensive)	
k	课 kè (lesson)	口 kǒu (mouth)	快 kuài (quick)	
h	喝 hē (to drink)	很 hěn (very)	黄 huáng (yellow)	like ch, as in Bach

PALATALS (tip of tongue behind lower front teeth)

j	鸡 jī (chicken)	家 jiā (family)	九 jiǔ (nine)	like j, as in **j**eep
q	七 qī (seven)	去 qù (to go)	钱 qián (money)	like ch, as in **ch**eap
x	西 xī (west)	谢 xiè (to thank)	想 xiǎng (to think)	like sh, as in **sh**eep

DENTAL SIBILANTS (tip of tongue behind upper front teeth)

z	字 zì (character)	脏 zāng (dirty)	走 zǒu (to walk)	like dz, as in Go**dz**illa
c	次 cì (occurrence)	菜 cài (vegetable)	从 cóng (from)	like ts, as in pi**zz**a
s	四 sì (four)	色 sè (color)	酸 suān (sour)	

RETROFLEXES (tip of tongue curled toward front of hard palate)

zh	只 zhǐ (only)	中 zhōng (center)	真 zhēn (really)	like dg, as in **j**erk
ch	吃 chī (to eat)	穿 chuān (to wear)	城 chéng (city)	
sh	十 shí (ten)	说 shuō (to speak)	少 shǎo (few)	
r	日 rì (day)	让 ràng (allow)	肉 ròu (meat)	like jh, as in **g**enre

Finals

Final	Examples			Pronunciation Notes
a	八 bā (eight)	大 dà (big)	法 fǎ (law)	
o	佛 Fó (Buddha)	末 mò (end)	伯 bó (uncle)	like wuh, as in **wha**t
e	喝 hē (to drink)	乐 lè (happy)	渴 kě (thirsty)	like uh, as in **huh**
i	四 sì (four)	你 nǐ (you)	比 bǐ (to compare)	(after dental sibilants and retroflexes e.g. sì): like ur, as in s**ir**
u	不 bù (not)	书 shū (book)	足 zú (foot)	
ü	女 nǚ (female)	绿 lǜ (green)	去 qù (to go)	like ü, as in German über, or u as in French tu

ai	爱 ài (to love)	买 mǎi (to buy)	来 lái (to come)	
ei	谁 shéi (who)	累 lèi (tired)	飞 fēi (to fly)	
ao	高 gāo (tall)	好 hǎo (good)	猫 māo (cat)	
ou	头 tóu (head)	走 zǒu (to walk)	都 dōu (all)	
er	二 èr (two)	儿 ér (child)	耳 ěr (ear)	
an	男 nán (male)	盘 pán (plate)	三 sān (three)	
en	很 hěn (very)	人 rén (person)	门 mén (door)	
ang	商 shāng (business)	帮 bāng (to help)	长 cháng (long)	
eng	梦 mèng (to dream)	等 děng (to wait)	城 chéng (city)	like ung, as in l**ung**
ong	龙 lóng (dragon)	东 dōng (east)	从 cóng (from)	like owng, as in **own** + **g**
ia	家 jiā (family)	下 xià (down)	恰 qià (appropriate)	
iao	笑 xiào (to smile)	秒 miǎo (second)	跳 tiào (to jump)	
ie	姐 jiě (older sister)	谢 xiè (to thank)	爹 diē (dad)	like yeh, as in **yes**
iu	六 liù (six)	丢 diū (to lose)	九 jiǔ (nine)	like eo, as in L**eo**
ian	店 diàn (store)	先 xiān (first)	天 tiān (sky)	like **Yen**
in	您 nín (you, polite)	今 jīn (now)	新 xīn (new)	
iang	两 liǎng (two)	象 xiàng (elephant)	讲 jiǎng (to speak)	
ing	名 míng (name)	英 yīng (hero)	星 xīng (star)	
iong	兄 xiōng (older brother)	窘 jiǒng (to embarrass)	穷 qióng (poor)	

ua	话 huà (speech)	刷 shuā (to brush)	挂 guà (to hang)	
uo	多 duō (many)	国 guó (country)	做 zuò (to do)	
uai	快 kuài (quick)	坏 huài (bad)	怪 guài (strange)	
ui	对 duì (correct)	水 shuǐ (water)	会 huì (to be able)	like **way**
uan	短 duǎn (short)	酸 suān (sour)	还 huán (to return)	
un	尊 zūn (to respect)	春 chūn (spring)	寸 cùn (inch)	like **won**
uang	黄 huáng (yellow)	光 guāng (light)	狂 kuáng (crazy)	
üe	学 xué (to study)	觉 jué (to feel)	缺 quē (to lack)	like weh, as in **wet**
üan	元 yuán (dollar)	选 xuǎn (to choose)	全 quán (complete)	like **when**
ün	云 yún (cloud)	裙 qún (skirt)	军 jūn (army)	

Special spelling rules

Rule 1: If no initial precedes i, the i is changed to y.

ia → ya
(e.g. 牙 yá: "tooth")

ie → ye
(e.g. 也 yě: "also")

iao → yao
(e.g. 要 yào: "to want")

iu → iou → you
(e.g. 有 yǒu: "to have")

ian → yan
(e.g. 言 yán: "speech")

iang → yang
(e.g. 羊 yáng: "sheep")

However, if no initial precedes i, in, or ing, simply add the initial y.

i → yi
(e.g. 一 yī: "one")

in → yin
(e.g. 因 yīn: "cause")

ing → ying
(e.g. 英 yīng: "hero")

Rule 2: The dots on the ü should be omitted, except following initial l or n.

jü → ju
(e.g. 句 jù: "sentence")

qü → qu
(e.g. 去 qù: "to go")

xü → xu
(e.g. 序 xù: "preface")

Rule 3: If no initial precedes ü, add the initial y and drop the umlaut.

ü → yu
(e.g. 鱼 yú: "fish")

üan → yuan
(e.g. 元 yuán: "dollar")

üe → yue
(e.g. 月 yuè: "month")

ün → yun
(e.g. 云 yún: cloud)

Rule 4: If no initial precedes u, change u to w.

ua → wa
(e.g. 娃 wá: "baby")

uo → wo
(e.g. 我 wǒ: "I, me")

uai → wai
(e.g. 外 wài: "outside")

uan → wan
(e.g. 玩 wán: "to play")

uang → wang   ui → uei → wei   uen → wen   ueng → weng
(e.g. 王 wáng: "king")   (e.g. 尾 wěi: "tail")   (e.g. 问 wèn: "to ask")   (e.g. 翁 wēng: "old man")

u on its own becomes wu.

u → wu
(e.g. 五 wǔ: "five")

Tones

All Mandarin syllables must include a tone. Mandarin has four primary tones, plus a neutral tone. The tone marks below are added to the main vowel in a syllable to indicate its tone.

一声 the first tone	二声 the second tone	三声 the third tone	四声 the fourth tone
—	´	ˇ	`

First tone is high and level, like opening your mouth for the doctor to say "ahhh."	
Second tone rises straight up in pitch, like asking a question.	
Third tone dips to the lowest point of your normal speaking range, and then comes back up, like saying "OK" in an uncertain tone of voice.	
The fourth tone falls quickly from the top to the bottom of your range, like you are angry.	

In addition to the four tones there is also a neutral tone that is written in pinyin without any tone marking. Neutral tone syllables are generally pronounced as light and unstressed.

Placement of tone marks

Tone marks always go over a vowel. When there is more than one vowel in a final, the tone mark goes over the "main" vowel (e.g., jiǎng, yǒu, guì). This happens to work out so that the tone mark goes over the letter that comes first in the alphabet (*a* before *i*, *o* before *u*, etc.), with the exception of *-iong*, where the mark goes over the *o*, and *-iu*, where the mark goes over the *u*.

Notes about tones

When a third tone occurs before other syllables, it becomes a half-third tone, meaning that only the first part of the dip is produced, and the pitch doesn't come all the way up. When two or three third tones occur in a row, with no natural pauses in between, the first third tone(s) transform into second tone, and the final syllable is pronounced with a complete third tone. This rule will be revisited in Unit 1.

ONLINE RESOURCES
Visit *http://college.betterchinese.com* for additional pinyin exercises.

Teacher's Expressions

Chinese	Pinyin	English
上课。	Shàng kè.	Let's begin class.
下课。	Xià kè.	Class dismissed.
请举手。	Qǐng jǔ shǒu.	Please raise your hand.
跟我念。	Gēn wǒ niàn.	Read aloud after me.
你来念。	Nǐ lái niàn.	Now you read it.
大声一点。	Dà shēng yì diǎn.	A little louder.
请看黑 / 白板。	Qǐng kàn hēi/báibǎn.	Please look at the black/white-board.
请翻到第___页。	Qǐng fāndào dì ___ yè.	Please turn to page ___.
请看第___段。	Qǐng kàn dì ___ duàn.	Please look at paragraph ___.
请看第___行。	Qǐng kàn dì ___ háng.	Please look at the ___ line.

Student's Expressions

Chinese	Pinyin	English
我没听清楚。	Wǒ méi tīng qīngchu.	I didn't hear it clearly.
可不可以再说一遍？	Kě bu kěyǐ zài shuō yí biàn?	Could you say it one more time?
可不可以说慢一点？	Kě bu kěyǐ shuō màn yì diǎn?	Could you speak more slowly?
我有一个问题。	Wǒ yǒu yí ge wèntí.	I have a question.
___是什么意思？	___ shì shénme yìsi?	What does ___ mean?
___中文怎么说？	___ Zhōngwén zěnme shuō?	How do you say ___ in Chinese?

Lesson Organization

Modern Chinese is organized by units, each representing a particular theme. In each unit, there are two lessons presenting different scenarios. The organization of each lesson is as follows:

Sections	Subsections	Description
Lesson Story		Lesson dialogue in illustrated format with simplified Chinese characters and pinyin for new vocabulary.
Lesson Text		Lesson dialogue text in simplified Chinese characters and pinyin.
Vocabulary	Lesson Vocabulary	Core new vocabulary with simplified Chinese characters, traditional Chinese characters (if different), pinyin, part of speech, and definition.
	Required Vocabulary	Related words and phrases that are not in the Lesson Text. Students are required to learn these words as core vocabulary. They will be used in the Structure Notes and Practice sections.
	Optional Vocabulary	Optional related words and phrases that are not in the Lesson Text. Students are not required to learn these words. They can be used for extended learning.
Pronunciation Notes		Details on the pronunciation of lesson words or phrases that are exceptions to general Chinese pronunciation rules.
Language Notes		Language and culture notes pertaining to the lesson theme and vocabulary.
Structure Notes		Grammar explanations, examples, and practices.
Practice	Speaking	Individual, partner, and group speaking exercises through conversations, presentations, and audio recordings.
	Writing and Typing	Stroke order is displayed for characters that students are required to be able to write for the lesson. These are the most frequently-used characters. Exercises that involve writing and typing Chinese characters are also provided.
	Reading	Reading comprehension sections contain vocabulary from the Lesson Vocabulary and Required Vocabulary sections.
Cultural Spotlight		Cultural information relevant to the lesson theme.
Text in English		Lesson dialogue text in simplified Chinese characters and English.
What Can You Do		Summary of interpretive, interpersonal, and presentational communication skills achieved by the student.
Unit Review		Found at the end of the second lesson per unit, this is a summary of all vocabulary and structure notes learned in the unit. To assess comprehension of the material from the two lessons, a short list of role-play suggestions are provided for extended communicative practice.

Abbreviations of Grammatical Terms

adj	Adjective
adv	Adverb
av	Auxiliary Verb
cj	Conjunction
ie	Idiomatic Expression
interj	Interjection
mw	Measure Word
n	Noun
nu	Number
on	Onomatopoeia
p	Particle
pr	Pronoun
prep	Preposition
qph	Question Phrase
qw	Question Word
rc	Resultative Complement
rv	Resultative Verb
v	Verb
dc	Directional Complement
vo	Verb-Object Compound

Icons

 Speaking Practice

 Reading Practice

Writing Practice

Audio component

Practice that requires making an audio recording

 Practice that requires using a computer

Character Profiles

孙玛丽
Sūn Mǎlì

An American student from Boston

Friendly, lively, and loves learning new things

In her sophomore year

Xiaomei's roommate

李中平
Lǐ Zhōngpíng

An American student from Texas

Cheerful and studious

Majors in mathematics but has broad interests, including Chinese

In his sophomore year

陈大东
Chén Dàdōng

A Canadian student from Montreal

Responsible and hard-working

Works at the campus coffee shop and likes studying languages

In his freshman year

Xiang'an's roommate

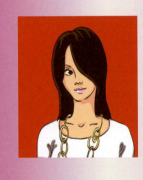

王小美
Wáng Xiǎoměi

An American student who was born in Beijing and raised in California

Artistic and a little shy

Loves humanities and the arts

In her freshman year

Mali's roommate

张安娜
Zhāng Ānnà

A Russian student from Moscow

Seems aloof, but has a sensitive side

In her sophomore year

Likes dancing and shopping

黄祥安
Huáng Xiáng'ān

A South African student from Johannesburg

Easygoing and kind-hearted

Loves music and soccer

In his freshman year

Dadong's roommate

我

Me

Communication Goals

Lesson 1: 你好! **Meeting People**
- Greet and say goodbye to people
- Introduce yourself and exchange names with others

Lesson 2: 你多大? 你是哪国人? **Age and Nationality**
- Ask and answer questions pertaining to age
- Ask and answer questions pertaining to nationality
- Count from 1 to 99

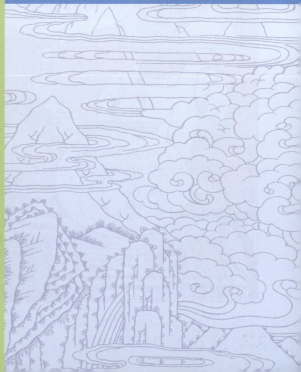

LESSON TEXT 1.1

Meeting People 你好！

Chen Dadong works at the campus coffee shop and greets his classmate and good friend, Sun Mali. Teacher Liu passes by and Sun Mali then tells their names to Teacher Liu.

孙玛丽：	大东，你好！	Dàdōng, nǐ hǎo!
陈大东：	玛丽，你好吗？	Mǎlì, nǐ hǎo ma?
孙玛丽：	我很好。你呢？	Wǒ hěn hǎo. Nǐ ne?
陈大东：	我也很好，谢谢。	Wǒ yě hěn hǎo, xièxie.
孙玛丽， 陈大东：	老师好！	Lǎoshī hǎo!
刘老师：	同学们好！	Tóngxuémen hǎo!

刘老师：	请问，你叫什么名字？	Qǐngwèn, nǐ jiào shénme míngzi?
孙玛丽：	我叫孙玛丽。	Wǒ jiào Sūn Mǎlì.
刘老师：	他叫什么名字？	Tā jiào shénme míngzi?
孙玛丽：	他叫陈大东。	Tā jiào Chén Dàdōng.
刘老师：	玛丽，大东，再见！	Mǎlì, Dàdōng, zàijiàn!
孙玛丽， 陈大东：	老师，再见！	Lǎoshī, zàijiàn!

字 词 VOCABULARY

LESSON VOCABULARY 1.1

	SIMPLIFIED	TRADITIONAL	PINYIN	WORD CATEGORY	DEFINITION
1.	你好		nǐ hǎo	*ie*	hello
	你		nǐ	*pr*	you
	好		hǎo	*adj*	good, well, fine
2.	吗	嗎	ma	*p*	(indicates a question)
3.	我		wǒ	*pr*	I
4.	很		hěn	*adv*	very
5.	呢		ne	*p*	(indicates "What about . . .?")
6.	也		yě	*adv*	also
7.	谢谢	謝謝	xièxie	*ie*	thank you
8.	老师	老師	lǎoshī	*n*	teacher
9.	同学们	同學們	tóngxuémen	*n*	classmates
	同学	同學	tóngxué	*n*	classmate
	们	們	men	*p*	(used after a pronoun or noun, referring to people, to indicate plural form)
10.	请问	請問	qǐngwèn	*ie*	excuse me; may I please ask
	请	請	qǐng	*v*	to request; to treat; please
	问	問	wèn	*v*	to ask
11.	叫		jiào	*v*	to call; to be called
12.	什么	甚麼	shénme	*qw*	what
13.	名字		míngzi	*n*	name
14.	他		tā	*pr*	he
15.	再见	再見	zàijiàn	*ie*	goodbye

NAMES

	SIMPLIFIED	TRADITIONAL	PINYIN	WORD CATEGORY	DEFINITION
16.	陈大东	陳大東	Chén Dàdōng	*name*	Chen Dadong
	陈	陳	Chén	*surname*	Chen
	大东	大東	Dàdōng	*given name*	Dadong
17.	孙玛丽	孫瑪麗	Sūn Mǎlì	*name*	Sun Mali
	孙	孫	Sūn	*surname*	Sun
	玛丽	瑪麗	Mǎlì	*given name*	Mali

REQUIRED VOCABULARY 1.1

	SIMPLIFIED	TRADITIONAL	PINYIN	WORD CATEGORY	DEFINITION
RELATED TO SCHOOL					
18.	学	學	xué	*v*	to learn
19.	学校	學校	xuéxiào	*n*	school
20.	姓		xìng	*v*	to be surnamed
PRONOUNS					
21.	您		nín	*pr*	you (polite form)
22.	她		tā	*pr*	she
23	它		tā	*pr*	it
TITLES					
24.	先生		xiānsheng	*n*	Mr.; husband; gentleman
25.	太太		tàitai	*n*	Mrs.; wife
26.	小姐		xiǎojie	*n*	Miss; young lady
27.	女士		nǔshì	*n*	Ms.; lady
SURNAME					
28.	刘	劉	Liú	*surname*	Liu

Pronunciation Notes

你 + 好 → 你 好
Nǐ + hǎo   Ní hǎo

In Chinese pinyin, syllables are conventionally labeled with the tone with which they are meant to be pronounced. However, there are some important exceptions. When a group of two or more third tone syllables appear consecutively in a single phrase, all of the third tones but the final one are changed to a second tone. We pronounce them as second tone even though they are marked as third tone. For example, in this lesson, when "nǐ" and "hǎo" are spoken together, "nǐ" is pronounced as "ní."

Greetings

The literal translation for the Chinese greeting 你好 (nǐ hǎo) is "you good." It is similar to "hello" in English.

Chinese people usually greet others by adding 你好 (nǐ hǎo) or just 好 (hǎo) after the names of the people they are addressing. They also sometimes use specific titles in their greetings. For example, when they greet a teacher, they normally say 老师 好 (lǎoshī hǎo), with a slight bow of the head to show respect. When students and teachers meet, students normally greet teachers first as another sign of respect.

The phrase 你好吗？ (nǐ hǎo ma?) is a common way to ask "how are you doing?"

How Chinese Names are Structured

In Chinese, the family name comes first, so someone named 陈大 东 (Chén Dàdōng) in Chinese would be called "Dadong Chen" in English. Most family names in Chinese consist of one character (example: 陈). Given names traditionally have two characters, but one-character names are popular in mainland China. Given names in Chinese normally carry special meanings. For instance, 大东 (Dàdōng) means "Great East."

陈　大　东
Family name　　Given Name

While there are standard Chinese equivalents for most common Western names, they sound a bit different in Chinese due to the common sounds used in each language. For example, the name "David" corresponds to the Chinese name 大卫 (Dàwèi). For a more authentic and unique effect, many students learning Chinese choose to take a new Chinese name that is different from the standard translation of their English name.

How Chinese People Address One Another

As a sign of respect, Chinese people often address others by their titles, such as 老师 (lǎoshī: Teacher), 先生 (xiānsheng: Mr.), 太太 (tàitai: Mrs.), and 小姐 (xiǎojie: Miss). In Chinese, titles are added after rather than before someone's name. For example, a teacher with the surname Liu is addressed as 刘老师 (Liú Lǎoshī: Teacher Liu); a man with the surname Chen is addressed as 陈先生 (Chén Xiānsheng: Mr. Chen).

When meeting someone for the first time on formal occasions, Chinese people normally use the expression 您贵姓 (Nín guì xìng?: "What is your honorable family name?") to politely ask for someone's surname. A more casual way to ask someone's surname is 您姓什么 (Nín xìng shénme?: "What is your family name?"). On informal occasions, 你叫什么名字？ (Nǐ jiào shénme míngzi?: "What is your name?") is commonly used to ask for others' full names or given names.

Online Resources

Visit *http://college.betterchinese.com* for the "Hundred Family Surnames," a list of the most commonly used family names in Chinese.

STRUCTURE NOTE 1.1
Use an adjective phrase to describe a subject

Chinese uses a special sentence pattern when describing a subject. In English, one would say, "He is very well." In Chinese, the adjective phrase still appears after the subject, but without a connecting verb, literally: "He very well."

When an adjective is used to describe a subject in an affirmative sentence, an adverb such as 很 (hěn) *is commonly used to modify the adjective.* 很 *can be translated into English as "very" but is usually omitted in the translation.*

> Subject + Adjective Phrase

From the Lesson Text:

我很好。
Wǒ hěn hǎo.
I am well.

Other examples:

刘太太很好。
Liú tàitai hěn hǎo.
Mrs. Liu is well.

他很好。
Tā hěn hǎo.
He is well.

Practice: Construct sentences using the information provided below.

Example: 我 → 我很好。

1. 她 _____
2. 老师 _____
3. 同学们 _____
4. 陈先生 _____
5. 孙小姐 _____

STRUCTURE NOTE 1.2
Use 们 *to convert a pronoun or noun (people only) to its plural form*

The conversion of singular nouns and pronouns to their respective plural forms using 们 (men) *can only be applied to nouns and pronouns regarding people.*

> Pronoun/Noun (people) + 们

From the Lesson Text:

同学 → 同学们
Tóngxuémen
Classmates (can also mean "students" when used by teachers)

Other examples:

我 → 我们
Wǒmen
We

老师 → 老师们
Lǎoshīmen
Teachers

Practice: Construct the plural forms of the nouns and pronouns below.

Example: 同学 → 同学们

1. 我 _____
2. 你 _____
3. 他 _____
4. 她 _____
5. 老师 _____

STRUCTURE NOTE 1.3

Use 也 to express "also"

也 (yě) *is placed in front of a verb phrase to express the meaning "also." In the absence of a verb,* 也 *is placed directly before the adjective phrase. While "also" can be moved around in an English sentence,* 也 *follows a fixed sentence pattern in Chinese.*

Subject + 也 + Verb/Adjective Phrase

From the Lesson Text: 我也很好。
Wǒ yě hěn hǎo.
I am also well.

Other examples: 他也很好。   孙玛丽也很好。
Tā yě hěn hǎo.   Sūn Mǎlì yě hěn hǎo.
He is also well.   Sun Mali is also well.

Practice: Transform each sentence by adding 也, according to the example given.

Example: 我很好。 → 我也很好。

1. 她很好。 _____
2. 老师很好。 _____
3. 同学们很好。 _____
4. 陈小姐很好。 _____
5. 孙女士很好。 _____

STRUCTURE NOTE 1.4
Use 吗 to turn a statement into a question
Adding the particle 吗 (ma) at the end of a statement turns that statement into a question.

Statement + 吗?

From the Lesson Text:

你好吗？
Nǐ hǎo ma?
Are you well? (equivalent to the English phrase "How are you?")

Other examples:

他好吗？
Tā hǎo ma?
Is he well?

孙玛丽好吗？
Sūn Mǎlì hǎo ma?
Is Sun Mali well?

Practice: Construct questions in Chinese using the information provided below.

Example: 你好 → 你好吗？
1. 她好 _____
2. 您好 _____
3. 老师好 _____
4. 同学们好 _____
5. 陈大东好 _____

STRUCTURE NOTE 1.5
Use 呢 to ask "What about . . . ?"
Following a statement about a person/object, 呢 (ne) can be added to ask about the status of another person/object regarding the same topic.

Statement + Noun/Pronoun + 呢?

From the Lesson Text:

我很好。你呢？
Wǒ hěn hǎo. Nǐ ne?
I am well. What about you?

Other examples:

我叫玛丽。你呢？
Wǒ jiào Mǎlì. Nǐ ne?
My name is Mali. What's yours?

陈大东呢？
Chén Dàdōng ne?
What about Chen Dadong?

Practice: Construct questions using the information provided below.

Example: 你 → 你呢？

1. 我 _____
2. 他 _____
3. 老师 _____
4. 同学们 _____
5. 孙太太 _____

STRUCTURE NOTE 1.6
Use 叫 to state one's name

The literal meaning of 叫 *(jiào) is "to be called." It is used to state one's name.*

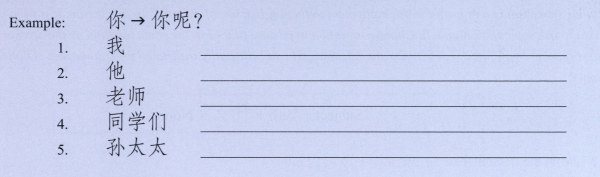

Subject + 叫 + Name

From the Lesson Text:　我叫孙玛丽。
Wǒ jiào Sūn Mǎlì.
I am (called) Sun Mali.

Other examples:　　他叫陈大东。　　　她叫孙玛丽。
Tā jiào Chén Dàdōng.　　Tā jiào Sūn Mǎlì.
He is (called) Chen Dadong.　She is (called) Sun Mali.

Practice: Create sentences using the phrases provided in the boxes below.

Example: 她叫孙玛丽。

我 他 你 她	叫	陈大东 孙玛丽 (your name) (your classmate's name)

_____
_____
_____
_____

STRUCTURE NOTE 1.7
Use 什么 *to ask "what?" questions*

什么 *(shénme) is a question word, equivalent to the English use of "what." In this lesson, it is used with* 叫 *(jiào) to ask someone's name. In Chinese, question words are placed in the same location as the answer would be in the response.* 叫什么名字 *(jiào shénme míngzi) can be literally translated as "(Someone) is called by what name?"*

Subject + Verb + 什么 + Noun?

From the Lesson Text:

你叫什么名字？
Nǐ jiào shénme míngzi?
What is your name?

Other examples:

他叫什么名字？
Tā jiào shénme míngzi?
What is his name?

老师叫什么名字？
Lǎoshī jiào shénme míngzi?
What is the teacher's name?

Practice: Construct complete questions using the information provided below.

Example: 你 → 你叫什么名字？
1. 他 _____
2. 她 _____
3. 他们 _____
4. 老师 _____
5. 你先生 _____

PRACTICE 1.1

Ask your teacher to give you a Chinese name. Write down the characters and the pinyin for your Chinese name below. Identify your surname and given name.

_____

PRACTICE 1.2

Greet your classmates using 你好 and ask 5 of them their names.

Example:

A: 我叫孙玛丽。你叫什么名字？

B: 我叫陈大东。你呢？

Full name	Family Name	Given Name

PRACTICE 1.3

Assign appropriate titles to the people shown in the pictures and then practice the greetings below with a partner.

Example:

A: 陈先生，你好吗？

B: 我很好，谢谢。你呢？

A: 我也很好，谢谢！

陈先生　刘老师　孙小姐　陈太太　孙丽

	Radical	Stroke Order
你	亻(人) rén person	ノ 亻 亻 伂 伱 你 你
好	女 nǚ woman	く 乂 女 妁 奵 好
我	戈 gē spear	丿 二 于 手 我 我 我
很	彳 chì step	丿 彳 彳 彳 彳 彳 很 很
也	乛 zhé bent	乛 か 也
老	老 lǎo old	一 十 土 耂 耂 老
师	巾 jīn cloth	丨 刂 𠂆 师 师 师
同	口 kǒu mouth	丨 冂 冂 同 同 同
学	子 zǐ child	丶 丷 丷 丷 兴 学 学
们	亻(人) rén person	丿 亻 亻 们 们
叫	口 kǒu mouth	丨 冂 口 叫 叫
名	口 kǒu mouth	丿 夕 夕 夕 名 名
字	宀 mián roof	丶 丷 宀 宁 宁 字
他	亻(人) rén person	丿 亻 亻 仲 他
见	见 jiàn see	丨 冂 贝 见

PRACTICE 1.5

Make an audio recording and send it to your teacher. In the recording, offer a greeting, give your name, and ask your teacher for his or her name.

PRACTICE 1.6

Send e-mails to your teacher and your classmates in Chinese. In the e-mails, greet them and introduce yourself.

Example: 老师好。我叫孙玛丽。

PRACTICE 1.7

陈大东：你们好！我叫陈大东。
同学们：陈大东，你好！
陈大东：老师姓什么？
孙玛丽：老师姓刘。

Read the dialogue and answer the following questions.
1. What is the surname of the teacher?
2. Who answers Chen Dadong's question?

PRACTICE 1.8

刘老师：陈大东，你好吗？
陈同学：我很好，谢谢老师。您呢？
刘老师：我也很好。大东，再见！
陈同学：老师，再见！

Read the dialogue and answer the following questions.
1. How does the teacher greet the student?
2. What does the student say when he is about to leave?

More on Addressing People in Chinese

In Chinese, there are numerous polite terms used to address people. The usage of these terms depends on the speaker's age and relationship with the people they are addressing, as well as the region the speaker is from. For example, children address their parents' friends as 叔叔 (shūshu: "uncle") and 阿姨 (āyí: "Aunt") and generally refer to elderly people as 爷爷 (yéye: "grandpa"), 奶奶 (nǎinai: "grandma"), or 老人家 (lǎo rénjiā: "old folks").

Calling a Person by His or Her Name

In China, do not be surprised when someone calls you by your full Chinese name. This is regarded as a more formal and respectful way of addressing others. First names are usually only used among family members and close friends.

In Western cultures, people older than you may have you call them by their given names. In China, however, one would never address a person of an older generation by his or her given name.

The Chinese Diaspora

There are over 40 million Chinese living outside of China, mainly in Southeast Asia, but sizable populations are found in North and South America, Europe, Africa, and Australia as well. These groups are referred to collectively as the Chinese Diaspora. Many of the Chinese that live overseas identify themselves as Chinese, retain their culture, and continue to follow Chinese traditions. Here are some examples of areas that have significant Chinese populations:

United States: There are about 3 million Chinese people living in the United States and Chinese is the third most spoken language in the country. From the 19th century onwards, immigration from China's southern provinces brought many Cantonese speakers to the US Since the 1980s, however, Mandarin speakers from the mainland have become increasingly prevalent. Immigration from Taiwan in the 1960s and 1970s also resulted in a number of Mandarin speakers entering the country. In many of the country's major cities, early Chinese settlers formed distinctive communities that came to be known as Chinatowns. San Francisco has one of the oldest Chinatowns in North America, which was established in the 1850s by immigrants who arrived during the California gold rush and the construction of transcontinental railroads. While Chinatowns are still an attractive feature of America's urban environments, these days skilled Chinese immigrants are spread out all across the US.

Canada: In Vancouver, roughly 18% of the total population is Chinese with Cantonese being the most popular Chinese dialect spoken, followed by Mandarin. Chinese characters are seen everywhere from grocery stores, shops, and restaurants to local banks. Vancouver and Toronto have the largest populations of immigrants and Canadians of Chinese origin.

United Kingdom: The earliest Chinese immigrants to the United Kingdom came from the cities of Tianjin and Shanghai in the early 19th century, which makes the Chinese community in the UK the oldest in Europe. As with the United States, many early Chinese immigrants to the UK were Cantonese speakers, but increasing numbers of Mandarin speakers have moved to the country since the 1980s.

孙玛丽：	大东，你好！	Dadong, hello!
陈大东：	玛丽，你好吗？	Mali, how are you?
孙玛丽：	我很好。你呢？	I'm well. And you?
陈大东：	我也很好，谢谢。	I'm very well too, thank you!
孙玛丽， 陈大东：	老师好！	Hello, Teacher!
刘老师：	同学们好！	Hello, students!

刘老师：	请问，你叫什么名字？	Excuse me, what is your name?
孙玛丽：	我叫孙玛丽。	My name is Sun Mali.
刘老师：	他叫什么名字？	What is his name?
孙玛丽：	他叫陈大东。	His name is Chen Dadong.
刘老师：	玛丽，大东，再见！	Mali, Dadong, goodbye!
孙玛丽， 陈大东：	老师，再见！	Teacher, goodbye!

What Can You Do?

INTERPRETIVE
- I can differentiate between a statement and a question.
- I can differentiate between singular and plural forms.

INTERPERSONAL
- I can exchange basic greetings, farewells, names, and expressions of courtesy.
- I can correctly address people by their Chinese names and titles.

PRESENTATIONAL
- I can present a basic introduction about myself or another person using culturally-appropriate expressions.

LESSON TEXT 1.2

Age and Nationality 你多大？你是哪国人？

Sun Mali meets Teacher Liu again a few days later. Teacher Liu asks Sun Mali about her age and nationality.

刘老师：	玛丽，你多大？	Mǎlì, nǐ duō dà?
孙玛丽：	我十九岁。	Wǒ shíjiǔ suì.
刘老师：	陈大东呢？	Chén Dàdōng ne?
孙玛丽：	他二十岁。	Tā èrshí suì.

刘老师：	你是哪国人？	Nǐ shì nǎ guó rén?
孙玛丽：	我是美国人。	Wǒ shì Měiguó rén.
刘老师：	陈大东是不是美国人？	Chén Dàdōng shì bu shì Měiguó rén?
孙玛丽：	不是，他不是美国人。他是加拿大人。	Bú shì, tā bú shì Měiguó rén. Tā shì Jiā'nádà rén.

字词 VOCABULARY

LESSON VOCABULARY 1.2

	SIMPLIFIED	TRADITIONAL	PINYIN	WORD CATEGORY	DEFINITION
1.	多		duō	*adj, qw*	many; how many
2.	大		dà	*adj*	big; old
3.	十九		shíjiǔ	*nu*	nineteen
4.	岁	歲	suì	*n, mw*	age; years old
5.	二十		èrshí	*nu*	twenty
6.	是		shì	*v*	to be
7.	哪		nǎ, něi	*qw*	which
8.	国	國	guó	*n*	country
9.	人		rén	*n*	person
10.	美国人	美國人	Měiguó rén	*n*	American
11.	美国	美國	Měiguó	*n*	United States
12.	不		bù	*adv*	not; no
13.	加拿大人		Jiā'nádà rén	*n*	Canadian
14.	加拿大		Jiā'nádà	*n*	Canada

REQUIRED VOCABULARY 1.2

NUMBERS

			PINYIN	WORD CATEGORY	DEFINITION
15.	一		yī	*nu*	one
16.	二		èr	*nu*	two
17.	三		sān	*nu*	three
18.	四		sì	*nu*	four
19.	五		wǔ	*nu*	five
20.	六		liù	*nu*	six
21.	七		qī	*nu*	seven
22.	八		bā	*nu*	eight
23.	九		jiǔ	*nu*	nine
24.	十		shí	*nu*	ten

	SIMPLIFIED	TRADITIONAL	PINYIN	WORD CATEGORY	DEFINITION

COUNTRIES AND CONTINENTS

	SIMPLIFIED	TRADITIONAL	PINYIN	WORD CATEGORY	DEFINITION
25.	国家	國家	guójiā	*n*	country
26.	非洲		Fēizhōu	*n*	Africa
27.	澳大利亚	澳大利亞	Àodàlìyà	*n*	Australia
28.	巴西		Bāxī	*n*	Brazil
29.	中国	中國	Zhōngguó	*n*	China
30.	英国	英國	Yīngguó	*n*	Britain; U.K.; England
31.	法国	法國	Fǎguó	*n*	France
32.	德国	德國	Déguó	*n*	Germany
33.	印度		Yìndù	*n*	India
34.	日本		Rìběn	*n*	Japan
35.	韩国	韓國	Hánguó	*n*	Korea
36.	墨西哥		Mòxīgē	*n*	Mexico
37.	俄罗斯	俄羅斯	Éluósī	*n*	Russia
38.	南非		Nánfēi	*n*	South Africa
39.	西班牙		Xībānyá	*n*	Spain
40.	越南		Yuènán	*n*	Vietnam
41.	意大利		Yìdàlì	*n*	Italy

ONLINE RESOURCES

Visit *http://college.betterchinese.com* for a complete list of the names of countries in Chinese.

Pronunciation Notes

不 + 是 → 不 是
bù + shì   bú shì

Tone change rule: By itself, 不 is pronounced with the fourth tone. But when 不 occurs in front of another fourth tone, it is pronounced with a second tone: "bú." Unlike the third tone rule we learned in Lesson 1, this fourth tone change rule is written as well as spoken.

In most cases when the first and third syllables in a phrase are the same, the second syllable is pronounced in the neutral tone.

是 + 不 + 是 → 是 不 是
shì + bú + shì   shì bu shì

Asking Someone's Age

Chinese people have different ways of asking someone his or her age, depending on whether the person is a child or an adult. When asking children their age, one says, "nǐ jǐ suì?" (你几岁?). However, when asking an adult his or her age, one should say, "nǐ duō dà?" (你多大?) or to be more respectful, "nín duō dà?" (您多大?)

Some Chinese speakers, especially those in Taiwan, use "nǐ jǐ suì?" (你几岁?) even for people older than the age of 10, such as teenagers and college students. Most Chinese adults, however, prefer to be asked "nín duō dà?" (您多大?)

Counting

Numbers from 11 – 19: The numbers between 10 and 20 follow a predictable pattern. The number 11 (十一: shíyī) is simply the number 10 (十: shí) followed by the number 1 (一: yī). As you can see, these two numbers add up to 11. The numbers 12 – 19 also follow this pattern.

11 – 19					
十一	shíyī	11	十六	shíliù	16
十二	shíèr	12	十七	shíqī	17
十三	shísān	13	十八	shíbā	18
十四	shísì	14	十九	shíjiǔ	19
十五	shíwǔ	15			

20 – 99		
二十	èrshí	20
二十一	èrshíyī	21
二十九	èrshíjiǔ	29
三十	sānshí	30
九十	jiǔshí	90
九十九	jiǔshíjiǔ	99

Numbers from 20 – 99: The numbers from 20 through 99 also follow a regular pattern. The number 20 (二十: èrshí) is composed of the number two (二: èr) followed by the number 10 (十: shí), literally "two tens." Now that we have a way to say 20, we can make the numbers 21 – 29 using the same pattern as in 11 – 19, by adding the numbers one through nine after 20. To say the number 21 (二十一: èrshíyī), for example, we say the number 20 (二十: èrshí) and then the number 1 (一: yī). The numbers up until the number 99 also follow this pattern.

The Chinese words for numbers are very simple, but it can be tricky to remember where the numbers are placed in relation to the 10. The number 19, for example, is 十九 (shíjiǔ), with the nine following the ten. The number 90 is 九十 (jiǔshí), with the nine coming first.

Chinese Names for Countries

中国 (Zhōngguó: China) means "Middle Kingdom" and reflects the ancient Chinese belief that their homeland was the center of the world. Many country names in Chinese sound similar to their native pronunciation and have meanings that describe the countries in a positive light. For example, 美国 (Měiguó: America) is literally "beautiful country," 英国 (Yīngguó: Britain; England) is "brave country," and 法国 (Fǎguó: France) is "lawful country."

It should be noted that not every country name includes the word 国 (guó: country) in its name. Examples: 日本 (Rìběn: Japan), 澳大利亚 (Àodàlìyà: Australia), 加拿大 (Jiā'nádà: Canada), and 俄罗斯 (Éluósī: Russia, although Russia is sometimes called 俄国). As a general rule, when the name of a country contains two or more characters, 国 is not used, unless it is in a formal (e.g., diplomatic) context.

STRUCTURE NOTE 1.8

Use 多大 to ask about someone's age

The type of question one uses to ask another about his or her age in Chinese varies according to the person's perceived age. As mentioned in Language Note 1.2:

> If the person's perceived age is ≤ ten years, use: 几岁？
> If the person's perceived age is > ten years, use: 多大？

多, in this context, acts as a question word, meaning "how much." So 多大 (duō dà) means "how old?"

Subject + 多大？

From the Lesson Text:

你多大？
Nǐ duō dà?
How old are you?

Other examples:

陈大东多大？　　　　　刘老师多大？
Chén Dàdōng duō dà?　　Liú lǎoshī duō dà?
How old is Chen Dadong?　How old is Teacher Liu?

Practice: Construct questions to ask about the ages of the following subjects.

Example:　你 → 你多大？

1.　他　　　＿＿＿＿＿＿＿＿＿＿＿＿＿＿＿＿＿＿＿
2.　你们　　＿＿＿＿＿＿＿＿＿＿＿＿＿＿＿＿＿＿＿
3.　老师　　＿＿＿＿＿＿＿＿＿＿＿＿＿＿＿＿＿＿＿
4.　孙小姐　＿＿＿＿＿＿＿＿＿＿＿＿＿＿＿＿＿＿＿
5.　陈先生　＿＿＿＿＿＿＿＿＿＿＿＿＿＿＿＿＿＿＿

STRUCTURE NOTE 1.9

Add 岁 after a number to state one's age

岁 (suì) is a unit of measure applied to age, equivalent to "years old." While in English, people sometimes omit the "years old," Chinese statements related to age is usually followed by 岁. It can be omitted in a conversation about one's age. The most common way to describe someone's age is to state the subject followed by their age, excluding the connecting verb, as if to say: "I nineteen years old."

Subject + Number + 岁

From the Lesson Text:

我十九岁。
Wǒ shíjiǔ suì.
I am 19 years old.

Other examples:

他二十岁。　　　　　刘老师三十岁。
Tā èrshí suì.　　　　　Liú lǎoshī sānshí suì.
He is 20 years old.　　Teacher Liu is 30 years old.

Practice: Create statements using the information provided below.

Example: 我 / 十九 → 我十九岁。

1. 他 / 五 _____

2. 她 / 十四 _____

3. 陈太太 / 六十 _____

4. 孙先生 / 七十一 _____

STRUCTURE NOTE 1.10

Use 是 to indicate equivalency

是 (shì) *is an equative verb (as in A=B) meaning "to be" and remains constant regardless of tense and subject. English has many forms of "to be," such as "am," "are," and "is," but Chinese encompasses all these forms in just* 是.

Subject + 是 + Predicate

From the Lesson Text:

我是美国人。
Wǒ shì Měiguó rén.
I am American.

Other examples:

他是加拿大人。
Tā shì Jiā'nádà rén.
He is Canadian.

陈老师是加拿大人。
Chén lǎoshī shì Jiā'nádà rén.
Teacher Chen is Canadian.

Practice: Create sentences using the phrases provided in the boxes below. Refer to the Optional Vocabulary if necessary.

刘太太		加拿大人
他们		老师
我	是	英国人
陈小姐		中国人
你们		墨西哥人

Example: 他们是英国人。

_____

_____

_____

_____

STRUCTURE NOTE 1.11

Use 哪国人 to ask about nationality and country + 人 to state nationality

哪国人 (nǎ guó rén) *is a question phrase used to ask about one's nationality.*

Subject + 是 + 哪国人?

To answer this question, apply the same sentence structure, replacing 哪国 *with the appropriate country and changing the subject if needed.*

Subject + 是 + Country + 人

From the Lesson Text:

你是哪国人？
Nǐ shì nǎ guó rén?
What is your nationality?

我是美国人。
Wǒ shì Měiguó rén.
I am American.

Other examples:

老师是哪国人？
Lǎoshī shì nǎ guó rén?
What is the teacher's nationality?

老师是加拿大人。
Lǎoshī shì Jiā'nádà rén.
The teacher is Canadian.

Practice: Use the given phrases to ask and answer questions about each subject's nationality. Refer to the Optional Vocabulary if necessary.

Example:　你(美国)→ 你是哪国人？我是美国人。

1. 您(韩国)　　　　　_____
2. 你们 (英国)　　　　_____
3. 他们 (德国)　　　　_____
4. 刘老师 (法国)　　　_____
5. 陈小姐 (日本)　　　_____

STRUCTURE NOTE 1.12

Use 不 to negate a verb

不 (bù) *means "no" or "not" and appears in front of most verbs to convert them into their negative form (recall the pronunciation note following the Vocabulary Section 1.2 about tone changes regarding* 不*).*

Subject + 不 + Verb Phrase

From the Lesson Text:

他不是美国人。
Tā bú shì Měiguó rén.
He is not American.

Other examples:

她不是老师。
Tā bú shì lǎoshī.
She is not a teacher.

我不叫陈大东。
Wǒ bú jiào Chén Dàdōng.
I am not called Chen Dadong.

Practice: Create sentences by applying the appropriate verb (叫, 姓, 是) and using the phrases provided below.

她		老师	Example: 他们不是老师。
他们		刘	
我	不 + Verb	美国人	_____
孙女士		加拿大人	_____
老师		孙玛丽	_____

STRUCTURE NOTE 1.13

Use Verb + 不 + Verb to form affirmative-negative questions

In addition to the 吗 pattern covered in Structure Note 1.4, statements with verbs can be transformed into questions by inserting 不 between the repeated verb. For example, a statement including the main verb 是 would transform into the phrase 是不是 (shì bu shì) literally meaning "are you or are you not."

> Subject + Verb + 不 + Verb + Noun Phrase

From the Lesson Text:

陈大东是不是美国人？
Chén Dàdōng shì bu shì Měiguó rén?
Is Chen Dadong American?

Other examples:

他是不是加拿大人？　　他是不是老师？
Tā shì bu shì Jiā'nádà rén?　　Tā shì bu shì lǎoshī?
Is he Canadian?　　Is he a teacher?

Practice: Apply the information provided below to create 是不是 questions. Refer to the Optional Vocabulary if necessary.

Example: 陈大东 / 美国人。 → 陈大东是不是美国人？

1. 刘先生 / 法国人。　_____
2. 你 / 加拿大人。　_____
3. 他 / 韩国人。　_____
4. 他们 / 法国人。　_____

STRUCTURE NOTE 1.14

Use Verb or 不 + Verb to answer affirmative-negative questions

Universal equivalents for "yes" and "no" do not exist in Chinese. Instead, responses repeat the corresponding verb in the question using the affirmative or negative form.

For "yes" replies, either repeat the verb followed by an affirmative statement or simply provide the affirmative statement.

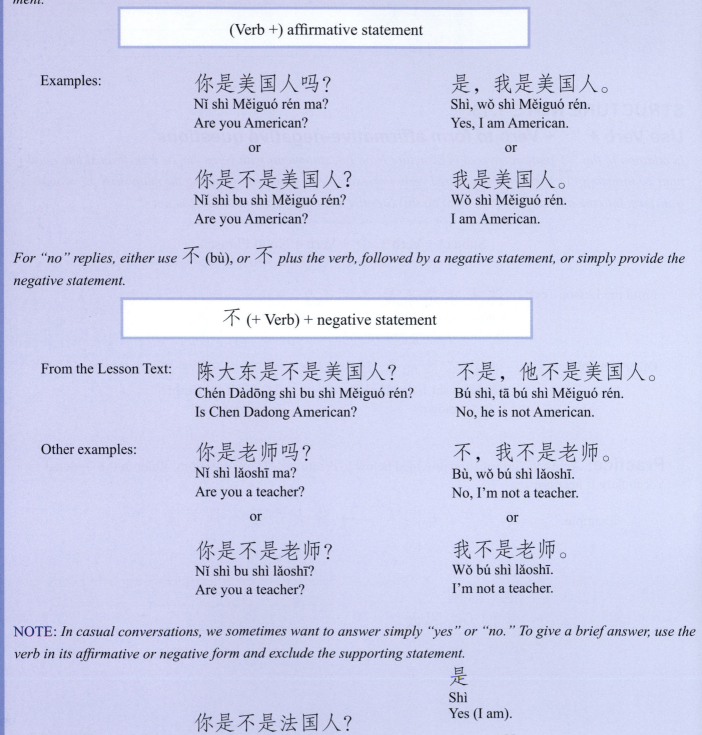

(Verb +) affirmative statement

Examples:

你是美国人吗?
Nǐ shì Měiguó rén ma?
Are you American?

是,我是美国人。
Shì, wǒ shì Měiguó rén.
Yes, I am American.

or

or

你是不是美国人?
Nǐ shì bu shì Měiguó rén?
Are you American?

我是美国人。
Wǒ shì Měiguó rén.
I am American.

For "no" replies, either use 不 (bù), or 不 plus the verb, followed by a negative statement, or simply provide the negative statement.

不 (+ Verb) + negative statement

From the Lesson Text:

陈大东是不是美国人?
Chén Dàdōng shì bu shì Měiguó rén?
Is Chen Dadong American?

不是,他不是美国人。
Bú shì, tā bú shì Měiguó rén.
No, he is not American.

Other examples:

你是老师吗?
Nǐ shì lǎoshī ma?
Are you a teacher?

不,我不是老师。
Bù, wǒ bú shì lǎoshī.
No, I'm not a teacher.

or

or

你是不是老师?
Nǐ shì bu shì lǎoshī?
Are you a teacher?

我不是老师。
Wǒ bú shì lǎoshī.
I'm not a teacher.

NOTE: *In casual conversations, we sometimes want to answer simply "yes" or "no." To give a brief answer, use the verb in its affirmative or negative form and exclude the supporting statement.*

Example:

你是不是法国人?
Nǐ shì bu shì Fǎguórén?
Are you French?

是
Shì
Yes (I am).

or

不是
Bú shì.
No (I am not).

Practice: Provide an answer to each question, using the information provided. Refer to the Optional Vocabulary if necessary.

Example:

你是不是美国人？ (negative) → 不是，我不是美国人。

Provide affirmative responses with supporting statements.

1. 他们是不是美国人？　　　_____

2. 老师是不是加拿大人？　　_____

3. 他是不是中国人？　　　　_____

Provide negative responses with supporting statements.

4. 刘先生是不是法国人？　　_____

5. 玛丽是不是日本人？　　　_____

PRACTICE 1.9

Working in groups of four or five, practice questions and answers pertaining to age and nationality. Write down your group members' responses. Appoint a group leader to introduce the ages and nationalities of everyone in the group.

Example:

A: 你多大？ 你是哪国人？

B: 我十八岁。 我是中国人。

Name	Age	Nationality

PRACTICE 1.10

Ask the other groups affirmative-negative questions pertaining to someone's nationality or age.

Example:

A: _____ 是不是美国人？

B: 不是，她不是美国人。她是中国人。

PRACTICE 1.11

Identify the correct word for each country below (using the Optional Vocabulary if necessary), and practice the dialogue shown in the example given.

Example:

A: 我是中国人。 你呢？你也是中国人吗？

B: 我也是中国人。／不是，我不是中国人。我是加拿大人。

1.

2.

3.

4.

	Radical	Stroke Order
多	夕 xī evening	ノ ク 夕 夕 多 多
大	大 dà big	一 十 大
一	一 yī one	一
二	一 yī one	一 二
三	一 yī one	一 二 三
四	囗 wéi enclosure	｜ 冂 冈 四 四
五	一 yī one	一 丆 五 五
六	八 bā eight	丶 一 六 六
七	一 yī one	一 七
八	八 bā eight	ノ 八
九	ノ piě slash	ノ 九
十	十 shí ten	一 十
岁	山 shān mountain	丨 屮 山 屶 岁 岁
是	日 rì sun	丨 冂 日 日 旦 早 旱 昇 是
人	人 rén person	ノ 人

PRACTICE 1.13

Make an audio recording and send it to your teacher. In the recording, state your age and nationality, and then ask your teacher about his or her nationality.

PRACTICE 1.14

Send e-mails to your teacher and your classmates in Chinese. In the e-mails, include a greeting, your name, age, and nationality.

Example:

老师好。我叫孙玛丽。我十九岁。我是美国人。

PRACTICE 1.15 (Use the Optional Vocabulary if necessary.)

陈大东： 我叫陈大东。我是加拿大人。
　　　　您也是加拿大人吗？

刘老师： 不是，我不是加拿大人。
　　　　我是中国人。

Read the dialogue and answer the following questions.
1. Is Chen Dadong Chinese?
2. Is the teacher the same nationality as Chen Dadong?

PRACTICE 1.16 (Use the Optional Vocabulary if necessary.)

陈大东： 他们是不是英国人？

孙玛丽： 不是，他们不是英国人。
　　　　他们是法国人。

陈大东： 他们多大？

孙玛丽： 刘先生四十二岁。
　　　　刘太太三十八岁。

Read the dialogue and answer the following questions.
1. Are Mr. and Mrs. Liu British?
2. How old is Mr. Liu?

PRACTICE 1.17 (Use the Optional Vocabulary if necessary.)

孙玛丽： 刘老师是哪国人？

陈大东： 刘老师是中国人。

孙玛丽： 她多大？

陈大东： 她三十岁。

Read the dialogue and answer the following questions.
1. What nationality is the teacher?
2. How old is she?

Hand Gestures for Numbers

People from different parts of the world use different hand gestures for counting. Chinese people count the numbers one through ten with a single hand. While numbers one through five are done in the same way as English speakers, the gestures for numbers six through ten differ because they are done on the same hand as well.

The Chinese play various fast-paced games using this method of counting that can be baffling to visitors upon first glance but are a lot of fun once you master the gestures. At a market in China, you can see vendors using these hand signs to indicate to customers how much they are being charged. These gestures are slightly different in different parts of China and Taiwan. The hand signs shown opposite are used mainly in northern Mainland China (including Beijing):

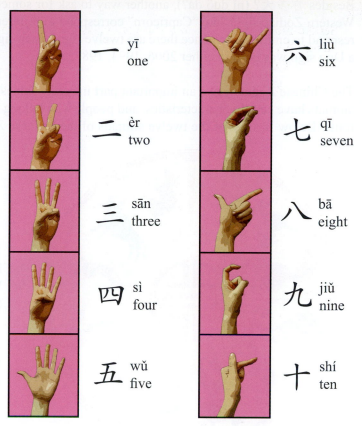

一 yī one	六 liù six
二 èr two	七 qī seven
三 sān three	八 bā eight
四 sì four	九 jiǔ nine
五 wǔ five	十 shí ten

The Symbolism of Numbers

In English-speaking culture, the number 13 is considered unlucky. Similarly, some numbers possess particular connotations in Chinese culture.

Four (四: sì): The Chinese have a great aversion to the number four because its pronunciation, "sì," sounds similar to the pronunciation of the word 死 (sǐ: "to die"). Because of this association with death, some people try to avoid having the number four in their address, phone number, and so on. For this reason, it should not be surprising that some buildings in China do not have a button for the fourth floor in their elevators.

Eight (八: bā): The number eight is considered to be a lucky number in Chinese culture because its pronunciation, "bā," sounds similar to 发 (fā: "prosperous"). In the opposite way to the number four, it is common for Chinese people to actively seek out the number eight for their phone numbers, license plates, and so on. It is believed that the more eights they have listed, the luckier they will be. When the Summer Olympic Games took place in China in 2008, the opening ceremony began at 8 p.m. on August 8, 2008.

Chinese Zodiac

Besides 你多大? (nǐ duō dà?), another way to ask for someone's age is to ask for their Chinese Zodiac sign. While Western Zodiac signs like "Capricorn" correspond to different times of the year, the signs of the Chinese Zodiac correspond to entire years. Since there are twelve signs, each sign has its turn once every twelve years. So, a person with a Dog sign was born in either 2006, 1994, 1982, etc.

The Chinese Zodiac plays an important part in some Chinese people's lives. It is traditionally believed that different animals have certain characteristics, and people who belong to the same Zodiac animal sign share similar personality traits. Below is a list of the twelve animals of the Chinese Zodiac in their typical order, starting clockwise with the Rat.

你属什么？
Nǐ shǔ shénme?
What is your Chinese Zodiac sign?
(literally: What [sign] do you belong to?)

我属龙。
Wǒ shǔ lóng.
I am a dragon (sign).

Zodiac Sign	Traditional	Pinyin	English	Corresponding Years
鼠（老鼠）		shǔ (lǎoshǔ)	Rat	1972, 1984, 1996, 2008
牛		niú	Ox	1973, 1985, 1997, 2009
虎（老虎）		hǔ (lǎohǔ)	Tiger	1974, 1986, 1998, 2010
兔（兔子）		tù (tùzi)	Rabbit	1975, 1987, 1999, 2011
龙	龍	lóng	Dragon	1976, 1988, 2000, 2012
蛇		shé	Snake	1977, 1989, 2001, 2013
马	馬	mǎ	Horse	1978, 1990, 2002, 2014
羊		yáng	Ram	1979, 1991, 2003, 2015
猴（猴子）		hóu (hóuzi)	Monkey	1980, 1992, 2004, 2016
鸡	鶏	jī	Chicken	1981, 1993, 2005, 2017
狗		gǒu	Dog	1982, 1994, 2006, 2018
猪	豬	zhū	Pig	1983, 1995, 2007, 2019

Online Resources

Visit *http://college.betterchinese.com* to learn about the origin of the Chinese Zodiac and the personality traits associated with each animal.

刘老师： 玛丽，你多大？

Mali, how old are you?

孙玛丽： 我十九岁。

I am 19 years old.

刘老师： 陈大东呢？

What about Chen Dadong?

孙玛丽： 他二十岁。

He is 20 years old.

刘老师： 你是哪国人？

What country are you from?

孙玛丽： 我是美国人。

I am American.

刘老师： 陈大东是不是美国人？

Is Chen Dadong American?

孙玛丽： 不是，他不是美国人。
他是加拿大人。

No, he is not American.

He is Canadian.

What Can You Do?

INTERPRETIVE
- I can recognize numbers from 1– 99 as they are said or written.
- I can figure out people's ages based on their Chinese Zodiac signs.
- I can distinguish between different types of affirmative-negative questions.
- I can differentiate between positive and negative statements.

INTERPERSONAL
- I can exchange information about age and nationality with others.

PRESENTATIONAL
- I can present a basic introduction about myself and others covering age and nationality.

ACT IT OUT

Working in groups, compose an original three-minute skit that utilizes the vocabulary and structures introduced in Unit 1. Each of you should assume a role and have a roughly equal number of lines in the skit. Be prepared to perform your skit in class. You can either come up with your own story or choose from one of the following situations:

a) You see some friends at a party on campus after the summer break and are introduced to some new people.

b) On a trip to Chinatown, you make friends with Mandarin-speaking store owners. You also happen to meet a few tourists who can speak Mandarin.

c) You attend a youth conference organized by the United Nations and have an opportunity to meet people from other countries who are also taking elementary Chinese.

CHECK WHAT YOU CAN DO

RECOGNIZE

Adjectives
- ☐ 好
- ☐ 大

Adverbs
- ☐ 很
- ☐ 也
- ☐ 不

Idiomatic Expressions
- ☐ 你好
- ☐ 请问
- ☐ 谢谢
- ☐ 再见

Measure words
- ☐ 岁

Names
- ☐ 孙玛丽
- ☐ 陈大东
- ☐ 刘

Nouns
- ☐ 老师
- ☐ 同学
- ☐ 名字
- ☐ 学校
- ☐ 先生
- ☐ 太太
- ☐ 小姐

- ☐ 女士
- ☐ 国人
- ☐ 美国
- ☐ 加拿大
- ☐ 美国人
- ☐ 加拿大人

Numbers
- ☐ 一二三
- ☐ 四五六

- ☐ 七八九
- ☐ 十
- ☐ 十九
- ☐ 二十

Particles
- ☐ 吗
- ☐ 呢
- ☐ 们

Pronouns
- ☐ 我
- ☐ 你

- ☐ 他
- ☐ 您
- ☐ 她
- ☐ 它

Question Words
- ☐ 什么
- ☐ 多
- ☐ 哪

Verbs
- ☐ 叫
- ☐ 学
- ☐ 姓
- ☐ 是

WRITE

- ☐ 你
- ☐ 好
- ☐ 我
- ☐ 很
- ☐ 也
- ☐ 老师
- ☐ 同学
- ☐ 们
- ☐ 叫
- ☐ 名字
- ☐ 他
- ☐ 见

- ☐ 多大
- ☐ 一二三
- ☐ 四五六
- ☐ 七八
- ☐ 九十
- ☐ 岁
- ☐ 是
- ☐ 人

USE

- ☐ An adjective phrase to describe a subject
- ☐ 们 to convert a pronoun or noun (people only) to its plural form
- ☐ 也 to express "also"
- ☐ 吗 to turn a statement into a question
- ☐ 呢 to ask "What about . . .?"
- ☐ 叫 to state one's name
- ☐ 什么 to ask "what?" questions

- ☐ 多大 to ask about someone's age
- ☐ 岁 after a number to state one's age
- ☐ 是 to indicate equivalency
- ☐ 哪国人 to ask about nationality and country + 人 to state nationality
- ☐ 不 to negate a verb
- ☐ Verb + 不 + Verb to form affirmative-negative questions
- ☐ Verb or 不 + Verb to answer affirmative-negative questions

Family

家

第二单元 UNIT 2

Communication Goals

Lesson 1: 家人和宠物 **Family and Pets**
- Identify family members and ask others about their families
- Ask whether someone has pets
- Ask and answer questions regarding quantity

Lesson 2: 工作和语言 **Jobs and Languages**
- Inquire about someone's occupation
- Ask and answer questions about what languages one can speak

LESSON TEXT 2.1

Family and Pets 家人和宠物

Wang Xiaomei meets Li Zhongping and his family outside of their dorm. Li Zhongping introduces his family members and asks Wang Xiaomei about her family and pets.

李中平： 小美，你好。这是我爸爸、妈妈和哥哥。你家有几个人？

Xiǎoměi, nǐ hǎo. Zhè shì wǒ bàba, māma, hé gēge. Nǐ jiā yǒu jǐ gè rén?

王小美： 我家有五个人：爸爸、妈妈、姐姐、妹妹和我。

Wǒ jiā yǒu wǔ gè rén: bàba, māma, jiějie, mèimei hé wǒ.

李中平： 这是我家的狗。你家有什么宠物？有没有狗？

Zhè shì wǒ jiā de gǒu. Nǐ jiā yǒu shénme chǒngwù? Yǒu méiyǒu gǒu?

王小美： 没有。我家有两只猫。我很喜欢狗，可是我妈妈喜欢猫。

Méiyǒu. Wǒ jiā yǒu liǎng zhī māo. Wǒ hěn xǐhuan gǒu, kěshì wǒ māma xǐhuan māo.

字 词 VOCABULARY

LESSON VOCABULARY 2.1

	SIMPLIFIED	TRADITIONAL	PINYIN	WORD CATEGORY	DEFINITION
1.	这	這	zhè, zhèi	*pr*	this
2.	爸爸		bàba	*n*	father
3.	妈妈	媽媽	māma	*n*	mother
4.	和		hé	*cj*	and, as well as
5.	哥哥		gēge	*n*	elder brother
6.	家		jiā	*n*	family, home
7.	有		yǒu	*v*	to have
8.	几	幾	jǐ	*qw*	how many
9.	个	個	gè	*mw*	(used for most nouns)
10.	姐姐		jiějie	*n*	elder sister
11.	妹妹		mèimei	*n*	younger sister
12.	的		de	*p*	(particle indicating possession)
13.	狗		gǒu	*n*	dog
14.	宠物	寵物	chǒngwù	*n*	pet
15.	没	沒	méi	*adv*	not
16.	可是		kěshì	*cj*	but
17.	两	兩	liǎng	*nu*	two (used before measure words)
18.	只	隻	zhī	*mw*	(used for most mammals and birds)
19.	猫	貓	māo	*n*	cat
20.	喜欢	喜歡	xǐhuan	*av*	to like

NAMES

			PINYIN	WORD CATEGORY	DEFINITION
21.	李中平		Lǐ Zhōngpíng	*name*	Li Zhongping
	李		Lǐ	*surname*	Li
	中平		Zhōngpíng	*given name*	Zhongping
22.	王小美		Wáng Xiǎoměi	*name*	Wang Xiaomei
	王		Wáng	*surname*	Wang

Simplified	Traditional	Pinyin	Word Category	Definition
小美		Xiǎoměi	*given name*	Xiaomei

REQUIRED VOCABULARY 2.1

Measure Words

23.	位		wèi	*mw*	(used formally for people)
24.	条	條	tiáo	*mw*	(used for fish, roads, and other long, thin animals and objects)
25.	口		kǒu	*n, mw*	mouth; (measure word for people)

Family Members

26.	家人		jiārén	*n*	family members
27.	兄弟姐妹		xiōngdì jiěmèi	*n*	siblings
28.	弟弟		dìdi	*n*	younger brother
29.	父亲	父親	fùqīn	*n*	father (formal)
30.	母亲	母親	mǔqīn	*n*	mother (formal)
31.	女儿	女兒	nǚér	*n*	daughter
32.	儿子	兒子	érzi	*n*	son
33.	孩子		háizi	*n*	child; children

OPTIONAL VOCABULARY 2.1

Animals

34.	鸟	鳥	niǎo	*n*	bird
35.	鱼	魚	yú	*n*	fish

Pronunciation Notes

Three pronunciations of 一: yī, yí or yì.

The number 1, 一, is pronounced differently depending on the tones that follow it.

When used in counting, 一 is pronounced "yī." However, if a fourth tone or a neutral tone character follows it, 一 is now pronounced "yí." Otherwise, it is pronounced "yì."

有一个人。
Yǒu yí gè rén.
There is one person.

我家有一只狗。
Wǒ jiā yǒu yì zhī gǒu.
I have a dog at home.

Chinese Titles of Family Members

In Chinese there are many more descriptive terms for family members than there are in English. In fact, your relationship to any member of the family can be immediately determined by what you call him or her. This concept can be tricky, but such specific titles reflect the importance that Chinese people place on familial relationships. Note also that different Chinese speaking regions use different terms, and that even within one region, multiple terms that differ in formality can be used to refer to the same individual.

Father's Side
父

Title	Pinyin	Meaning
爷爷	yéye	Grandfather
奶奶	nǎinai	Grandmother
伯伯	bóbo	Elder uncle
叔叔	shūshu	Younger uncle
姑姑	gūgu	Aunt
表/堂哥*	biǎo/tánggē	Elder male cousin
表/堂姐*	biǎo/tángjiě	Elder female cousin
表/堂弟*	biǎo/tángdì	Younger male cousin
表/堂妹*	biǎo/tángmèi	Younger female cousin

* Use 堂 only for cousins with the same surname as you

Mother's Side
母

Title	Pinyin	Meaning
外公	wàigōng	Grandfather
外婆	wàipó	Grandmother
舅舅	jiùjiu	Uncle (both elder and younger)
阿姨	āyí	Aunt (both elder and younger)
表哥	biǎogē	Elder male cousin
表姐	biǎojiě	Elder female cousin
表弟	biǎodì	Younger male cousin
表妹	biǎomèi	Younger female cousin

ONLINE RESOURCES

Visit *http://college.betterchinese.com* to learn more titles for relatives in a Chinese family.

STRUCTURE NOTE 2.1
Use 有 to express possession

有 (yǒu) means "has" or "to have." In this lesson, 有 is used to describe how many people are in a family. While an English speaker would say, "There are four people in my family," a Chinese speaker would say, "My family has four people." Unlike English, Chinese verbs are not conjugated, so "have" and "has" are both expressed by 有.

Subject + 有 + Noun Phrase

From the Lesson Text:

我家有五个人。
Wǒ jiā yǒu wǔ gè rén.
There are five people in my family.

Other examples:

老师家有八个人。
Lǎoshī jiā yǒu bā gè rén
There are eight people in the teacher's family.

他有两只猫。
Tā yǒu liǎng zhī māo.
He has two cats.

Practice: Create sentences by applying the appropriate verb and using the information provided below.

他家		四个人
她们家		三只狗
老师家	有	五只猫
你		两个姐姐
王小美		一个哥哥

Example: 他家有四个人。

_____

_____

_____

_____

STRUCTURE NOTE 2.2

Use 没有 to express "not have"

As discussed in Structure Note 1.14, most verbs are negated using 不. To negate the verb 有, a special adverb, 没 (méi), is applied before 有. Like 不 + verb, 没有 can be used to respond negatively to a question involving 有.

Subject + 没有 + Noun Phrase

From the Lesson Text:

没有。我家有两只猫。
Méiyǒu. Wǒ jiā yǒu liǎng zhī māo.
No (I do not have). My family has two cats.

Other examples:

他家没有狗。
Tā jiā méiyǒu gǒu.
His family doesn't have a dog.

我没有弟弟。
Wǒ méiyǒu dìdi.
I do not have a younger brother.

Practice: Answer each question using the structure 没有.

Example: 你家有猫吗？ → 没有，可是我家有狗。

1. 他家有狗吗？ _____
2. 王老师家有猫吗？ _____
3. 王先生有妹妹吗？ _____
4. 李太太家有宠物吗？ _____
5. 陈大东家有猫吗？ _____

STRUCTURE NOTE 2.3

Use 有没有 to form a "have or not have" question

Recall from Structure Note 1.13, affirmative-negative questions are formed using the pattern Verb + 不 + Verb. When constructing a 'have or not have' question, 没 replaces 不, as in 有没有.

> Subject + 有没有 + Noun Phrase?

From the Lesson Text:
你家有什么宠物？有没有狗？
Nǐ jiā yǒu shénme chǒngwù? Yǒu méiyǒu gǒu?
What pets do you have at home? Do you have a dog?

Other examples:
他有没有猫？　　　　　你有没有兄弟姐妹？
Tā yǒu méiyǒu māo?　　　Nǐ yǒu méiyǒu xiōngdì jiěmèi?
Does he have a cat?　　　Do you have siblings?

NOTE: *Another way to form a Yes-No question involving* 有 *is to use the particle* 吗.

Example:
你家有猫吗？
Nǐ jiā yǒu māo ma?
Do you have cats at home?

To casually answer "yes" or "no," use 有 *or* 没有 *without the optional supporting statement.*

Example:
你家有宠物吗？　　　　　有。
Nǐ jiā yǒu chǒngwù ma?　　Yǒu.
Do you have pets at home?　Yes (I have).

or　　　　　　　　　　　　or

你家有没有宠物？　　　　没有。
Nǐ jiā yǒu méiyǒu chǒngwù?　Méiyǒu.
Do you have pets at home?　No (I do not have).

Practice: Use the information provided below to create 有没有 questions.

Example: 他家／猫 → 他家有没有猫？
1.   陈大东家／宠物   _____
2.   她／妹妹   _____
3.   他／兄弟姐妹   _____
4.   王太太家／猫   _____
5.   小美／姐姐   _____

STRUCTURE NOTE 2.4
Use 有什么 to ask what one has

In this lesson, the verb 有 is used with 什么 to form a "what" question.

$$\text{Subject} + 有 + 什么 + \text{Noun?}$$

From the Lesson Text: 你家有什么宠物？
                               Nǐ jiā yǒu shénme chǒngwù?
                               What pets do you have at home?

Other examples: 你家有什么人？   老师有什么宠物？
                       Nǐ jiā yǒu shénme rén?   Lǎoshī yǒu shénme chǒngwù?
                       What people are in your family?   What pets does the teacher have?

NOTE: *When using a question phrase such as* 什么*,* 几*, or* 哪国人*, it is incorrect to add the question particle* 吗 *at the end because these phrases already imply questions. As a rule, only use* 吗 *for affirmative-negative questions.*

Practice: Create questions using 有什么 and the information provided below.

小美的家		人	Example: 他家有什么人？
你同学的家	有什么	狗	_____
你们家		猫	_____
他家		宠物	_____

STRUCTURE NOTE 2.5
Use 的 to indicate possession

的 (de) *is a particle that has several uses. In this lesson,* 的 *is used between a noun or pronoun and another noun to indicate a possessive relationship. For nouns,* 的 *functions similar to " 's " in English. For instance, "Teacher Wang's home" translates to* 王老师的家*. Unlike English, Chinese does not have special possessive pronouns like "my," so* 的 *also appears after pronouns to indicate possessive relationships. For example, "my classmate" is translated as* 我的同学*.*

Noun / Pronoun + 的 + Noun

From the Lesson Text: 这是我家的狗。

Zhè shì wǒ jiā de gǒu.

This is my family's dog.

Other examples:

他的名字

Tā de míngzi

His name

王先生的弟弟

Wáng Xiānsheng de dìdi

Mr. Wang's younger brother

NOTE: 的 *is usually omitted when using pronoun phrases to describe close family members or personal relationships and is therefore commonly omitted with nouns like* 家, *as in* 我家有三个人. *Similarly,* 我的 爸爸 *is normally stated as* 我爸爸 *because of the implied proximity of the relationship. Note, however, that this rule does not apply to all pronouns. For example, it is incorrect to say* *我们爸爸.

Even if the relationship between the two nouns is close, the 的 *cannot be omitted when describing a possession belonging to a noun. For example, the* 的 *in* 王老师的爸爸 *must be present because* 王老师 *is a noun and not a pronoun.*

Practice: Insert 的 to create phrases indicating possession, using the information provided below.

Example: 你 / 哥哥 → 你的哥哥

1. 他 / 老师 _____
2. 你们家 / 狗 _____
3. 李中平 / 爸爸 _____
4. 王小美 / 妈妈 _____
5. 刘老师 / 妹妹 _____

STRUCTURE NOTE 2.6
Use number + measure word to quantify a noun

Similar to how English uses measure words, like "piece" or "cup" (as in "a cup of water"), Chinese nouns are typically quantified using a special grammatical classifier, or "measure word," which must be placed between the number and the noun.

Number + Measure Word + Noun

From the Lesson Text: 我家有两只猫。

Wǒ jiā yǒu liǎng zhī māo.

My family has two cats.

Other examples:

她有三个妹妹。 我家有一只狗。
Tā yǒu sān gè mèimei. Wǒ jiā yǒu yì zhī gǒu.
She has three younger sisters. My family has a dog.

In Chinese, 一 is used in place of indefinite articles found in English like "a" or "an," as in "a dog." In the example above, one says 我家有一只狗 rather than 我家有一狗, where 只 is inserted as the measure word. However, when talking about a noun more generally or hypothetically, 一 and the associated measure word are omitted, as in 我家有狗, equivalent to "my family has dogs." Note that when talking about two of a particular noun, 两 (liǎng) replaces 二, as seen from the Lesson Text example above: 我家有两只猫. 二 is only used when talking about the number two in the abstract.

Measure words are categorized and assigned according to characteristics of the associated nouns. Below are some common measure words and their corresponding nouns:

Measure Word	Used For	Example Nouns
只 (zhī)	most mammals and birds	dogs, cats, birds
条 (tiáo)	long, flexible things	fish, roads, pants
位 (wèi)	people (polite form)	teachers, doctors
口 (kǒu)	people	people

In addition to the list above, 个 (gè) is considered a default measure word and can be attached to many nouns. For example, the measure word used for family members is 个, as in 一个哥哥.

NOTE: Different dialects and regions apply varying measure words for some nouns. For example, some people say 一条狗 rather than 一只狗. Similarly, some may prefer to ask 你家有几口人？ instead of 你家有几个人？

Practice: Create short phrases by selecting the appropriate measure word(s) to accompany the provided nouns and respective quantities (numbers noted in parentheses).

Measure Word	Noun (Quantity)
个	狗 (3)
位	兄弟姐妹 (5)
只	猫 (1)
条	同学 (20)
	先生 (1)
	老师 (2)

Example: 三只狗

_____

_____

_____

_____

STRUCTURE NOTE 2.7

Use 几 + measure word to ask how many and number + measure word to answer

几 (jǐ) *is used to ask "how many" and can be answered by simply replacing the question word,* 几, *with a number.* 几 *is generally used when the expected amount is less than 10.*

> Subject + Verb + 几 + Measure Word + Noun?

From the Lesson Text:	你家有几个人？ Nǐ jiā yǒu jǐ gè rén? How many people are in your family?	我家有五个人：爸爸、妈妈、姐姐、妹妹和我。 Wǒ jiā yǒu wǔ gè rén: bàba, māma, jiějie, mèimei hé wǒ. I have five people in my family: father, mother, elder sister, younger sister, and me.
Other example:	她家有几只宠物？ Tā jiā yǒu jǐ zhī chǒngwù? How many pets does her family have?	她家有五只宠物：两只猫和三只狗。 Tā jiā yǒu wǔ zhī chǒngwù: liǎng zhī māo hé sān zhī gǒu. Her family has five pets: two cats and three dogs.

Practice: Create question and answer pairs by applying the appropriate measure word to accompany the provided nouns and respective quantities (numbers noted in parentheses).

Noun (Quantity)

Example: 他家 / 人 (4)　　　你家有几个人？　我家有四个人。

　　　她家 / 狗 (3)

　　　老师家 / 人 (6)　　_____　_____

　　　小美家 / 宠物 (2)

　　　你家 / 姐姐 (1)　　_____　_____

　　　中平家 / 人 (4)　　_____　_____

PRACTICE 2.1

Fill in your details in the space provided below. Then, working with a partner, ask how many people there are in your partner's family and fill in her his or her details.

Example:

A: 你家有几个人？

B: 我家有四个人：爸爸、妈妈、哥哥和我。你家呢？

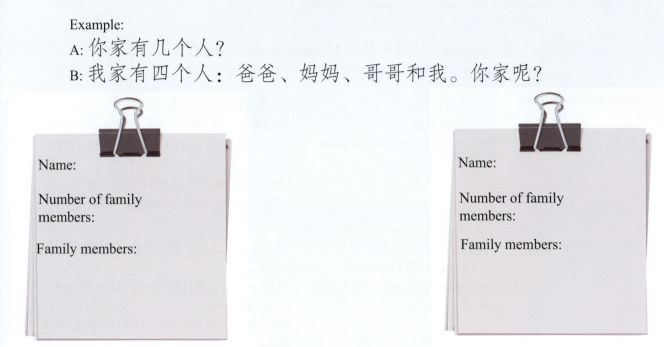

Name:

Number of family members:

Family members:

Name:

Number of family members:

Family members:

PRACTICE 2.2

Working with a partner, ask and answer questions about siblings. Introduce your siblings by telling your partner their names and ages.

Example:

A: 你有没有兄弟姐妹？

B: 有。我有一个弟弟。他叫李中平。他二十岁。

PRACTICE 2.3

Practice the above conversation using the information provided below.

1. 姐姐 / 二十六岁

2. 哥哥 / 三十岁

3. 弟弟 / 五岁

4. 姐姐 / 十九岁
妹妹 / 十四岁

5. 哥哥 / 二十八岁
弟弟 / 九岁

PRACTICE 2.4

Draw your family tree with Chinese titles. Put names of family members under their appropriate Chinese titles. Expand your tree by referring to the Language Notes section for the titles of family members.

PRACTICE 2.5

Using the dialogue pattern below, take a survey of the class to determine what the most common pet among your classmates is. Record your answers in the table below.

Example:

A: 你家有没有宠物？

B: 有。

A: 有什么宠物？

B: 我家有猫。

A: 有几只猫？

B: 有两只猫。

Pet	Number

	Radical	Stroke Order
这	辶 chuò walk	丶 ㇐ 亠 文 ì文 这 这
爸	父 fù father	丿 八 丷 父 爷 爷 爸 爸
妈	女 nǚ woman	乚 乆 女 妈 妈 妈
和	口 kǒu mouth	丿 二 千 禾 禾 禾 和 和
家	宀 mián roof	丶 丷 宀 宀 宇 宇 家 家 家
有	月 yuè moon	一 ナ 才 有 有 有
几	几 jī table	丿 几
个	人 rén person	丿 人 个
的	白 bái white	丿 亻 白 白 白 的 的 的
宠	宀 mián roof	丶 丷 宀 宀 宇 宠 宠 宠
物	牛 niú cow	丿 ㇇ 牛 牛 牪 物 物 物
没	氵(水) shuǐ water	丶 冫 氵 氵 沪 沪 没
可	口 kǒu mouth	一 ㇀ 丆 口 可
两	一 yī one	一 ㇀ 冂 丙 丙 两 两
只	口 kǒu mouth	丶 丷 口 口 尸 只

🗨️ **PRACTICE 2.7**

Make an audio recording and send it to your teacher. In the recording, talk about how many people there are in your family and who they are. In addition, say if you own any pets. If you do, say what kind of and how many pets you have.

PRACTICE 2.8

Send e-mails to your teacher and your classmates in Chinese. In the e-mails, include an introduction to your family members and any pets you may have.

Example: 我家有四个人：爸爸、妈妈、哥哥和我。我爸爸五十岁。我妈妈四十岁。我弟弟十岁。我家有两只猫。我们很喜欢猫。

PRACTICE 2.9

李中平：陈老师家有几个人？

王小美：陈老师家有五个人：爸爸、妈妈、哥哥、姐姐和她。

李中平：她家有没有宠物？

王小美：有。她家有一只猫和两只狗。

Provide details about Teacher Chen's family and pets in the space below.
Number of family members:
Family members:
Animals:

PRACTICE 2.10

孙玛丽：陈大东，你家有没有宠物？

陈大东：没有，我不喜欢宠物。你家呢？

孙玛丽：我家有很多宠物。

陈大东：有什么宠物？

孙玛丽：有三只狗和四只猫。

Read the dialogue and answer the following questions.
1. Does Chen Dadong keep pets at home?
2. What kind of and how many pets does Sun Mali have?

Evolution of the Traditional Chinese Family

In traditional Chinese society, many people's ideal household was a large family with many grandchildren. The structure of a traditional Chinese family was much like a pyramid and typically spanned four generations, all of which would live in the same household with the younger generations subservient to the older generations. In modern China, with the advent of the one-child policy, the configuration of the Chinese family has undergone major changes. There are now two pairs of grandparents looking after one grandchild in a reverse-pyramid structure. Being at the center of the family, the child is often referred to as 小皇帝 (xiǎo huángdì: "little emperor") or 小公主 (xiǎo gōngzhǔ: "little princess"). In recent years, local regulations regarding the one-child policy have eased somewhat. For instance, if both parents are single children themselves, then they are allowed to have a second child.

Pets in Chinese Culture

Traditionally, imperial gentry households kept fish, turtles, and birds as pets. Goldfish in particular have long been popular as they symbolize wealth in Chinese culture. More recently, dogs and cats have increased in popularity, especially among people living in cities.

Many Chinese people also "walk birds" as a hobby. This is an age-old custom that is still around today. If you visit a park or a wooded area in Beijing in the early morning, you will see people, mostly elderly, leisurely strolling around holding bird cages or carrying poles on their shoulders with bird cages hanging at both ends. Many older people enjoy gathering together to show one another their birds and chat about their bird-raising experiences and current events.

Giant Pandas

The most famous of all of China's animals is the giant panda. Giant pandas are native to the mountainous regions of western China and have been in existence for 2 – 3 million years. Pandas are one of China's national treasures and have been presented to many countries around the world as a symbol of peace and friendship.

At present, there are only about 1000 – 2000 pandas in the world, almost all living within the borders of China. The Chinese government has taken many measures to protect these endangered animals. The three provinces of Sichuan, Gansu, and Shanxi have formed a joint natural habitat for pandas, while the government has also stipulated in its Constitution that pandas be treated as rare and protected animals. When the Olympic Games took place in China in 2008, the giant panda was chosen as one of the five mascots, representing the animal's important symbolic role in Chinese culture.

李中平： 小美，你好。这是我爸爸、妈妈和哥哥。你家有几个人？

Hello Xiaomei. This is my dad, mom and older brother. How many people are there in your family?

王小美： 我家有五个人：爸爸、妈妈、姐姐、妹妹和我。

There are five people in my family: my dad, mom, elder sister, younger sister, and me.

李中平： 这是我家的狗。你家有什么宠物？有没有狗？

This is my family's dog. What pets do you have at home? Do you have a dog?

王小美： 没有。我家有两只猫。我很喜欢狗，可是我妈妈喜欢猫。

No. I have two cats at home. I like dogs, but my mom likes cats.

What Can You Do?

INTERPRETIVE
- I can understand the specific titles for family members.
- I can understand who is in a person's family tree.
- I can understand expressions that indicate possession.

INTERPERSONAL
- I can exchange information about families, pets, and quantities with others.

PRESENTATIONAL
- I can present a basic introduction about my family and pets using culturally-appropriate expressions.

工作和语言
Jobs and Languages

LESSON TEXT 2.2

Jobs and Languages　工作和语言

Li Zhongping and Wang Xiaomei walk back to the dorms. Li Zhongping invites Wang Xiaomei to visit his room and they talk about Chen Dadong.

王小美：	这个男孩是谁？	Zhèige nánhái shì shéi?
李中平：	他是我的朋友陈大东。那个女孩是他妹妹。	Tā shì wǒ de péngyou Chén Dàdōng. Nèige nǚhái shì tā mèimei.
王小美：	他做什么工作？	Tā zuò shénme gōngzuò?
李中平：	他是学生，也是咖啡店的服务员。	Tā shì xuéshēng, yě shì kāfēi diàn de fúwùyuán.

王小美：	他会说什么语言？	Tā huì shuō shénme yǔyán?
李中平：	他会说英语、法语，还会说一点儿汉语。	Tā huì shuō Yīngyǔ, Fǎyǔ, hái huì shuō yì diǎnr Hànyǔ.
王小美：	他会不会写汉字？	Tā huì bu huì xiě Hànzì?
李中平：	他只会写简单的汉字。	Tā zhǐ huì xiě jiǎndān de Hànzì.

LESSON VOCABULARY 2.2

	SIMPLIFIED	TRADITIONAL	PINYIN	WORD CATEGORY	DEFINITION
1.	男孩（子）		nánhái(zi)	*n*	boy
	男		nán	*n*	male
2.	谁	誰	shéi	*qw*	who
3.	那		nà, nèi	*pr*	that
4.	朋友		péngyou	*n*	friend
5.	女孩（子）		nǔhái(zi)	*n*	girl
	女		nǔ	*n*	female
6.	做		zuò	*v*	to do
7.	工作		gōngzuò	*n, v*	work, job; to work
8.	学生	學生	xuéshēng	*n*	student
9.	咖啡店		kāfēi diàn	*n*	coffee shop
	咖啡		kāfēi	*n*	coffee
	店		diàn	*n*	shop, store
10.	服务员	服務員	fúwùyuán	*n*	waiter, server
11.	会	會	huì	*av*	to know how; can
12.	说	說	shuō	*v*	to speak
13.	语言	語言	yǔyán	*n*	language
14.	英语	英語	yīngyǔ	*n*	English language (spoken)
15.	法语	法語	fǎyǔ	*n*	French language (spoken)
16.	还	還	hái	*adv*	also
17.	一点（儿）	一點（兒）	yì diǎn(r)	*n*	a little, some (see Pronunciation Notes)
18.	汉语	漢語	hànyǔ	*n*	Chinese language (spoken)
19.	写	寫	xiě	*v*	write
20.	只		zhǐ	*adv*	only, just
21.	简单	簡單	jiǎndān	*adj*	simple
22.	汉字	漢字	hànzì	*n*	Chinese characters

	SIMPLIFIED	TRADITIONAL	PINYIN	WORD CATEGORY	DEFINITION
OCCUPATIONS					
23.	商人		shāngrén	n	businessman
24.	大学生	大學生	dàxuéshēng	n	college student
	大学	大學	dàxué	n	college, university
25.	教授		jiàoshòu	n	professor
26.	律师	律師	lǜshī	n	lawyer
LANGUAGES					
27.	中文		Zhōngwén	n	Chinese language
	文		wén	n	written language; culture

OPTIONAL VOCABULARY 2.2

	SIMPLIFIED	TRADITIONAL	PINYIN	WORD CATEGORY	DEFINITION
LANGUAGES					
28.	英文		Yīngwén	n	English language (written)
29.	法文		Fǎwén	n	French language (written)
30.	西班牙语	西班牙語	Xībānyáyǔ	n	Spanish language (spoken)
31.	日语	日語	Rìyǔ	n	Japanese language (spoken)
CHINESE DIALECTS					
32.	普通话	普通話	Pǔtōnghuà	n	Mandarin
33.	广东话	廣東話	Guǎngdōng huà	n	Cantonese
34.	上海话	上海話	Shànghǎi huà	n	Shanghainese
35.	台湾话	臺灣話	Táiwān huà	n	Taiwanese

Pronunciation Notes

一点 ＋ 儿 → 一点儿
yì diǎn ＋ ér   yì diǎnr

The suffix 儿 (r)
In some regions of China, especially in Beijing, the suffix 儿 (r) is attached to the end of some finals. This causes a change in the pronunciation of the original finals, but the meaning and usage of the words are still the same.

The Difference between 语 (yǔ) and 文 (wén)

语 (yǔ) specifies spoken language while 文 (wén) means written language. In colloquial Chinese, this line has become blurred: for instance, 中文 (Zhōngwén) is used to refer to both spoken and written Chinese.

In mainland China, Mandarin is also referred to as 汉语 (Hànyǔ) or 普通话 (Pǔtōnghuà), while Chinese communities outside mainland China refer to it as 华语 (Huáyǔ) or 国语 (Guóyǔ).

Studying Chinese as a Foreign Language

People all over the world are now studying Chinese. As our global community expands, more people around the world are becoming interested in learning Chinese language and culture. Students studying Chinese range from preschoolers to professionals to senior citizens and come from a variety of backgrounds.

It is very common in China, especially in Beijing, to meet students from various countries studying Chinese language and culture at universities. It is not unusual to see people from countries as different as Nigeria and Korea talking to each other in Chinese.

Other Spoken Chinese Dialects

Wu (吴语: Wúyǔ)

After Mandarin, the second most spoken dialect family in China is Wu, with an estimated 90 million speakers in China. Wu is spoken in the city of Shanghai as well as in the provinces of Zhejiang and Jiangsu. 上海话 (Shànghǎi huà: Shanghainese), which literally means "Shanghai talk," is regarded as the most notable representative of all the Wu dialects.

Cantonese (粤语: Yuèyǔ)

The third most spoken Chinese dialect is Cantonese, with an estimated 71 million speakers, mainly in Guangdong province and the Guangxi region of China as well as in Hong Kong, Macau, Southeast Asia, Australia, the United Kingdom, Canada, and the United States. Cantonese is commonly known as 广东话 (Guǎngdōng huà), which literally means "Guangdong talk."

Historically, the majority of overseas Chinese emigrated from the provinces of Guangdong and Fujian. As a result, there are many Cantonese speakers in Chinatowns all around the world.

Min Nan (闽南语: Mǐnnányǔ)

The Southern Min dialect family includes the dialects spoken in the southern province of Fujian (called 福建话 Fújiàn huà) and in Taiwan (called 台湾话 Táiwān huà). This dialect has an estimated 49 million speakers total. Along with Mandarin, Taiwanese (sometimes called Hokkien in English) is a major language of Taiwan and can be seen on television programs and other media there.

ONLINE RESOURCES

Visit *http://college.betterchinese.com* for a list of the Chinese words for other languages as well as occupations.

STRUCTURE NOTE 2.8

Use 这 or 那 to express "this" or "that"

这 (zhè, zhèi) and 那 (nà, nèi) are demonstratives; 这 means "this" and 那 means "that." Measure words and corresponding nouns can be inserted after 这/那 to create an expanded subject phrase, emphasizing the object being described. In Northern China, when 这 and 那 precede a measure word, they are conventionally pronounced as zhèi and nèi.

> 这 / 那 (+ Number) + Measure Word + Noun

From the Lesson Text:

那个女孩是他的妹妹。
Nèige nǚhái shì tā de mèimei.
That girl is his younger sister.

Other examples:

这两个男孩是你的同学吗？
Zhè liǎng gè nánhái shì nǐ de tóngxué ma?
Are these two boys your classmates?

那位女士是我的教授。
Nèi wèi nǚshì shì wǒ de jiàoshòu.
That lady is my professor.

这 and 那 can also be used like "this" or "that" as pronouns that replace entire noun phrases, as in "this is my friend."

> 这 / 那 + 是 + Noun Phrase

Other examples:

这是你弟弟吗？
Zhè shì nǐ dìdi ma?
Is this your younger brother?

那是我的老师。
Nà shì wǒ de lǎoshī.
That is my teacher.

Practice: Create questions or sentences using each of the noun phrases provided below.

Subject		Noun Phrase	Example: 那是陈大东吗？
这个人		陈大东	_____
这		商人	_____
那个服务员	是	他的朋友	_____
那		她的妹妹	_____
那位先生		我的狗	_____

STRUCTURE NOTE 2.9
Use 谁 to ask "who?"

谁 (shéi) means "who" or "whom." Similar to the possessive pronoun 他的, 谁 can also be combined with 的 to form the question phrase, "whose." To answer a question regarding possession, apply either the expanded or abridged pattern introduced in Structure Note 2.8 and replace 谁 with the appropriate noun phrase.

Subject + 是 + 谁？

From the Lesson Text:

这个男孩是谁？
Zhège nánhái shì shéi?
Who is this boy?

他是我的朋友陈大东。
Tā shì wǒ de péngyou Chén Dàdōng.
He is my friend Chen Dadong.

Other examples:

那个人是谁？
Nèige rén shì shéi?
Who is that person?

那是谁？
Nà shì shéi?
Who is that?

Practice: Construct questions in Chinese using the information provided below.

Example: 他 → 他是谁？

1. 这 _____
2. 那 _____
3. 他们 _____
4. 那位先生 _____
5. 你的老师 _____

STRUCTURE NOTE 2.10
Use 还 to express "also"

还 means "also," "in addition," or "as well as." It is inserted before the last item in a list of verb phrases, as in "我会说汉语，还会说英语。" Remember that 还 must always be followed by a verb — when making a list of nouns, 还 can only be used when followed by the verb 有, as in "我会说汉语、英语还有法语。"

Verb Phrase + 、 + Verb Phrase ... + 还 + Verb Phrase

From the Lesson Text:

他会说英语、法语，还会说一点儿汉语。
Tā huì shuō Yīngyǔ, Fǎyǔ, hái huì shuō yì diǎnr Hànyǔ.
He can speak English, French, and also a little bit of Chinese.

Other example:

我家有三个人：爸爸、妈妈，还有我。
Wǒ jiā yǒu sān gè rén: bàba, māma, háiyǒu wǒ.
There are three people in my family: my dad, my mom, and me.

NOTE: For lists, Chinese uses the enumeration or listing comma (顿号: dùnhào): 、. It is only used when separating elements in a list that are not marked by 还 or any other conjunctions. In other situations, the regular comma (逗号: dòuhào) is used.

Practice: Create sentences using the provided lists and 还有.

Example: Chinese, French, Japanese → 汉语、法语，还有日语

1. One elder brother, one younger brother, one younger sister

   _____

2. Chinese people, American people, Canadian people

   _____

3. Businessmen, professors, lawyers, teachers, students

   _____

STRUCTURE NOTE 2.11
Use 会 to state what one knows how to do

会 (huì) *is equivalent to the English "know how to" or "can" and functions as an auxiliary verb to state one's abil-ity to perform an action.*

Subject + 会 + Verb Phrase

From the Lesson Text: 他会说英语、法语，还会说一点儿汉语。
Tā huì shuō Yīngyǔ, Fǎyǔ, hái huì shuō yì diǎnr Hànyǔ.
He can speak English, French, and also a little bit of Chinese.

Other examples: 我会说法语。   我不会写法文。
Wǒ huì shuō Fǎyǔ.   Wǒ bú huì xiě Fǎwén.
I can speak French.   I cannot write in French.

Practice: Choose the appropriate verb (说, 写) to construct sentences, using the information below.

我们		汉语
他的爸爸	会	英语
我的律师	不会	法语
你		汉字
她的老师		英文

Example: 我们会说汉语。

_____

_____

_____

_____

STRUCTURE NOTE 2.12
Use 会不会 to ask whether or not one knows how to do something

The Verb 不 *Verb pattern* 会不会 *(huì bu huì) can be used when asking if someone knows how to do something.*

Subject + 会不会 + Verb Phrase?

From the Lesson Text: 他会不会写汉字?

Tā huì bu huì xiě Hànzì?

Can he write Chinese characters?

In sentences that utilize 会 *(huì),* use 会 *(huì) to answer "yes" and* 不会 *(bú huì) to answer "no."*

Examples: 你的同学会不会说英语?   会。

Nǐ de tóngxué huì bu huì shuō Yīngyǔ?   Huì.

Can your classmate speak English?   Yes.

你会不会写法文?   不会。

Nǐ huì bu huì xiě Fǎwén?   Bú huì.

Can you write in French?   No.

Practice: Construct questions using 会不会 and the information provided.

Example: 他 / 写汉字 → 他会不会写汉字?

1. 我 / 说英语   _____
2. 他们 / 说法语   _____
3. 老师 / 说中文   _____
4. 王小姐 / 写英文   _____
5. 李先生 / 写汉字   _____

STRUCTURE NOTE 2.13

Use 只 *to express "only"*

只 *(zhǐ) is placed between the subject and the verb to express the meaning "only."*

Subject + 只 + Verb Phrase

From the Lesson Text: 他只会写简单的汉字。

Tā zhǐ huì xiě jiǎndān de Hànzì.

He can only write simple Chinese.

Other examples: 她只有一只狗。   我只有一个哥哥。

Tā zhǐ yǒu yì zhī gǒu.   Wǒ zhǐ yǒu yí gè gēge.

She only has a dog.   I only have an elder brother.

Practice: Create sentences by adding 只 and the appropriate verb(s) to the phrases below.

Example: 我家 / 三个人 → 我家只有三个人。

1. 他家 / 两个人   _____
2. 你 / 一个弟弟   _____
3. 玛丽 / 一只猫   _____
4. 李太太 / 汉字   _____
5. 王老师 / 法语   _____

PRACTICE 2.11

Bring a picture of your family to class. Working with a partner, select people from your partner's picture and ask who they are, what their occupations are, and what languages they can speak. Respond to your partner's questions as well.

Example:

A: 那个女孩是谁？

B: 那是我的妹妹。

A: 她做什么工作？

B: 她是学生。

A: 她会说什么语言？

B: 她会说英语。

PRACTICE 2.12

Working in groups of four or five, practice asking someone what languages they can speak and write and record the information in the chart below. Practice answering these questions as well. Appoint a group leader to present to the rest of the class the different languages everyone in the group can speak and write.

Example:

A: 你会说什么语言？

B: 我会说英语和汉语。

C: 你会不会写汉字？

D: 我只会一点儿。你们呢？

Name	Spoken Language(s)	Written Langauge(s)

PRACTICE 2.13

Take a survey of the class to determine what language is most commonly studied among your classmates. Record the most popular answer below.

Language	Number of Students

PRACTICE 2.14

Match the information provided with the pictures below. Describe each person's details on the card that corresponds to the image.

Example: 他是我爸爸。他五十一岁。他是商人。他会说英语和日语。

爸爸	十八岁	老师	英语
姐姐	二十五岁	律师	法语
妈妈	四十七岁	服务员	中文
弟弟	五十一岁	商人	日语

PRACTICE 2.15

	Radical	Stroke Order
孩	子 zǐ child	フ 了 子 孑 孑 孖 孩 孩 孩
子	子 zǐ child	フ 了 子
谁	讠(言) yán speech	丶 讠 讠 讠 讠 讠 讠 谁 谁
做	亻(人) rén person	ノ 亻 亻 什 什 估 估 做 做 做
作	亻(人) rén person	ノ 亻 亻 亻 亻 作 作
言	言 yán speech	丶 二 亠 言 言 言 言
生	生 shēng life	ノ 亻 牛 牛 生
员	口 kǒu mouth	丶 口 口 尸 员 员 员
会	人 rén person	ノ 人 人 会 会 会
中	丨 gǔn line	丶 口 口 中
英	⺿ (草) cǎo grass	一 十 艹 艹 苁 苹 英 英
文	文 wén script	丶 二 亠 文
还	辶 chuò walk	一 丆 不 不 不 还 还
点	灬 (火) huǒ fire	丨 卜 上 占 占 占 点 点
那	阝 (邑) yì city	刀 刁 刃 那 那 那

PRACTICE 2.16

Make an audio recording and send it to your teacher. In the recording, include an introduction to your family members, along with information about their jobs and the languages they can speak and write.

PRACTICE 2.17

Send e-mails to your teacher and your classmates in Chinese. In the e-mails, introduce a family member. Indicate what his or her job is, and what languages he or she can speak and write.

Example:

我爸爸是律师。他会说英语。他也会说中文，可是他不会写汉字。

PRACTICE 2.18

王小美：你爸爸做什么工作？
李中平：他是老师。你爸爸呢？
王小美：我爸爸是商人。

Read the dialogue and answer the following questions.
1. What does Wang Xiaomei's father do?
2. What does Li Zhongping's father do?

PRACTICE 2.19

我的中文老师是刘老师。她六十岁。她是语言教授。她只会说一点儿法语。她会写汉字和英文。

Read the passage and answer the following questions.
1. How old is the teacher?
2. Which languages does she know how to write?

PRACTICE 2.20

孙玛丽：那个男孩是谁？
王小美：那是我的同学。他叫李中平。
孙玛丽：他是美国人吗？
王小美：是，他是美国人，
　　　　可是他也会说中文。

Read the dialogue and answer the following questions.
1. What is the name of Wang Xiaomei's classmate?
2. Which language does he know how to speak?

The Classification of Professions

In China it is customary to divide professions into four broad categories, a system of classification that dates back as far as the Zhou Dynasty (1045 – 256 BC). Similar to European feudalism, there was traditionally a hierarchical ranking of these occupations, with one's social status dependant on which class one belonged to. Below is a brief decsription of each of the class categories.

Shì

The landed gentry class (士) were first renowned for their skills on the battlefield but this gave way over time to intellectual pursuits with the advent of philosophical schools of thought. They made up the ruling class and served the emperors by performing administrative and military duties.

Nóng

The agricultural class (农) in ancient China was regarded socially as being second only to the scholar class. Since agriculture was essential for sustaining the growth of ancient Chinese society, farmers were respected for their abilities to cultivate the land and produce food.

Gōng

The artisan class (工) was also deemed important in ancient China. This class was composed of skilled laborers, such as carpenters and architects, who produced essential goods. Often, the skills were passed on from generation to generation within the same family, from father to son. As their businesses grew, highly skilled and successful artisans would build trade guilds and take on apprentices.

Shāng

The merchant class (商), which was composed of merchants such as traders and bankers, assumed the lowest rank of the four occupations. Although they also benefited society by bringing vital goods and services to the public, they were often depicted as greedy and as having lower intellectual and moral aspirations than other classes.

王小美：	这个男孩是谁？	Who is this guy?
李中平：	他是我的朋友陈大东。那个女孩是他妹妹。	He's my friend Chen Dadong. That girl is his younger sister.
王小美：	他做什么工作？	What kind of work does he do?
李中平：	他是学生，也是咖啡店的服务员。	He is a student, and he also works as a waiter at a coffee shop.

王小美：	他会说什么语言？	What languages can he speak?
李中平：	他会说英语、法语，还会说一点儿汉语。	He can speak English, French, and also a little bit of Chinese.
王小美：	他会不会写汉字？	Can he write Chinese characters?
李中平：	他只会写简单的汉字。	He can only write simple Chinese.

What Can You Do?

INTERPRETIVE
- I can understand different terms for occupations and languages.
- I can understand different types of affirmative-negative questions.

INTERPERSONAL
- I can exchange information about occupations and language abilities with others.
- I can inquire about someone's identity and provide my own when asked.

PRESENTATIONAL
- I can present a basic introduction about my or another's occupation and language abilities.

ACT IT OUT

Working in groups, compose an original three-minute skit that utilizes the vocabulary and structures introduced in Unit 2. Each of you should assume a role and have a roughly equal number of lines in the skit. Be prepared to perform your skit in class. You can either come up with your own story or choose from one of the following situations:

a) You visit a Chinese friend's home and meet the friend's family.

b) You interview for a job that requires knowledge of several languages.

c) Your family cannot decide what pet to get, so you take a vote of what each member wants.

CHECK WHAT YOU CAN DO

RECOGNIZE

Adjective
- □ 简单

Adverbs
- □ 没
- □ 只
- □ 还

Auxiliary Verbs
- □ 喜欢
- □ 会

Conjunctions
- □ 和
- □ 可是

Measure Words
- □ 个
- □ 只
- □ 位
- □ 条
- □ 口

Names
- □ 李中平
- □ 王小美

Nouns
- □ 家
- □ 家人
- □ 爸爸
- □ 妈妈
- □ 哥哥
- □ 姐姐
- □ 妹妹
- □ 狗
- □ 宠物
- □ 猫
- □ 兄弟姐妹
- □ 弟弟
- □ 父亲
- □ 母亲
- □ 女儿
- □ 儿子
- □ 孩子
- □ 男孩
- □ 朋友
- □ 女孩
- □ 工作
- □ 语言
- □ 学生
- □ 咖啡店
- □ 服务员
- □ 英语
- □ 法语
- □ 汉字
- □ 一点(儿)
- □ 汉语
- □ 商人
- □ 大学生
- □ 教授
- □ 律师
- □ 中文

Number
- □ 两

Particle
- □ 的

Pronouns
- □ 这
- □ 那

Question Words
- □ 几
- □ 谁

Verbs
- □ 有
- □ 做
- □ 工作
- □ 说
- □ 写

WRITE
- □ 这
- □ 爸
- □ 妈
- □ 和
- □ 家
- □ 有
- □ 几
- □ 个
- □ 的
- □ 宠
- □ 物
- □ 没
- □ 可
- □ 两
- □ 只
- □ 孩
- □ 子
- □ 谁
- □ 做
- □ 作
- □ 言
- □ 生
- □ 员
- □ 会
- □ 中
- □ 英
- □ 文
- □ 还
- □ 点
- □ 那

USE
- □ 有 to express possession
- □ 没有 to express "not have"
- □ 有没有 to form a "have or not have" question
- □ 有什么 to ask what one has
- □ 的 to indicate possession
- □ Number + measure word to quantify a noun
- □ 几 + measure word to ask how many and number + measure word to answer
- □ 这 or 那 to express "this" or "that"
- □ 谁 to ask "who?"
- □ 还 to express "also"
- □ 会 to state what one knows how to do
- □ 会不会 to ask whether or not one knows how to do something
- □ 只 to express "only"

时

Time

第三单元
UNIT 3

Communication Goals

Lesson 1: 星期几？几点？ **Days of the Week and Time**
- State and ask the time
- Talk about future events
- Make appointments
- Apologize for tardiness

Lesson 2: 生日快乐！ **Happy Birthday!**
- Ask and answer questions about days of the week and months
- State and ask for the date
- Wish someone "happy birthday" and offer gifts

LESSON TEXT 3.1

Days of the Week and Time　星期几？几点？

Chen Dadong, Sun Mali, and Huang Xiang'an decide to go to a soccer game. Once at the stadium, Dadong and Xiang'an wait for Mali.

黄祥安：	这个星期有足球比赛，你会去看吗？	Zhèige xīngqī yǒu zúqiú bǐsài, nǐ huì qù kàn ma?
陈大东：	星期几？什么时候？	Xīngqī jǐ? Shénme shíhou?
黄祥安：	星期三晚上六点半。	Xīngqīsān wǎnshang liù diǎn bàn.
陈大东：	好，我去。玛丽，你呢？	Hǎo, wǒ qù. Mǎlì, nǐ ne?
孙玛丽：	我也会去。我们六点见吧。	Wǒ yě huì qù. Wǒmen liù diǎn jiàn ba.

黄祥安：	现在几点？玛丽还没有来！	Xiànzài jǐ diǎn? Mǎlì hái méiyǒu lái!
陈大东：	现在差不多六点一刻。	Xiànzài chàbuduō liù diǎn yí kè.
孙玛丽：	对不起！	Duìbuqǐ!
陈大东	没关系，比赛还没开始呢！	Méi guānxi, bǐsài hái méi kāishǐ ne!
黄祥安：	我们走吧。	Wǒmen zǒu ba.

字 词 VOCABULARY

LESSON VOCABULARY 3.1

	SIMPLIFIED	TRADITIONAL	PINYIN	WORD CATEGORY	DEFINITION
1.	星期		xīngqī	n	week
2.	足球		zúqiú	n	soccer
3.	比赛	比賽	bǐsài	n	match; competition
4.	去		qù	v	to go
5.	看		kàn	v	to look at; to see; to read
6.	星期几	星期幾	xīngqī jǐ	qph	what day is it?
7.	什么时候	什麼時候	shénme shíhou	qph	when?
	时候	時候	shíhou	n	time
8.	星期三		Xīngqīsān	n	Wednesday
9.	晚上		wǎnshang	n	night; p.m.
	晚		wǎn	adj	late
10.	点（钟）	點（鐘）	diǎn (zhōng)	n	o'clock (hour unit of time)
11.	半		bàn	n	half
12.	见	見	jiàn	v	to meet, to see
13.	吧		ba	p	(indicates suggestion)
14.	现在	現在	xiànzài	n	now
15.	还没（有）	還沒（有）	hái méi (yǒu)	adv	not yet, still have not
	还	還	hái	adv	still
16.	来	來	lái	v	to come
17.	差不多		chàbuduō	adv, adj	almost; about; around
18.	刻		kè	n	quarter of an hour
19.	对不起	對不起	duìbuqǐ	ie	sorry
20.	没关系	沒關係	méi guānxi	ie	it's ok; it doesn't matter
21.	开始	開始	kāishǐ	v, n	to begin; beginning
22.	走		zǒu	v	to go; to leave

NAMES

	SIMPLIFIED	TRADITIONAL	PINYIN	WORD CATEGORY	DEFINITION
23.	黄祥安	黃祥安	Huáng Xiáng'ān	name	Huang Xiang'an
	黄	黃	Huáng	surname	Huang

Simplified	Traditional	Pinyin	Word Catgory	Definition
祥安		Xiáng'ān	*given name*	Xiang'an

REQUIRED VOCABULARY 3.1

Time

	Simplified	Traditional	Pinyin	Word Catgory	Definition
24.	分		fēn	*n*	minute
25.	秒		miǎo	*n*	second
26.	早上		zǎoshang	*n*	early morning; a.m.
	早		zǎo	*adj*	early
27.	上午		shàngwǔ	*n*	morning
28.	中午		zhōngwǔ	*n*	noon, midday
29.	下午		xiàwǔ	*n*	afternoon; p.m.
30.	小时	小時	xiǎoshí	*n*	hour
31.	钟头	鐘頭	zhōngtóu	*n*	hour (colloquial)
32.	时间	時間	shíjiān	*n*	time
33.	零		líng	*nu*	zero

OPTIONAL VOCABULARY 3.1

Common Expressions

	Simplified	Traditional	Pinyin	Word Catgory	Definition
34.	不好意思		bù hǎoyìsi	*ie*	sorry; excuse me (when used for minor inconveniences)
35.	没(有)问题	沒(有)問題	méi (yǒu) wèntí	*ie*	no problem
36.	没事	沒事	méi shì	*ie*	no problem; not a bother
37.	不客气	不客氣	bú kèqi	*ie*	you're welcome

Sports

	Simplified	Traditional	Pinyin	Word Catgory	Definition
38.	篮球	籃球	lánqiú	*n*	basketball
39.	橄榄球	橄欖球	gǎnlǎnqiú	*n*	rugby; football (American)
40.	棒球		bàngqiú	*n*	baseball

Days of the Week

Chinese has several words for week: 星期 (xīngqī) is the most common. Words for Monday through Saturday are formed using 星期 followed by numbers one to six, starting with Monday (星期一). Sunday can be called 星期日 (Xīngqī rì) (more formal) or 星期天 (Xīngqī tiān) (more casual).

Day of the Week	Pinyin	English
星期一	Xīngqīyī	Monday
星期二	Xīngqīèr	Tuesday
星期三	Xīngqīsān	Wednesday
星期四	Xīngqīsì	Thursday
星期五	Xīngqīwǔ	Friday
星期六	Xīngqīliù	Saturday
星期天（日）	Xīngqītiān (rì)	Sunday

Stating the Time

The basic format for expressing a time in Chinese is to use 点 to mark the hour, and 分 to mark the minutes. 5:30, for example, would be 五点三十分.

To specify a.m. or p.m., add 上午 or 下午 before the time: 5:00 p.m.下午五点.

Just as in English, where 5:30 can be expressed as "half-past five" or "five thirty," there are a number of alternate ways to express the same time in Chinese. The table below presents these options and how they are used.

Unit	Definition	Usage
点(钟)	hour	times that are exactly on the hour can optionally end with 钟: 5:00 五点 or 五点钟
半	half	added after the hour to express half-hours: 5:30 五点半 (same as 五点三十分)
一刻	15 minutes	indicates quarters: 5:15 五点一刻 (same as, 五点十五分)
三刻	45 minutes	three quarters, 45 minutes: 5:45 五点三刻 (same as, 五点四十五分)
分	minute	this unit is optional in casual speech when it follows a two-character minute: 5:20 五点二十分 or 五点二十. Minutes below 10 can be expressed with a preceding 0 or on their own: 12:01 十二点零一(分) or 十二点一分.

Note: most speakers prefer to use 两点 rather than 二点 when talking about times that start with two. Two's that do not come at the beginning of a time, however, are always 二, so 3:02 would be 三点零二(分).

语法

STRUCTURE NOTE 3.1

Use 会 to indicate the possibility of an action taking place in the future

In Structure Note 2.11, 会 (huì) was introduced to express one's ability to do something. 会 can also be used to denote an action that will occur in the future. This is similar to the use of "will" in English, as in, "I will go." Note, however, that unlike the use of "will" in English, 会 is not necessarily required to refer to future actions in Chinese.

> Subject + 会 + Verb

From the Lesson Text:

你会去看吗？
Nǐ huì qù kàn ma?
Are you going to see it?

Other examples:

你会去咖啡店吗？
Nǐ huì qù kāfēi diàn ma?
Will you go to the coffee shop?

会，大东也会去咖啡店。
Huì, Dàdōng yě huì qù kāfēi diàn.
Yes (I will go), Dadong will also go to the coffee shop.

Practice: Transform the sentences below using 会, following the given example.

Example: 我去中国。→ 我会去中国。
1. 他去看足球比赛。 _____
2. 我们星期天去加拿大吗？ _____
3. 你七点去看足球比赛吗？ _____
4. 你什么时候来？ _____
5. 老师星期三不去中国吗？ _____

STRUCTURE NOTE 3.2

Use 什么时候 to ask "when"

In Chinese, time phrases precede the verb phrase. Usually, time expressions such as 什么时候 (shénme shíhou) appear between the subject and the verb phrase. When the subject is clear, the subject can be dropped, resulting in a more colloquial "when" phrase.

> Subject + 什么时候 + Verb Phrase?

From the Lesson Text:

什么时候？
Shénme shíhou?
When? (What time?)

Other examples:

你什么时候去看足球比赛？
Nǐ shénme shíhou qù kàn zúqiú bǐsài?
When will you go to the soccer game?

我三点半去。
Wǒ sān diǎn bàn qù.
I'm going at 3:30.

什么时候去咖啡店？　　　　　　　星期四。
Shénme shíhou qù kāfēi diàn?　　　　Xīngqī sì.
When will (you) go to the coffee shop?　　(I am going to the coffee shop on)
　　　　　　　　　　　　　　　　　　Thursday.

Practice: Create questions including 什么时候 and the information provided.

Example:　　去法国 → 你什么时候去法国？

1.　来　　　　　　_____

2.　去中国　　　　_____

3.　开始　　　　　_____

4.　来美国　　　　_____

5.　去看足球比赛　_____

STRUCTURE NOTE 3.3

Use 星期几 *to ask "what day of the week" and* 星期 *+ number to state the day of the week*

To ask the day of the week, use the question phrase 星期几 (xīngqī jǐ).

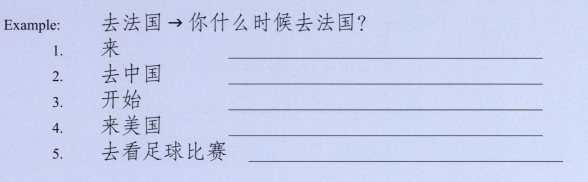

星期几？

To state the day of the week, replace 几 *with the appropriate number.*

星期 + Number

From the Lesson Text:　　星期几？　　　　　　星期三晚上六点半。
　　　　　　　　　　　　Xīngqī jǐ?　　　　　　Xīngqīsān wǎnshang liù diǎn bàn.
　　　　　　　　　　　　What day is it?　　　　Wednesday evening at 6:30.

Other examples:　　　　你星期几走？　　　　我星期六走。
　　　　　　　　　　　　Nǐ xīngqī jǐ zǒu?　　　Wǒ Xīngqīliù zǒu.
　　　　　　　　　　　　What day of the week will you leave?　I will leave on Saturday.

　　　　　　　　　　　　你星期几去加拿大？　　我星期五去加拿大。
　　　　　　　　　　　　Nǐ xīngqī jǐ qù Jiā'nádà?　Wǒ Xīngqīwǔ qù Jiā'nádà.
　　　　　　　　　　　　What day of the week will you go to　I will go to Canada on Friday.
　　　　　　　　　　　　Canada?

Practice: Rewrite the sentences below in Chinese.

Example: What day of the week is he going to America? → 他星期几去美国？

1. What day of the week are you going to Canada?

   _____

2. Teacher Chen is leaving for China on Tuesday.

   _____

3. What day of the week is the soccer match?

   _____

4. The match starts on Saturday morning at 11 a.m.

   _____

5. On Sunday, my father will come to America.

   _____

STRUCTURE NOTE 3.4

Use 几点 *to discuss time*

几点 (jǐ diǎn) *is a question phrase used to ask what time something is happening. It is used in a manner similar to* 什么时候 *but is a specific request for the time.* 几点 *appears after the subject phrase and before the verb phrase.*

> Subject + 几点 + Verb

To answer, replace 几点 *with the actual time, as in* 下午五点半 *(see Language Notes for details on stating time).*

> Subject + Time + Verb

From the Lesson Text:

现在几点？
Xiànzài jǐ diǎn?
What time is it now?

现在差不多六点一刻。
Xiànzài chàbuduō liù diǎn yí kè.
It's about 6:15 (right now).

Other examples:

比赛几点开始？
Bǐsài jǐ diǎn kāishǐ?
What time does the game start?

比赛四点开始。
Bǐsài sì diǎn kāishǐ.
The game starts at 4.

请问，现在几点？
Qǐngwèn, xiànzài jǐ diǎn?
Excuse me, what time is it?

现在三点二十三分。
Xiànzài sān diǎn èr shí sān fēn.
It's 3:23 (right now).

Practice: 现在几点？ Answer the question using the times provided below.

Example: 6:20 p.m. → 现在下午六点二十分。

1. 8:45 a.m. _____
2. 11:00 p.m. _____
3. 12:02 a.m. _____
4. 3:30 p.m. _____
5. 7:53 a.m. _____

STRUCTURE NOTE 3.5

Use 差不多 to express "almost"

差不多 (chàbuduō) *literally means "the difference is not great." It is a phrase used to indicate an approximation or rough estimate, as in* 差不多八个人, *"around eight people." However, when used with ages and times of day, as it is in this lesson,* 差不多 *means "almost."*

$$差不多 + Number$$

From the Lesson Text: 现在差不多六点一刻。
Xiànzài chàbuduō liù diǎn yí kè.
It's about 6:15 (right now).

Other examples: 陈大东差不多二十岁。　现在差不多七点半。
Chén Dàdōng chàbuduō èr shí suì.　Xiànzài chàbuduō qī diǎn bàn.
Chen Dadong is almost 20 years old.　It's almost 7:30 now.

Practice: Transform the sentences below using 差不多, following the example provided.

Example: 孙玛丽十九岁。 → 孙玛丽差不多十九岁。

1. 我妈妈五十岁。 _____
2. 我妹妹八岁。 _____
3. 现在九点一刻。 _____
4. 现在八点半。 _____
5. 现在三点十四分。 _____

STRUCTURE NOTE 3.6
Use 还没(有) to express "not yet" or "still have not"

When 还 is used with 没有, it means the action has not yet occurred but is anticipated. The 有 in 没有 is optional and may be omitted. 还没有 appears before the verb.

Subject + 还没（有）+ Verb

From the Lesson Text:

比赛还没开始呢！
Bǐsài hái méi kāishǐ ne!
The game hasn't started yet!

Other examples:

你还没有去美国吗？
Nǐ hái méi yǒu qù Měiguó ma?
You haven't gone to America yet?
(implies "Why are you still here?")

大东还没来咖啡店。
Dàdōng hái méi lái kāfēi diàn.
Dadong has not arrived at the coffee shop yet.

Practice: Create questions or sentences using the given words and 还没(有).

陈老师		去美国	Example: 他还没有去美国。
我姐姐		开始	_____
他	还没有	去学校	_____
我们		去加拿大	_____
比赛		去咖啡店	

STRUCTURE NOTE 3.7
Use 吧 to make a suggestion

吧 (ba) is a sentence-final particle that turns a statement into a suggestion and/or lightens the tone of the statement. The 吧 construction can be loosely translated as "let us . . .," "shall we . .," or "how about . . ." and is used in colloquial speech.

Sentence + 吧

From the Lesson Text:

我们走吧。
Wǒmen zǒu ba.
Let's go.

我们六点见吧。
Wǒmen liù diǎn jiàn ba.
Let's meet at 6:00.

Other examples:

我们开始吧。
Wǒmen kāishǐ ba.
Shall we begin?

同学们，我们说汉语吧。
Tóngxuémen, wǒmen shuō Hànyǔ ba.
Classmates, how about we speak Chinese?

Practice: Create sentences by inserting the correct verb and 吧.

我们	英语
你	中国
你们	足球比赛
同学们	咖啡店
妹妹你	学校的比赛

吧

Example: 我们说英语吧。

_____

_____

_____

_____

PRACTICE 3.1

Working with a partner, ask for the time, then ask when a sports game will start. You should base your dialogue on the images below. Refer to the chart in the Language Notes for more information on descriptions related to time.

Example:

A: 现在几点？

B: 现在差不多六点一刻。

A: 比赛几点开始？

B: 比赛七点开始。

A: 比赛差不多开始了，我们走吧。 / 没关系，比赛还没开始。

PRACTICE 3.2

With a partner, ask about the day of the week and time for the following events. Write the name of each sport beneath the pictures below. Refer to the Optional Vocabulary if necessary.

Example:

A: 足球比赛是星期几？几点开始？

B: 足球比赛星期日下午三点半开始。

星期/时间	日	一	二	三	四	五	六
11:00		棒球 (bàngqiú) 比赛					网球 (wǎngqiú) 比赛
15:30	足球 比赛			橄榄球 (gǎnlǎnqiú) 比赛			
20:45						篮球 (lánqiú) 比赛	

1.

3.

5.

2.

4.

PRACTICE 3.3

Given the choice, which match would you go to see? Ask your classmates and record the most popular result below.

Most Popular Sport	Number of Students

	Radical	Stroke Order
什	亻(人) rén person	丿 亻 仁 什
么	丿 piě slash	丿 厶 么
星	日 rì sun	丶 冂 冂 日 旦 旦 晃 星 星
期	月 yuè moon	一 十 艹 艹 甘 其 其 其 期 期 期 期
时	日 rì sun	丨 冂 日 日 旷 时 时
上	一 yī one	丨 卜 上
钟	钅(金) jīn gold	丿 钅 钅 钅 钅 钅 钊 钊 钟
半	丶 diǎn dot	丶 丷 丷 芈 半
在	土 tǔ earth	一 ナ 才 右 在 在
来	一 yī one	一 冖 冖 平 来 来
去	厶 sī private	一 十 土 去 去
对	寸 cùn inch	丁 又 又 对 对
起	走 zǒu walk	一 十 土 丰 丰 走 走 起 起 起
开	廾 gǒng hands joined	一 二 开 开
始	女 nǚ woman	乚 乆 女 妒 妒 姶 始 始

💻 **PRACTICE 3.5**

Type the following sentences on your computer and provide answers to the questions.

1. 现在下午两点一刻。

2. 现在几点?

3. 这个星期的足球比赛是什么时候?

PRACTICE 3.6

Make an audio recording and send it to your teacher. In the recording, invite your friends to watch a sports game. Include the date and time of the event.

PRACTICE 3.7

黄祥安：你会去看星期三的足球比赛吗？

陈大东：比赛几点开始？

黄祥安：比赛下午三点半开始。

陈大东：我会去。

Read the dialogue and answer the following questions.
1. On what day and at what time is the soccer match?
2. Will Chen Dadong go to watch the match?

PRACTICE 3.8

孙玛丽：现在几点？

陈大东：现在两点五十八分。

孙玛丽：比赛四点开始。

陈大东：好，我们走吧。

Read the dialogue and answer the following questions.
1. What time is now?
2. What time will the match begin?

PRACTICE 3.9

李中平：现在几点？

陈大东：现在三点五十分。

李中平：孙玛丽还没有来。

孙玛丽：对不起！

陈大东：没关系。

黄祥安：我们走吧。

Read the dialogue and answer the following questions.
1. Who is late?
2. How did Chen Dadong respond to Sun Mali's apology?

The Chinese Calendar

While people in China use the Western Gregorian calendar in their everyday lives, there is also a traditional Chinese calendar that follows the phases of the moon and the sun. This calendar is referred to as 农历 (nónglì: "the agricultural calendar") or 旧历 (jiùlì: "the old calendar"). The Chinese calendar uses the lunar cycles not only to indicate the length of the month but also to denote seasonal festivals or holidays, hence why Chinese New Year falls on a different date each year.

The calendar contains a number of seasonal markers, originally included in order to help farmers to make decisions about planting crops. Nowadays, these seasonal markers often denote a time for celebration. For example, 冬至 (Dōngzhì: "Winter Solstice") is a time for family members to get together and eat dumplings or balls of glutinous rice called 汤圆 (tāngyuán), which symbolize reunion. As this time of year is usually cold, it is also traditional to eat hot pot (meats and vegetables simmered in a clay pot) to ward off the chills from the winter season.

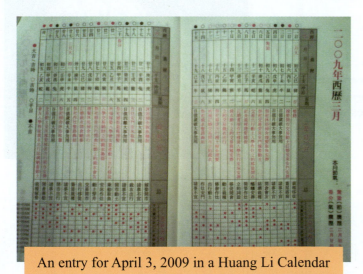

An entry for April 3, 2009 in a Huang Li Calendar

Auspicious Dates

For many Chinese people, auspicious and inauspicious dates play an important role in organizing events. This system of what one should (or should not) do on certain days is dictated by another specific calendar known as 黄历 (Huánglì: "the Imperial Calendar").

The first Imperial Calendar was printed in the Tang Dynasty over 1000 years ago and continues to be produced today. It contains a record of solar and lunar cycles and uses astrology to predict auspicious dates. Thus, the almanac can be consulted for the best day to hold a wedding, banquet, or any other large event. To give an example, the entry for January 1st, 2008 in the Imperial Calendar states:

"DO: Tame the cattle.
DON'T: Move into a new house, break ground for construction or graves."

黄祥安：	这个星期有足球比赛，你会去看吗？	There is a soccer game this week; are you going to go see it?
陈大东：	星期几？什么时候？	What day is it? And what time?
黄祥安：	星期三晚上六点半。	Wednesday evening at 6:30.
陈大东：	好，我去。玛丽，你呢？	OK, I'll go. Mali, how about you?
孙玛丽：	我也会去。我们六点见吧。	I'll go too. Let's meet at 6:00.

黄祥安：	现在几点？玛丽还没有来！	What time is it now? Mali's still not here!
陈大东：	现在差不多六点一刻。	It's about 6:15.
孙玛丽：	对不起！	I'm sorry!
陈大东：	没关系，比赛还没开始呢！	That's OK. The game hasn't started yet!
黄祥安：	我们走吧。	Let's go.

What Can You Do?

INTERPRETIVE
- I can understand and distinguish the time.
- I can understand and interpret information about the date, time or day of an appointment.

INTERPERSONAL
- I can exchange information about the time or day related to an appointment.
- I can make appointments and invite people to events.

PRESENTATIONAL
- I can present an invitation to others, giving the time and day of the event.

LESSON TEXT 3.2

Happy Birthday! 生日快乐!

Li Zhongping and Wang Xiaomei are studying in the library when Sun Mali walks by. Zhongping asks Xiaomei about Mali's birthday, and Xiaomei tells him there is a birthday party for Mali tomorrow. The next day, Mali arrives at her dorm to find a surprise party.

李中平:	玛丽的生日是几月几号？是今天还是明天？	Mǎlì de shēngrì shì jǐ yuè jǐ hào? Shì jīntiān háishì míngtiān?
王小美:	是明天。她的生日是十月三号。	Shì míngtiān. Tā de shēngrì shì Shíyuè sān hào.
李中平:	是吗？有生日派对吗？	Shì ma? Yǒu shēngrì pàiduì ma?
王小美:	有！明天下午玛丽家有派对。	Yǒu! Míngtiān xiàwǔ Mǎlì jiā yǒu pàiduì.

大家:	玛丽，生日快乐！	Mǎlì, shēngrì kuàilè!
孙玛丽:	你们都来了！我真高兴！	Nǐmen dōu lái le! Wǒ zhēn gāoxìng!
王小美:	大家吃蛋糕吧！	Dàjiā chī dàngāo ba!
李中平:	这是我送你的生日礼物，祝你生日快乐！	Zhè shì wǒ sòng nǐ de shēngrì lǐwù, zhù nǐ shēngrì kuàilè!
孙玛丽:	谢谢你！	Xièxie nǐ!

LESSON VOCABULARY 3.2

	SIMPLIFIED	TRADITIONAL	PINYIN	WORD CATEGORY	DEFINITION
1.	生日		shēngrì	*n*	birthday
2.	月		yuè	*n*	month
3.	号	號	hào	*n*	day; number
4.	今天		jīntiān	*n*	today
	今		jīn	*n*	today; now
	天		tiān	*n*	day; sky; heaven
5.	还是	還是	háishì	*cj*	or
6.	明天		míngtiān	*n*	tomorrow
7.	十月		Shíyuè	*n*	October
8.	生日派对	生日派對	shēngrì pàiduì	*n*	birthday party
	派对	派對	pàiduì	*n*	party
9	生日快乐	生日快樂	shēngrì kuàilè	*ie*	happy birthday
	快乐	快樂	kuàilè	*adj, n*	happy; happiness
10.	都		dōu	*adv*	both; all
11.	了		le	*p*	(indicates change of state or action completion)
12.	真		zhēn	*adv*	really, truly
13.	高兴	高興	gāoxìng	*adj*	pleased; happy
14.	大家		dàjiā	*pr*	everyone
15.	吃		chī	*v*	to eat
16.	蛋糕		dàngāo	*n*	cake
17.	送		sòng	*v*	to give (as a gift)
18.	礼物	禮物	lǐwù	*n*	present
19.	祝		zhù	*v*	to wish

REQUIRED VOCABULARY 3.2

Simplified	Traditional	Pinyin	Word Cateogry	Definition
Days of the week				
20. 日		rì	*n*	day
Year				
21. 年		nián	*n*	year
Day relative to today				
22. 昨天		zuótiān	*n*	yesterday
Months				
23. 一月		Yīyuè	*n*	January
24. 二月		Èryuè	*n*	February
25. 三月		Sānyuè	*n*	March
26. 四月		Sìyuè	*n*	April
27. 五月		Wǔyuè	*n*	May
28. 六月		Liùyuè	*n*	June
29. 七月		Qīyuè	*n*	July
30. 八月		Bāyuè	*n*	August
31. 九月		Jiǔyuè	*n*	September
32. 十一月		Shíyīyuè	*n*	November
33. 十二月		Shí'èryuè	*n*	December

* Refer to the Language Notes for more vocabulary on expressions of time and the months in a year.

The Chinese Calendar

In Chinese, the full date is stated in the following order: year, month, then day. For example, May 24th, 2012 would be 二零一二年五月二十四号.

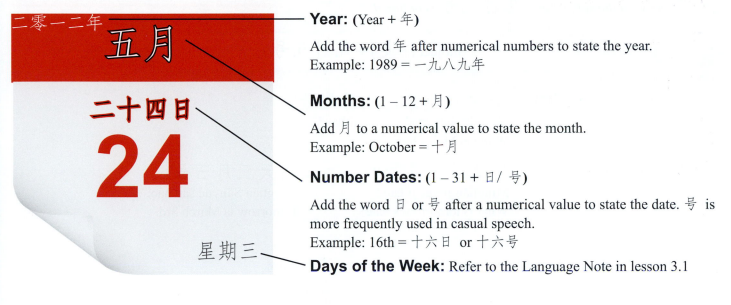

Year: (Year + 年)

Add the word 年 after numerical numbers to state the year.
Example: 1989 = 一九八九年

Months: (1 – 12 + 月)

Add 月 to a numerical value to state the month.
Example: October = 十月

Number Dates: (1 – 31 + 日 / 号)

Add the word 日 or 号 after a numerical value to state the date. 号 is more frequently used in casual speech.
Example: 16th = 十六日 or 十六号

Days of the Week: Refer to the Language Note in lesson 3.1

Time Expressions: Past, Present, Future

Because Chinese does not indicate tense in the same way as European languages (i.e., verbs are not conjugated to show whether something happened in the past or will happen in the future), providing a timeframe can be a very useful way of filling in the context. Below is a table with the units of reference for the day, week, month, and year.

Day and Year

大前天	前天	昨天	今天	明天	后天	大后天
dà qiántiān	qiántiān	zuótiān	jīntiān	míngtiān	hòutiān	dà hòutiān
three days ago	day before yesterday	yesterday	today	tomorrow	day after tomorrow	three days later
大前年	前年	去年	今年	明年	后年	大后年
dà qiánnián	qiánnián	qùnián	jīnnián	míngnián	hòunián	dà hòunián
three years ago	year before last	last year	this year	next year	year after next	three years from now

Week and Month

上上(个)星期	上(个)星期	这(个)星期	下(个)星期	下下(个)星期
shàngshàng (ge) xīngqī	shàng (ge) xīngqī	zhè(i)(ge) xīngqī	xià (ge) xīngqī	xiàxià (ge) xīngqī
two weeks ago	last week	this week	next week	two weeks from now
上上个月	上个月	这个月	下个月	下下个月
shàngshàng ge yuè	shàng ge yuè	zhè(i)ge yuè	xià ge yuè	xiàxià ge yuè
two months ago	last month	this month	next month	two months from now

STRUCTURE NOTE 3.8

Use 几 to ask "what month" and "what day"

In Structure Note 3.4 , 几 was used to ask for time. In this lesson, 几 is used in a similar fashion to inquire about calendar months and days, with numbers replacing 几 when providing a response. For this structure, the insertion of 是 between the subject and 几月几号 is optional.

Subject (+ 是) + 几月几号？

From the Lesson Text:　　玛丽的生日是几月几号？
Mǎlì de shēngrì shì jǐ yuè jǐ hào?
When is Mali's birthday?

Other examples:　　明天几月几号？　　　　明天三月三号。
Míngtiān jǐ yuè jǐ hào?　　Míngtiān Sānyuè sān hào.
What is tomorrow's date?　　Tomorrow is March 3rd.

Practice: Create questions using the information provided below.

Example:　　你的生日 → 你的生日是几月几号？
1.　昨天　　　　　_____
2.　下个星期三　　_____
3.　他们的派对　　_____
4.　你妈妈的生日　_____
5.　明天　　　　　_____

STRUCTURE NOTE 3.9

Use 都 to mean "both" or "all"

When using a plural subject, 都 (dōu), meaning "both" or "all," indicates that the adjacent verb phrase applies to everyone included in the subject. Unlike English, where "we can all" or "we all can" are used interchangeably, 都 must appear before an auxiliary verb and after the subject.

Subject + 都 + Verb Phrase

From the Lesson Text:　　你们都来了！
Nǐmen dōu lái le!
You all came! (implies: I'm glad you're here)

Other examples:　　他们都是日本人。　　　他们都会说中文。
Tāmen dōu shì Rìběn rén.　　Tāmen dōu huì shuō Zhōngwén.
They are all Japanese.　　They can all speak Chinese.

NOTE: *To create a negative statement,* 不 *is coupled with* 都. *However, the placement of* 不 *with respect to* 都 *can change the meaning of the sentence. When* 不 *precedes* 都, *it has the meaning of "not all" while* 不 *following* 都 *means "none" or "no one."*

Examples:

我们不都是老师。
Wǒmen bù dōu shì lǎoshī.
Not all of us are teachers.

他们不都是美国人。
Tāmen bù dōu shì Měiguó rén.
Not all of them are American.

我们都不是老师。
Wǒmen dōu bú shì lǎoshī.
None of us are teachers.

他们都不是美国人。
Tāmen dōu bú shì Měiguó rén.
None of them are American.

Practice: Create complete Chinese sentences with 都, 都不, or 不都 using the information below.

他们		会说法语
老师们	都	明天去美国
同学们	都不	是美国人
我们	不都	没有狗
她们		很好

Example: 他们不都会说法语。

_____

_____

_____

_____

STRUCTURE NOTE 3.10

Use 了 *to indicate a change of state or situation*

Chinese does not conjugate verbs to indicate tense as English does ("I cooked," "I cook," "I will cook."). Instead, Chinese uses particles that indicate "aspect," which gives information about the time structure of an event. The particle 了 *(le) is the most common aspect marker in Chinese. It does not directly correspond to any grammatical form in English. While there are a few different ways to use* 了, *its basic usage is to denote some change (of state) associated with the action in the sentence. In this lesson,* 了 *appears at the end of a sentence to mean that the situation has changed from its previous state.*

> Sentence + 了

From the Lesson Text:

你们都来了！
Nǐmen dōu lái le!
You all came!

Other examples:

比赛开始了。
Bǐsài kāishǐ le.
The game has started.

Since 了 *indicates a change of state, it is normally not used with verbs like* 是 *because they indicate states of being. When* 了 *does occur with such verbs, it often adds a change-of-state meaning to the sentence. For example, when* 了 *occurs at the end of a negative statement containing* 是, *it means "this is not the case anymore."*

Examples:　　我们不是朋友了。　　　　　玛丽没有工作了。
　　　　　　　Wǒmen bú shì péngyou le.　　Mǎlì méiyǒu gōngzuò le.
　　　　　　　We are not friends anymore.　　Mali does not have a job anymore.

Practice: Rewrite the sentences below using 了, following the example given.

Example:　　他们的派对开始。 → 他们的派对开始了。
　1.　　她们开始吃蛋糕。　　＿＿＿＿＿＿＿＿＿＿＿＿＿＿
　2.　　妈妈来。　　　　　　＿＿＿＿＿＿＿＿＿＿＿＿＿＿
　3.　　他现在没有狗。　　　＿＿＿＿＿＿＿＿＿＿＿＿＿＿
　4.　　她会说中文。　　　　＿＿＿＿＿＿＿＿＿＿＿＿＿＿
　5.　　我不吃。　　　　　　＿＿＿＿＿＿＿＿＿＿＿＿＿＿

STRUCTURE NOTE 3.11

Use the verb 送 *in the context of gift giving*

In this lesson, 送 (sòng) *means "to give"and can only be applied to objects that are presented as gifts.*

Subject + 送 + Recipient + Object

From the Lesson Text:　　这是我送你的生日礼物。
　　　　　　　　　　　Zhè shì wǒ sòng nǐ de shēngrì lǐwù.
　　　　　　　　　　　This is my birthday present for you.

Other Examples:　　她送我一只狗。
　　　　　　　　　Tā sòng wǒ yì zhī gǒu.
　　　　　　　　　She is giving me a dog.

　　　　　　　　　这是爸爸送我的礼物。
　　　　　　　　　Zhè shì bàba sòng wǒ de lǐwù.
　　　　　　　　　This is a present that dad gave me.

Practice: Create sentences using 送 and the given words, following the example given.

Example:　　我 / 妈妈 / 生日蛋糕 → 我送妈妈生日蛋糕。
　1.　　他 / 老师 / 生日礼物　　＿＿＿＿＿＿＿＿＿＿＿＿＿＿
　2.　　我 / 妹妹 / 一只狗　　　＿＿＿＿＿＿＿＿＿＿＿＿＿＿
　3.　　爸爸 / 我 / 一个蛋糕　　＿＿＿＿＿＿＿＿＿＿＿＿＿＿
　4.　　我 / 我的朋友 / 两只猫　＿＿＿＿＿＿＿＿＿＿＿＿＿＿
　5.　　我哥哥 / 我 / 生日礼物　＿＿＿＿＿＿＿＿＿＿＿＿＿＿

STRUCTURE NOTE 3.12
Use 的 *to modify nouns*

In Structure Note 2.5, 的 was used to indicate possession. In this lesson, 的 is used to link a modifying verb phrase to a noun. In English, a modifying verb phrase appears after the main noun, but in Chinese, all modifiers come before the main noun.

> Modifier + 的 + Noun

From the Lesson Text:

我送你的生日礼物
wǒ sòng nǐ de shēngrì lǐwù
the birthday present I gave you

Other examples:

我会说的语言
wǒ huì shuō de yǔyán
the language that I can speak

加拿大来的同学
Jiā'nádà lái de tóngxué
the classmate from Canada

The modified noun phrase is then inserted into a sentence to create a larger, complete statement.

From the Lesson Text:

这是我送你的生日礼物。
Zhè shì wǒ sòng nǐ de shēngrì lǐwù.
This is the birthday present I got for you.

Practice: Construct Chinese phrases using the information provided below.

Example: The present I gave her → 我送她的礼物

1. My family's dog   _____
2. The cake I ate   _____
3. The party I will be going to   _____
4. The Chinese characters I can write   _____
5. The cat that my mother gave me   _____

PRACTICE 3.10

Ask six of your classmates for the dates of their birthdays and on which days of the week they fell this year. Record their details in the following chart. Present your findings to the class.

Example:

A: 你的生日是几月几号？

B: 我的生日是七月十号。

A: 你的生日是星期几？

B: 我的生日是星期二。

Name	Birthday	What day of the week is/ was his/her birthday?

PRACTICE 3.11

Do a survey to determine which month has the highest number of students' birthdays in the class. Record your findings below.

Month	Number of students

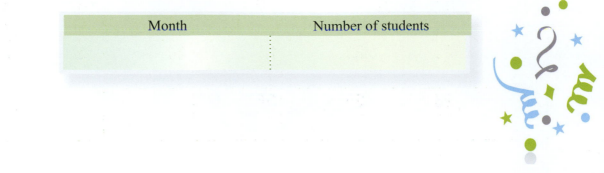

PRACTICE 3.12

Sing the "Happy Birthday" song in Chinese.

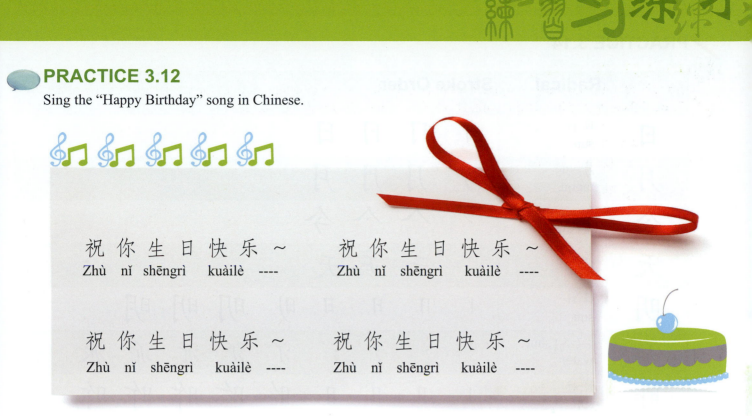

祝 你 生 日 快 乐 ～
Zhù nǐ shēngrì kuàilè ----

祝 你 生 日 快 乐 ～
Zhù nǐ shēngrì kuàilè ----

祝 你 生 日 快 乐 ～
Zhù nǐ shēngrì kuàilè ----

祝 你 生 日 快 乐 ～
Zhù nǐ shēngrì kuàilè ----

PRACTICE 3.13

Imagine that today is July 11. Working with a partner, ask questions about the dates of the events on the calendar below and respond accordingly.

Example:

小美的生日是几月几号？

小美的生日是星期几？

小美的生日是今天还是昨天？

七月

日	一	二	三	四	五	六
		1	2	3	4	5
6	7	8	9	10 小美生日	11	12 足球比赛
13	14 篮球比赛	15	16	17	18	19 生日派对
20	21	22	23 祥安生日	24	25	26
27	28	29	30			

	Radical	Stroke Order
日	日 rì sun	丨 冂 日 日
月	月 yuè moon	丿 刀 月 月
今	人 rén person	丿 人 亼 今
天	大 dà big	一 二 于 天
明	日 rì sun	丨 冂 日 日 日 明 明 明
派	氵(水) shuǐ water	丶 冫 氵 汇 汇 沪 派 派 派
昨	日 rì sun	丨 冂 日 日 旷 昨 昨 昨 昨
快	忄(心) xīn heart	丶 丷 忄 忄 忤 快 快
乐	丿 piě slash	一 二 乐 乐 乐
都	阝(邑) yì city	一 十 土 耂 者 者 者 都 都
了	⁷ zhé bent	⁷ 了
吃	口 kǒu mouth	丨 口 口 吃 吃 吃
送	辶 chuò walk	丶 丷 半 关 关 关 送 送
礼	礻(示) shì show	丶 ⁷ 礻 礻 礼
祝	礻(示) shì show	丶 ⁷ 礻 礻 礻 祀 祀 祀 祝

![speech bubble] **PRACTICE 3.15**

![microphone] Make an audio recording and send it to your teacher. In the recording, state the date of your birthday and ask your teacher when his or her birthday is.

PRACTICE 3.16

Type the following sentences on your computer and provide answers to the questions.

1. 大东的生日是几月几号？
2. 今天早上有生日派对。
3. 你们都来了！我真高兴！
4. 这是我送你的生日礼物。
5. 玛丽的生日派对是几月几号？

PRACTICE 3.17

王小美：大东的生日是什么时候？
孙玛丽：他的生日是三月二十七号。
王小美：他的生日是星期几？
孙玛丽：是星期六。

Read the dialogue and answer the following questions.
1. What is the date of Chen Dadong's birthday?
2. What day of the week is it?

PRACTICE 3.18

李中平：大东，生日快乐！
陈大东：这是你送我的礼物吗？
李中平：是。吃蛋糕吧！
陈大东：好，谢谢你！

Read the dialogue and answer the following questions.
1. Who's birthday is it?
2. What is the birthday present?

PRACTICE 3.19

下星期五是我的生日派对。我很高兴。朋友们会来我的生日派对。生日派对会有蛋糕。祥安和大东也会送我生日礼物。

Read Sun Mali's diary and answer the following questions.
1. Why is Sun Mali so happy?
2. What are Xiang'an and Dadong going to give Sun Mali?

Chinese Birthdays

The system of determining age in China differs to that in the West. When a baby is born, it is already one 岁 (sùi: "year of age") and becomes a year older after the passing of Chinese New Year, rather than his or her birthday. This method of reckoning age is still used in China, thus a Chinese person's age according to this system can be quite different to their age according to the Western system.

In traditional Chinese culture, a baby's one-month birthday also merits special celebration and calls for the serving of symbolic foods. These "red egg and ginger ceremonies," as they are called, are an opportunity to introduce the baby to relatives and friends, as well as to announce the infant's name. Eggs, representing fertility and unity, are dyed red (the color of good luck) and passed out to guests; the ginger is believed to restore strength to the mother that she lost during childbirth.

Although birthday cakes have become popular in today's China, noodles are the traditional food served to celebrate a birthday. 长寿面 (cháng-shòu miàn: "longevity noodles") are considered to represent long life and to bring good luck due to their literally extended length. At a Chinese birthday one might also find 寿桃 (shòutáo: the "Chinese birthday bun"), a peach-shaped bun filled with lotus or red bean paste.

Gift-Giving

There are a few important things to remember when it comes to Chinese gift-giving etiquette. Firstly, one should present a gift with both hands as a sign of respect. The recipient should in turn accept the gift with both hands and may also make a show of refusing to accept the present so as not to appear greedy. Lastly, in order to avoid seeming eager, the recipient may not immediately open the gift in the presence of the giver.

It is also worth noting what kinds of presents are appropriate and inappropriate to give in Chinese culture:

What to Give

Giving presents to children is fairly simple: money wrapped in 红包 (hóngbāo: "red envelopes") is frequently given to the younger generations by their older relatives on special occasions or holidays. When going to a Chinese person's house or staying with a Chinese host, it is customary to bring a gift such as fruit or houseplants.

What Not to Give

There are some gifts that are considered inauspicious. Giving someone a clock, for example, is to be avoided, because the Chinese 送钟 (sòng zhōng: "to give a clock") sounds identical to 送终 (sòng zhōng: "to send off the deceased"). Similarly, pears are not given because the Chinese name for the fruit, 梨 (lí), has the same sound as the word for "separation," 离 (lí).

李中平： 玛丽的生日是几月几号？ 是今天还是明天？

When is Mali's birthday? Is it today or tomorrow?

王小美： 是明天。她的生日是十月三号。

It's tomorrow. Her birthday is October 3.

李中平： 是吗？有生日派对吗？

Really? Will there be a birthday party?

王小美： 有！明天下午玛丽家有派对。

Yeah! There's a party tomorrow afternoon at Mali's house.

大家： 玛丽，生日快乐！

Happy birthday, Mali!

孙玛丽： 你们都来了！我真高兴！

You all came! I'm really happy!

王小美： 大家吃蛋糕吧！

Let's have cake!

李中平： 这是我送你的生日礼物，祝你生日快乐！

This is my birthday present to you. Happy Birthday!

孙玛丽： 谢谢你！

Thank you!

What Can You Do?

INTERPRETIVE
- I can understand the terms for the different days of the week and months of the year.
- I can understand birthday greetings and express thanks.

INTERPERSONAL
- I can exchange information about the days of the week and months.
- I can state and ask for the date.

PRESENTATIONAL
- I can share birthday greetings and present gifts.
- I can present information on the time and date of occasions relative to today.

ACT IT OUT

Working in groups, compose an original three-minute skit that utilizes the vocabulary and structures introduced in Unit 3. Each of you should assume a role and have a roughly equal number of lines in the skit. Be prepared to perform your skit in class. You can either come up with your own story or choose from one of the following situations:

a) You and friends want to attend an athletic event at your university but everyone has different plans.

b) You are planing a birthday party for a friend and ask what your friends are planning to get him or her for a present.

c) You and some friends schedule a time to go to see a soccer match.

CHECK WHAT YOU CAN DO

RECOGNIZE

Adjective
- □ 高兴

Adverbs
- □ 还没(有)
- □ 差不多
- □ 都
- □ 真

Conjunction
- □ 还是

Idiomatic Expressions
- □ 对不起
- □ 没关系
- □ 生日快乐

Months
- □ 一月
- □ 二月
- □ 三月
- □ 四月
- □ 五月
- □ 六月
- □ 七月
- □ 八月
- □ 九月
- □ 十月
- □ 十一月
- □ 十二月

Name
- □ 黄祥安

Nouns
- □ 星期
- □ 星期三
- □ 足球
- □ 比赛
- □ 晚上
- □ 点(钟)
- □ 半
- □ 现在
- □ 刻
- □ 分
- □ 秒
- □ 早上
- □ 上午
- □ 中午
- □ 下午
- □ 小时
- □ 钟头
- □ 时间
- □ 零
- □ 生日
- □ 月
- □ 号
- □ 今天
- □ 明天
- □ 生日派对
- □ 蛋糕
- □ 礼物
- □ 日
- □ 年
- □ 昨天

Particles
- □ 吧
- □ 了

Pronoun
- □ 大家

Question Phrases
- □ 星期几
- □ 甚么时候

Verbs
- □ 去
- □ 看
- □ 开始
- □ 见
- □ 走
- □ 来
- □ 吃
- □ 送
- □ 祝

WRITE
- □ 什么
- □ 星期
- □ 时
- □ 上
- □ 钟
- □ 半
- □ 在
- □ 来
- □ 去
- □ 对
- □ 起
- □ 开
- □ 始
- □ 日
- □ 月
- □ 今天
- □ 明
- □ 派
- □ 昨
- □ 快
- □ 乐
- □ 都
- □ 了
- □ 吃
- □ 送
- □ 礼
- □ 祝

USE

- □ 会 to indicate the possibility of an action taking place in the future
- □ 什么时候 to ask "when"
- □ 星期几 to ask "what day of the week" and 星期 + number to state the day of the week
- □ 几点 to discuss time
- □ 差不多 to express "almost"
- □ 还没(有) to express "not yet" or "still have not"
- □ 吧 to make a suggestion

- □ 几 to ask "what month" and "what day"
- □ 都 to mean "both" or "all"
- □ 了 to indicate a change of state or stituation
- □ The verb 送 in the context of gift giving
- □ 的 to modify nouns

食

Food

第四单元
UNIT 4

Communication Goals

Lesson 1: 点菜 **Ordering Food**
- Inquire and express preferences for food and drink
- Express hunger
- Order food and drinks at a restaurant

Lesson 2: 味道怎么样? **How Does It Taste?**
- Discuss various dishes and their flavors
- Offer to pay for a meal

点菜
Ordering Food

huān yíng guāng lín
欢迎光临！
jǐ wèi
请问，几位？

三位。

zuò
请坐。
xiǎng hē
请问想喝什么？

gěi
请给我们
bēi chá
三杯茶。

好。这是我们
cài dān
的菜单。

LESSON TEXT 4.1

Ordering Food 点菜

Chen Dadong, Li Zhongping, and Sun Mali go out to eat at a Chinese restaurant. While there, Mali spots a new student, Zhang Anna, at the next table. They invite Anna over to eat with them.

服务员：	欢迎光临！请问，几位？	Huānyíng guānglín! Qǐngwèn, jǐ wèi?
陈大东：	三位。	Sān wèi.
服务员：	请坐。请问想喝什么？	Qǐng zuò. Qǐngwèn xiǎng hē shénme?
孙玛丽：	请给我们三杯茶。	Qǐng gěi wǒmen sān bēi chá.
服务员：	好。这是我们的菜单。	Hǎo. Zhè shì wǒmen de càidān.

孙玛丽：	那是不是安娜？她是个新同学。	Nà shì bu shì Ānnà? Tā shì gè xīn tóngxué.
李中平：	安娜！——安娜，你喜欢不喜欢吃中国菜？	Ānnà! – Ānnà, nǐ xǐhuan bu xǐhuan chī Zhōngguó cài?
张安娜：	我只喜欢吃饺子。	Wǒ zhǐ xǐhuan chī jiǎozi.
陈大东：	那，我们点一盘饺子，一只烧鸡，一份青菜和一碗酸辣汤。好不好？	Nà, wǒmen diǎn yì pán jiǎozi, yì zhī shāojī, yí fèn qīngcài hé yì wǎn Suānlàtāng. Hǎo bu hǎo?
孙玛丽：	好。这家饭馆的烧鸡很好吃。我饿了，我们点菜吧！	Hǎo. Zhèi jiā fànguǎn de shāojī hěn hǎo chī. Wǒ è le, wǒmen diǎn cài ba!

字 词 VOCABULARY

LESSON VOCABULARY 4.1

	SIMPLIFIED	TRADITIONAL	PINYIN	WORD CATEGORY	DEFINITION
1.	欢迎光临	歡迎光臨	huānyíng guānglín	ie	welcome (to a store/restaurant)
	欢迎	歡迎	huānyíng	v	to welcome
2.	几位	幾位	jǐ wèi	qph	how many (people)
3.	坐		zuò	v	to sit
4.	想		xiǎng	av	would like to (do something)
5.	喝		hē	v	to drink; to eat (soup)
6.	给	給	gěi	v	to give
7.	杯		bēi	n, mw	cup; (used for liquid)
8.	茶		chá	n	tea
9.	菜单	菜單	càidān	n	menu
10.	新		xīn	adj	new
11.	中国菜	中國菜	Zhōngguó cài	n	Chinese food
	中国	中國	Zhōngguó	n	China
	菜		cài	n	dish, food
12.	饺子	餃子	jiǎozi	n	dumplings
13.	那（么）	那（麼）	nà (me)	cj	then; in that case
14.	点（菜）	點（菜）	diǎn (cài)	v	to order (food)
15.	盘	盤	pán	n, mw	plate; (used for plates of food)
16.	烧鸡	燒雞	shāojī	n	roasted chicken
17.	份		fèn	mw	(used for portions of food; measure word for gifts)
18.	青菜		qīngcài	n	green vegetables
19.	碗		wǎn	n, mw	bowl; (used for bowls of food)
20.	酸辣汤	酸辣湯	Suānlàtāng	n	Hot and Sour Soup
21.	家		jiā	mw	(used for restaurants and companies)
22.	饭馆	飯館	fànguǎn	n	restaurant

LESSON VOCABULARY 4.1 (continued)

	SIMPLIFIED	TRADITIONAL	PINYIN	WORD CATEGORY	DEFINITION
23.	好吃		hǎo chī	*adj*	tasty (of solid food)
24.	饿	餓	è	*adj*	hungry
NAMES					
25.	张安娜	張安娜	Zhāng Ānnà	*name*	Zhang Anna
	张	張	Zhāng	*surname*	Zhang
	安娜		Ānnà	*given name*	Anna

REQUIRED VOCABULARY 4.1

EATING

26.	吃饭	吃飯	chī fàn	*vo*	to eat
	饭	飯	fàn	*n*	meal; rice
27.	做饭	做飯	zuò fàn	*vo*	to cook
28.	渴		kě	*adj*	thirsty
29.	水		shuǐ	*n*	water

OPTIONAL VOCABULARY 4.1

FOODS

30.	麻婆豆腐		Mápó Dòufu	*n*	Mapo Tofu
31.	北京烤鸭	北京烤鴨	Běijīng Kǎoyā	*n*	Peking Duck
32.	汽水		qìshuǐ	*n*	soft drink
33.	果汁		guǒzhī	*n*	fruit juice
34.	饮料	飲料	yǐnliào	*n*	beverage
35.	瓶		píng	*n, mw*	bottle; (used for bottles)

Pronouns: He, She, It

Mandarin Chinese originally possessed no gender-specific third-person pronouns such as "she" or "he." It was only after Western influence in the 20th century that 他 (tā), 她 (tā), and 它 (tā) were introduced to differentiate between "he," "she," and "it." In the spoken language, however, the difference is inaudible. Written (traditional) Chinese also possesses special pronouns for animals and deities, 牠 tā and 祂 tā.

Traditional Chinese does possess both masculine and feminine forms of the word "you," 你 (nǐ) and 妳 (nǐ). In colloquial communication, 你 is the most frequently used form, and one will always write "你好" rather than "妳好."

Use of Nin 您

The second-person pronoun 您 (nín) is generally used to address one's elders or people of a higher social station. As a customer, you would also frequently hear it used by employees in restaurants or stores. You might use 您 (nín) to address a peer in a formal situation, but only at the first meeting. 您 (nín) is never used in the plural: if addressing more than one elder or superior, 你们 (nǐmen) is always used rather than 您们 (nínmen).

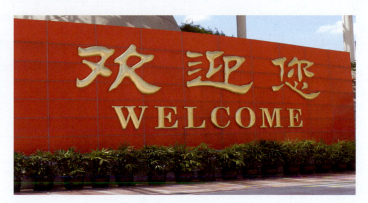

Omitting Pronouns

In Chinese, certain words may be left out when there is sufficient information in the context to make the meaning clear. This is the case for pronouns such as 我 (wǒ), "I/me"; the "I" subject in the sentence is implied. In this lesson, for example, the sentence 请你给我们三杯茶 is shortened to 请给我们三杯茶 by omitting the subject 你 (nǐ). With the continued study of Chinese, more confident intuition will develop about when it is appropriate to omit pronouns and other words.

STRUCTURE NOTE 4.1
Use 想 to indicate a desired action

The auxiliary verb 想 (xiǎng) *means "would like to." In this pattern,* 想 *must be followed by a verb phrase and cannot be directly followed by an object to express a desire for something as in "I would like tea."*

Subject + 想 + Verb + Object

From the Lesson Text:　请问想喝什么？
Qǐngwèn xiǎng hē shénme?
What would you like to drink?

Other examples:　我想去中国。
Wǒ xiǎng qù Zhōngguó.
I would like to go to China.

他想喝水。
Tā xiǎng hē shuǐ.
He would like to drink water.

Practice: Create complete sentences using the above structure and the information provided below.

Example:　我 / 看足球比赛 → 我想去看足球比赛。
1. 玛丽 / 咖啡 _____
2. 他 / 学校 _____
3. 老师 / 青菜 _____
4. 大东 / 茶 _____
5. 祥安 / 水 _____

STRUCTURE NOTE 4.2
Use 给 to mean "to give"

In Structure Note 3.11, 送 *was introduced as a verb associated with the giving of a gift. In this lesson,* 给 (gěi) *is also introduced as "to give" but is typically used for non-gift items. Similar to* 送, *the verb* 给 *must appear between the subject and recipient; however, the subject can be omitted if its presence is implied.*

Subject + 给 + Recipient + Object

From the Lesson Text:　请给我们三杯茶。
Qǐng gěi wǒmen sān bēi chá.
Please give us three cups of tea.

Other examples:　我想给玛丽一份生日礼物。
Wǒ xiǎng gěi Mǎlì yí fèn shēngrì lǐwù.
I would like to give Mali a birthday present.

请你给我一份菜单。
Qǐng nǐ gěi wǒ yí fèn càidān.
Please can you give me a menu.

Practice: Create complete sentences with 给, using the information below.

我的同学		我	一杯茶	Example: 他给我一杯茶。
我妹妹		祥安	一个足球	_____
他	给	他们	三盘饺子	_____
大东		玛丽	两杯水	_____
服务员		我们	一份礼物	_____

STRUCTURE NOTE 4.3

Use 喜欢 to express liking something or someone

喜欢 (xǐhuan) *means "like" or "enjoy" and is usually followed by the noun or action of preference. To negate the sentence, add* 不 *in front of* 喜欢 *to mean "dislike." Other adverbs such as* 只 *and* 很 *can be added in front of* 喜欢 *to indicate "only like" or "really like," respectively.*

> Subject + 喜欢 + Verb Phrase/Noun

From the Lesson Text: 我只喜欢吃饺子。
Wǒ zhǐ xǐhuan chī jiǎozi.
I only like to eat dumplings.

Other examples: 他不喜欢猫，只喜欢狗。 我们都很喜欢说中文。
Tā bù xǐhuan māo, zhǐ xǐhuan gǒu. Wǒmen dōu hěn xǐhuan shuō Zhōngwén.
He doesn't like cats, he only likes dogs. We all really like to speak Chinese.

Practice: Create sentences using 喜欢 and the information provided below, inserting verbs where appropriate.

Example: 我 / 青菜 (doesn't like) → 我不喜欢吃青菜。

1. 他 / 安娜 (really likes) _____
2. 老师 / 咖啡 (doesn't like) _____
3. 中平 / 他的哥哥 (only like) _____
4. 祥安 / 看足球比赛 (like) _____
5. 玛丽 / 中国菜 (only like) _____

STRUCTURE NOTE 4.4

Use Verb + 不 + Verb with two-character verbs to form affirmative-negative questions

To use the Verb 不 *Verb pattern (see Structure Notes 1.13 and 1.14) with two-character verbs like* 喜欢, *simply repeat the entire verb.*

2-Character Verb + 不 + 2-Character Verb

For certain two-character verbs, such as 喜欢, the second character is often omitted before the 不 followed by the full two-character verb, as in 喜不喜欢. The full two-character verb is often repeated in formal written Chinese.

1st Character of 2-Character Verb + 不 + 2-Character Verb

From the Lesson Text: 你喜欢不喜欢吃中国菜？
Nǐ xǐhuan bu xǐhuan chī Zhōngguó cài?
Do you (or do you not) like to eat Chinese food?

Other examples: 你喜不喜欢喝茶？ 她喜不喜欢我？
Nǐ xǐ bu xǐhuan hē chá? Tā xǐ bu xǐhuan wǒ?
Do you (or do you not) like to drink tea? Does she (or does she not) like me?

Practice: Create complete sentences including 喜欢不喜欢 or 喜不喜欢 and the information provided below.

你	吃饺子
他们	新的菜单
大东	做饭
老师	说汉语
她	去看足球比赛

Example: 大东喜不喜欢吃饺子？

_____

_____

_____

_____

STRUCTURE NOTE 4.5
Use 那(么) to mean "Well then" or "In that case"

The demonstrative pronoun 那 (nà) can also be used as a conjunction meaning "Well then" or "In that case." It serves as a transition word from one thought to another, addressing an already established fact or statement. 那 and 那么 can be used interchangeably.

那（么）+ Statement/Question

From the Lesson Text: 我只喜欢吃饺子。 那，我们点一盘饺子……
Wǒ zhǐ xǐhuan chī jiǎozi. Nà, wǒmen diǎn yì pán jiǎozi……
I only like to eat dumplings. Then let's get a plate of dumplings . . .

Other examples: 我不想去饭馆。 那，我们去咖啡店吧。
Wǒ bù xiǎng qù fànguǎn. Nà, wǒmen qù kāfēi diàn ba.
I don't want to go to the restaurant. In that case, let's go to the coffee shop.

我不会说法语。
Wǒ bú huì shuō Fǎyǔ.
I don't know how to speak French.

那么，你会说什么语言呢？
Nàme, nǐ huì shuō shénme yǔyán ne?
Well then, what languages can you speak?

Practice: Respond to the provided statements with sentences beginning with 那（么）.

Example: 我不是美国人。→ 那，你是哪国人？

1. 我不想去加拿大。 _____
2. 我不会说英语。 _____
3. 我不是大东的朋友。 _____
4. 我很想吃饺子。 _____
5. 我不想喝咖啡。 _____

STRUCTURE NOTE 4.6

Use 好 + Verb to form a compound adjective

The adjective 好 and its negative 不好, when combined with certain verbs, create compound adjectives that express positive or negative attributes, as in 好吃 (hǎo chī: "delicious"). When it is used with verbs such as 做 and 写, the 好/不好 pattern means "easy/difficult (to do something)."

好 + Verb

From the Lesson Text:
这家饭馆的烧鸡很好吃。
Zhèi jiā fànguǎn de shāojī hěn hǎo chī.
The roast chicken at this restaurant is really good.

Other examples:
中国菜好吃吗？
Zhōngguó cài hǎo chī ma?
Does Chinese food taste good?

咖啡很好喝！
Kāfēi hěn hǎo hē!
The coffee is very tasty!

Practice: Create complete sentences expressing your opinion of the items listed below, combining the appropriate intensifiers (很好, 好, 不好) and verbs.

Example: 饺子 (eat) → 饺子很好吃。

1. 汉字 (write) _____
2. 法国菜 (make) _____
3. 青菜 (eat) _____
4. 茶 (drink) _____
5. 饭馆的菜 (eat) _____

ONLINE RESOURCES

Visit *http://college.betterchinese.com* for more examples of compound adjectives.

PRACTICE 4.1

Working with a partner, practice the questions and answers below. When you are finished, you may switch roles.

Example:

A: 欢迎光临！请问，几位？

B: 我们三个人。

A: 请坐。你们想喝什么？

B: 请给我们三杯茶。

A: 好。请看我们的菜单。

PRACTICE 4.2

Working with a partner, ask whether each character likes the following foods. Answer accordingly.

Example:

A: 小美喜欢不喜欢吃麻婆豆腐？

B: 她喜欢吃麻婆豆腐。

1. 酸辣汤

2. 青菜

3. 饺子

4. 烧鸡

PRACTICE 4.3

Working in groups of three or four, act out a restaurant scenario with a waiter or waitress and customers looking at a menu. Discuss food and drink preferences and then order the food. You may use the additional dishes below to help you.

1. 北京烤鸭

Běijīng Kǎoyā

Peking Duck

2. 春卷

Chūnjuǎn

Spring Rolls

3. 宫保鸡丁

Gōngbǎo Jīdīng

Kung Pao Chicken

4. 炒面

chǎomiàn

fried noodles

5. 清炒白菜

qīng chǎo báicài

stir-fried Chinese cabbage

6. 炒饭

chǎofàn

fried rice

PRACTICE 4.4

Take a survey of the class to find out which Chinese dish students like the most. Record the most popular response below.

Dish	Number of students

	Radical	Stroke Order
国	囗 wéi enclosure	丨 冂 冂 冃 冃 国 国 国
杯	木 mù wood	一 十 才 木 朾 杯 杯 杯
饿	饣 (食) shí eat	丿 𠂊 饣 饣 饣 饣 饿 饿 饿
光	儿 rén person	丨 丬 丬 业 光 光
位	亻 (人) rén person	丿 亻 亻 仁 伫 位 位
坐	土 tǔ earth	丿 人 𠆢 从 丛 坐 坐
想	心 xīn heart	一 十 才 木 札 相 相 相 相 想 想 想
喝	口 kǒu mouth	丨 口 口 叩 叩 呵 呵 呵 呵 喝 喝 喝
给	纟 (丝) sī silk	乙 纟 纟 纟 纠 纠 纷 给 给
新	斤 jīn axe	丶 亠 立 立 立 辛 辛 亲 亲 新 新 新
份	亻 (人) rén person	丿 亻 亻 份 份 份
青	青 qīng blue	一 二 丰 圭 青 青 青 青
菜	艹 (草) cǎo grass	一 十 艹 艹 芯 芯 莁 莁 莁 菜 菜
饭	饣 (食) shí eat	丿 𠂊 饣 饣 饣 饭 饭
馆	饣 (食) shí eat	丿 𠂊 饣 饣 饣 馆 馆 馆 馆 馆 馆

💬 **PRACTICE 4.6**

🎤 Make an audio recording and send it to your teacher. In the recording, state what foods you would like to order at a Chinese restaurant and state the reason for your preferences.

PRACTICE 4.7

Type the following sentences on your computer and provide answers to the questions.

1. 欢迎光临！
2. 请问您想喝什么？
3. 请坐，这是我们饭馆的菜单。
4. 她是不是新同学？
5. 我饿了，我们点菜吧！

PRACTICE 4.8

服务员：欢迎光临！请问，几位？
孙玛丽：五位。
服务员：请坐。请问想喝什么？
孙玛丽：你们有咖啡吗？
服务员：有。要几杯？
孙玛丽：五杯。
服务员：好。

Read the dialogue and answer the following questions.
1. How many people are at the restaurant with Sun Mali?
2. What do they order?

PRACTICE 4.9

孙玛丽：我饿了，我们去吃晚饭吧！
陈大东：你想吃什么？
孙玛丽：我今天想吃中国菜。
陈大东：我们吃饺子吧！
孙玛丽：好！我还想喝酸辣汤。

Read the dialogue and answer the following questions.
1. Are they going to have lunch or dinner?
2. What do you think they are going to order?

PRACTICE 4.10

我和陈大东、张安娜、孙玛丽星期五晚上会去中国饭馆吃饭。朋友说那家饭馆的烧鸡很不错。我想吃烧鸡、饺子和青菜。

Read Huang Xiang'an's diary and answer the following questions.
1. When do they plan to go to the Chinese Restaurant?
2. What does Huang Xiang'an want to eat?

Cuisine Across China

Chinese cuisine is as rich and varied as its culture, peoples, and dialects. A lot of the differences between China's cuisines have been brought about by variations in local resources, geography, and traditions. There are eight major types of regional cuisine, each possessing its own distinctive characteristics. Below are four of the most well known of these styles.

四川 **Sìchuān**	Sichuan cuisine is characterized by its spicy and strong flavors, making use of garlic, chili, and other peppers, often in great quantities. 麻婆豆腐 (Mápó Dòufu: "Pockmarked Lady's Tofu") and 宫保鸡丁 (Gōngbǎo Jīdīng: "Kung Pao Chicken") are two Sichuanese favorites.
广东 **Guǎngdōng**	Guangdong cuisine is often described as "light" or "fresh," with attention paid to releasing the natural flavors of the ingredients. Among the region's specialties are 冬瓜盅 (Dōngguāzhōng: "Winter Melon Cup") and 烧乳猪 (Shāo Rǔ Zhū: "Roast Suckling Pig").
上海 **Shànghǎi**	Shanghai's cuisine is known for its smaller portions than the average Chinese fare and its propensity toward "drunken" foods, which are prepared by soaking alcohol into the food before cooking in order to alter the flavoring.
东北 **Dōngběi**	Northeastern cuisine is a product of its environment: its hearty steamed buns and hot pot are a great way to fight the winter chills. The staple food in Northeastern cuisine is noodles, and in addition it is also famed for its pickles.

Symbolism in Chinese Food

Foods endowed with special symbolic significance are an essential part of any Chinese festival. Some foods gain their importance through the linguistic link of homophones. Fish, for instance, is considered auspicious because the word for fish, 鱼 (yú), sounds the same as the word meaning "abundance," 余 (yú). Similarly, in the Guangdong and Guangxi regions, the pomelo fruit is a symbol of abundance due to the similarity of its Chinese name 柚 (yòu) to the word "to have" 有 (yǒu). There are also a number of other foods that have metaphorical significance, such as pastries containing a seed filling: the seeds represent fertility and the promise of a large family. Round foods such as rice cakes symbolize family unity, as does the serving of whole chicken. All these dishes may be found at various Chinese festival celebrations, occasions rich in family reunion, well-wishes and, of course, food.

服务员：	欢迎光临！请问，几位？	Welcome! How many are you?
陈大东：	三位。	Three.
服务员：	请坐。请问想喝什么？	Please sit. What you would like to drink?
孙玛丽：	请给我们三杯茶。	Please bring us three cups of tea.
服务员：	好。这是我们的菜单。	Sure. This is our menu.

孙玛丽：	那是不是安娜？她是个新同学。	Isn't that Anna? She's a new student.
李中平：	安娜！——安娜，你喜欢不喜欢吃中国菜？	Anna! – Anna, do you like to eat Chinese food?
张安娜：	我只喜欢吃饺子。	I only like to eat dumplings.
陈大东：	那，我们点一盘饺子，一只烧鸡，一份青菜和一碗酸辣汤。好不好？	Then let's get a plate of dumplings, one roast chicken, an order of vegetables, and a bowl of Hot and Sour Soup. OK?
孙玛丽：	好。这家饭馆的烧鸡很好吃。我饿了，我们点菜吧！	OK. The roast chicken at this restaurant is really good. I'm hungry; let's order!

What Can You Do?

INTERPRETIVE
- I can recognize the terms for several Chinese dishes.

INTERPERSONAL
- I can exchange my preferences for various foods with others.
- I can order food and drinks at a restaurant
- I can express hunger and order food in a restaurant.

PRESENTATIONAL
- I can list Chinese dishes and present others with choices.

安娜，你不会
yòng kuài zi
用筷子吗？

不会。

我只会
yòng dāo zi
用刀子、
chā zi
叉子……

shì yí xià
试一下吧！
jiāo
我教你。

ò yòng kuài zi
哦，用筷子
a
很简单啊！

chī bǎo
大家吃饱了吗？
wǎn fàn   qǐng kè
今天晚饭我请客！

LESSON TEXT 4.2

How Does It Taste?　味道怎么样?

Chen Dadong, Sun Mali, and Li Zhongping discuss their food and teach Zhang Anna how to use chopsticks.

陈大东:	酸辣汤真好喝！我喜欢酸辣的味道。	Suānlàtāng zhēn hǎo hē! Wǒ xǐhuan suān là de wèidào.
孙玛丽:	烧鸡也不错。中平，青菜的味道怎么样?	Shāojī yě bú cuò. Zhōngpíng, qīngcài de wèidào zěnmeyàng?
李中平:	太咸了。我要叫一碗米饭。	Tài xián le. Wǒ yào jiào yì wǎn mǐfàn.
陈大东:	中平，你为什么不吃肉?	Zhōngpíng, nǐ wèishénme bù chī ròu?
李中平:	因为我吃素。	Yīnwèi wǒ chī sù.

孙玛丽:	安娜，你不会用筷子吗?	Ānnà, nǐ bú huì yòng kuàizi ma?
张安娜:	不会。我只会用刀子，叉子……	Bú huì. Wǒ zhǐ huì yòng dāozi, chāzi …
李中平:	试一下吧！我教你。	Shì yí xià ba! Wǒ jiāo nǐ.
张安娜:	哦，用筷子很简单啊！	Ò, yòng kuàizi hěn jiǎndān a!
陈大东:	大家吃饱了吗? 今天晚饭我请客!	Dàjiā chī bǎo le ma? Jīntiān wǎnfàn wǒ qǐng kè!

LESSON VOCABULARY 4.2

	SIMPLIFIED	TRADITIONAL	PINYIN	WORD CATEGORY	DEFINITION
1.	好喝		hǎo hē	*adj*	tasty (of liquids)
2.	酸		suān	*adj*	sour
3.	辣		là	*adj*	spicy
4.	味道		wèidào	*n*	taste, flavor
	不错	不錯	bú cuò	*adj*	not bad, pretty good
5.	错	錯	cuò	*adj*	wrong
6.	怎么样	怎麼樣	zěnmeyàng	*qw*	how is it
7.	太		tài	*adv*	too, excessively, extremely
8.	咸	鹹	xián	*adj*	salty
9	要		yào	*av*	to want; must; will; should
10.	叫		jiào	*v*	to order
11.	米饭	米飯	mǐfàn	*n*	rice
12.	为什么	爲甚麼	wèishénme	*qw*	why
13.	肉		ròu	*n*	meat
14.	因为	因爲	yīnwèi	*cj*	because
15.	吃素		chī sù	*vo*	to be vegetarian
16.	用		yòng	*v*	to use
17.	筷子		kuàizi	*n*	chopsticks
18.	刀子		dāozi	*n*	knife
19.	叉子		chāzi	*n*	fork
20.	试	試	shì	*v*	to try
21.	一下		yí xià	*mw*	a bit
22.	教		jiāo	*v*	to teach
23.	哦		ò	*p*	oh! (interjection)
24.	啊		a	*p*	(used to make a question less abrupt)
25.	吃饱	吃飽	chī bǎo	*rv*	to be full
26.	晚饭	晚飯	wǎnfàn	*n*	dinner
27.	请客	請客	qǐng kè	*vo*	to treat one's guests (i.e. to pay for others)

REQUIRED VOCABULARY 4.2

	SIMPLIFIED	TRADITIONAL	PINYIN	WORD CATEGORY	DEFINITION
MEALS					
28.	早饭	早飯	zǎofàn	*n*	breakfast
29.	午饭	午飯	wǔfàn	*n*	lunch
FLAVORS					
30.	甜		tián	*adj*	sweet
31.	苦		kǔ	*adj*	bitter

OPTIONAL VOCABULARY 4.2

	SIMPLIFIED	TRADITIONAL	PINYIN	WORD CATEGORY	DEFINITION
AT THE RESTAURANT					
32.	买单	買單	mǎidān	*n, vo*	check; to pay the bill; "check, please."
33.	结帐	結帳	jié zhàng	*vo*	to pay the bill
FOODS					
34.	白饭	白飯	báifàn	*n*	white rice (alternate term for 米饭)
35.	水果		shuǐguǒ	*n*	fruit
36.	海鲜	海鮮	hǎixiān	*n*	seafood
37.	鸡肉	鷄肉	jī ròu	*n*	chicken
38.	猪肉	豬肉	zhū ròu	*n*	pork
39.	牛肉		niú ròu	*n*	beef

ONLINE RESOURCES
Visit *http://college.betterchinese.com* for a list of other Chinese foods.

Onomatopoeia

It can be fun to look at how other cultures represent certain sounds in their language. Onomatopoeia refers to words that sound like the thing they describe (for instance, "buzz" or "whoosh"). Chinese possesses many such words: to represent the sound of laughter, Chinese has the words 嘻嘻 xīxī or 哈哈 hāhā, very like the English "hee hee" and "ha ha."

There are interesting similarities and differences in the representation of animal noises: the word for the sound a cat makes is 喵 miāo, virtually identical to the English "meow." The noise made by a dog, however, is 汪 wāng rather than "woof," and a bird's twittering is 叽叽喳喳 jījī zhāzhā. Often, but not always, an onomatopoeic character has a "mouth" (口) radical to indicate that it is a "sound" character.

Foreign Names in Chinese

As mentioned in Language Notes 1.1, Chinese names are chosen with care for their meaning, even in transliterations, which often reveal something about the person or thing they describe. This is particularly true with the Chinese names for certain Western celebrities. For instance, the name for Audrey Hepburn is 奥黛丽赫本 Àodàilì Hèběn. The three characters of the given name mean, in turn, "profound," "dark eyebrow pigment used by women in ancient times," and "beautiful," words specifically chosen for the actress famed for her beauty and darkly penciled brows. Marilyn Monroe is referred to as 玛丽 (beauty) 莲 (lotus) 梦 (dream) 露 (dew) Mǎlìlián Mènglù, and Brad Pitt is 布拉德 (virtuous) 皮特 (special) Bùlādé Pítè.

It is good to remember, though, that Chinese equivalents of foreign names are not always consistent, especially between different Chinese speaking regions. Vincent van Gogh's name, for example, could be rendered as either 文森特·梵高 Wénsēntè · Fàngāo or 温森特·梵谷 Wēnsēntè · Fàngǔ, while Picasso is transliterated as both 毕加索 Bìjiāsuǒ and 毕卡索 Bìkǎsuǒ.

Place Names in Chinese

Foreign place names in Chinese are also represented by characters that approximate the sound of the original; the Chinese name for Berlin, for instance, is 柏林 Bólín. Because many Western place names were originally translated from Cantonese, however, they may sound quite unlike their English versions in Mandarin. New York, for example, is 纽约 Niǔyuē in Mandarin, because the Cantonese pronunciation of these characters more closely resembles the English.

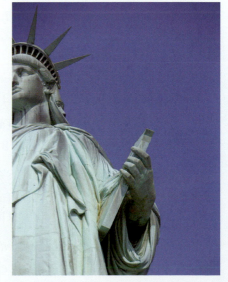

Just as with people's names, the characters for place names are often chosen to convey a positive meaning. The transliteration of London is 伦敦 Lúndūn, the two characters meaning "human relationships" (or "ethics") and "sincere" respectively, while Delhi is rendered as 德里 Délǐ, again making use of the character for "virtue."

STRUCTURE NOTE 4.7
Use 怎么样 to ask for an opinion of something

To ask someone what his or her opinion about something is, simply state the subject followed by 怎么样 (zěnmeyàng), meaning "how is (it)?"

Subject + 怎么样?

From the Lesson Text:

青菜的味道怎么样?
Qīngcài de wèidào zěnmeyàng?
How do the vegetables taste?

Other examples:

妹妹的生日派对怎么样?
Mèimei de shēngrì pàiduì zěnmeyàng?
How was your younger sister's birthday party?

你的工作怎么样?
Nǐ de gōngzuò zěnmeyàng?
How's your job?

Practice: Use the English phrases with 怎么样 to create questions in Chinese.

Example: Mrs. Liu's cake   → 刘太太做的蛋糕怎么样?

1.   Yesterday's soccer game   _____
2.   This cafe's coffee   _____
3.   This Hot and Sour Soup   _____
4.   His spoken French   _____
5.   This restaurant   _____

STRUCTURE NOTE 4.8
Use 太……了 to describe an exaggerated attribute

太 *(tài) is an adverb that means "too" or "extremely." Similar to* 很, 太 *appears before the adjective and expresses a great degree of the adjective of reference.* 太 *can be distinguished from other adverbs as it connotes excess beyond expectation and it typically appears with* 了 *for further emphasis.*

太 + Adjective + 了

From the Lesson Text: 太咸了。
Tài xián le.
(It is) Too salty.

Other examples: 汤太辣了。
Tāng tài là le.
The soup is too spicy.

妈妈今天晚上要做饺子,太好了!
Māma jīntiān wǎnshang yào zuò jiǎozi, tài hǎo le!
Mom is making dumplings tonight, great!

NOTE: 太……了 *can be used in a positive or negative context. While the literal translation may appear negative, as with* 太好了*, or "excessively good," colloquially, this is actually a positive remark meaning "Great!" or "Awesome!"*

144   第四单元 ▪ 第二课 ▪ 食

Practice: Create sentences using the 太……了 pattern and the provided phrases.

蛋糕		大	Example: 你写的字太大了！
她的英语		好吃	
妈妈做的饭	太	甜	_____
这碗酸辣汤		好	_____
你写的字		辣	_____

STRUCTURE NOTE 4.9
Use 要 to indicate desire

In Structure Note 4.1, 想 *was introduced to express a desire or inclination to perform an action. In contrast,* 要 *(yào), meaning "want," can be applied to objects as well as actions.*

> Subject + 要 + Noun/Verb Phrase

From the Lesson Text:

我要叫一碗米饭。
Wǒ yào jiào yì wǎn mǐfàn.
I want to order a bowl of rice.

Other examples:

她要去中国。
Tā yào qù Zhōngguó.
She wants to go to China.

他不要咖啡。
Tā bú yào kāfēi.
He doesn't want coffee.

Practice: Create complete sentences including 要 and the provided information.

Example: 小美 / 两杯茶 → 小美要两杯茶。

1. 大东 / 去加拿大 _____
2. 玛丽 / 蛋糕 _____
3. 祥安 / 看足球比赛 _____
4. 中平 / 一份青菜 _____
5. 安娜 / 两盘饺子 _____

STRUCTURE NOTE 4.10
Use 为什么 and 因为 to ask questions and give explanations respectively

为什么 *(wèishénme) is a question phrase meaning "why" and typically appears between the subject and verb phrase.*

> Subject + 为什么 + Verb Phrase

In addition, 为什么 can also be placed before the subject and verb phrase.

为什么 + Subject + Verb Phrase

The difference between the two structures above is that the emphasis is placed on the verb phrase or subject immediately following 为什么. To answer a "why" question, 因为 (yīnwèi), meaning "because," is followed by the supporting reason, as in English.

因为 + Supporting Reason

From the Lesson Text:

你为什么不吃肉？
Nǐ wèishénme bù chī ròu?
Why don't you eat meat?

因为我吃素。
Yīnwèi wǒ chī sù.
Because I'm a vegetarian.

Other examples:

她为什么不吃午饭？
Tā wèishénme bù chī wǔfàn?
Why doesn't she have lunch?

因为她不饿。
Yīnwèi tā bú è.
Because she is not hungry.

你家为什么没有猫？
Nǐ jiā wèishénme méiyǒu māo?
Why don't you have cats at home?

因为我妈妈不喜欢猫。
Yīnwèi wǒ māma bù xǐhuan māo.
Because my mother doesn't like cats.

Practice: Create questions and answers using the 为什么 and 因为 patterns.

Example:　你 / 要去这家饭馆 → 你为什么要去这家饭馆？
　　　　　　　　　　　　　　 因为我喜欢吃中国菜。

1.　你 / 要点饺子 　＿＿＿＿＿＿＿＿＿＿＿＿＿＿＿＿＿
　　　　　　　　　　＿＿＿＿＿＿＿＿＿＿＿＿＿＿＿＿＿

2.　她 / 不去看比赛 　＿＿＿＿＿＿＿＿＿＿＿＿＿＿＿＿＿
　　　　　　　　　　　＿＿＿＿＿＿＿＿＿＿＿＿＿＿＿＿＿

3.　大东 / 会说汉语 　＿＿＿＿＿＿＿＿＿＿＿＿＿＿＿＿＿
　　　　　　　　　　　＿＿＿＿＿＿＿＿＿＿＿＿＿＿＿＿＿

4.　安娜 / 不会用筷子 　＿＿＿＿＿＿＿＿＿＿＿＿＿＿＿＿＿
　　　　　　　　　　　　＿＿＿＿＿＿＿＿＿＿＿＿＿＿＿＿＿

5.　老师 / 四点半吃晚饭 ＿＿＿＿＿＿＿＿＿＿＿＿＿＿＿＿＿
　　　　　　　　　　　　＿＿＿＿＿＿＿＿＿＿＿＿＿＿＿＿＿

STRUCTURE NOTE 4.11

Use 一下 to express the brevity of an action

The use of 一下 *(yí xià) following a verb has the same effect as the English equivalent "for a moment" or "for a bit." It indicates the informality or brevity of an action. Some verbs, such as* 试 *(shì), are conventionally used with* 一下 *. When the verb is followed by an object,* 一下 *(yí xià) comes between the verb and the object. Note that* 一下 *cannot follow auxiliary verbs, such as* 要 *or* 想*.*

> Subject + Verb + 一下 (+ Object)

From the Lesson Text:

试一下吧！
Shì yí xià ba!
Give it a try!

Other examples:

看一下菜单吧。
Kàn yí xià càidān ba.
Take a look at the menu.

请坐一下。
Qǐng zuò yí xià.
Please sit for a bit.

NOTE: 一下 *describes the short length of time taken for an action, while* 一点儿 *(yìdiǎnr) describes the small quantity of an object. For example,* 喝一下茶 *means "drink tea for a moment," while* 喝一点儿茶*, means "drink a bit of tea."*

Practice: Transform each sentence using 一下, following the example.

Example: 请看 → 请看一下。

1. 请试味道 _____

2. 我问老师 _____

3. 你要试吗 _____

4. 你们坐 _____

5. 请来学校 _____

✏ PRACTICE 4.11

Determine the most appropriate adjectives to describe the tastes of the foods below and record them in Chinese in the spaces provided.

💬 PRACTICE 4.12

Working with a partner, act out dialogues about the foods shown below. Ask each other about the food and how it tastes. Elaborate on the conversation if you can.

Example:

A：酸辣汤的味道怎么样？
B：很好喝，我很喜欢酸辣的味道。
A：我不喜欢。我要一碗米饭。

1.

2.

3.

PRACTICE 4.13

Working with a partner, act out a dialogue in which Partner A does not know how to use chopsticks and Partner B teaches him or her to use them.

Example:

A: 你会不会用筷子？

B: 不会。我们西班牙人用刀子叉子。

A: 试一下吧！我教你。

B: 哦，用筷子很简单啊！

PRACTICE 4.14

Working in groups of three to four, imagine that you are in a restaurant. The waiter has brought you your food, but none of you enjoys the taste. Discuss why you do not like the dishes and what you will eat instead.

Example:

A: 这家饭馆的酸辣汤太辣了！

B: 烧鸡太咸了！我要喝点儿水。

PRACTICE 4.15

Work with a partner to complete and act out the following dialogues in Chinese. Present your dialogues to the class.

A: 你吃饱了吗？

B: (Yes, I am.) _____

A: 今天晚饭我请客。

B: (Thank you!) _____

A: (You're welcome!) _____

B: (Why did you treat me to dinner?) _____

A: 因为今天是我的生日！

B: (Happy Birthday to you!) _____

✏ PRACTICE 4.16

	Radical	Stroke Order
请	讠(言) yán speech	`、` `讠` `讠` `讠` `讠` `请` `请` `请` `请`
晚	日 rì sun	`丨` `丨` `日` `日` `日'` `日̂` `日̂` `昡` `晚` `晚`
不	一 yī one	`一` `丆` `不` `不`
错	钅(金) jīn gold	`丿` `𠂉` `𠂉` `钅` `钅` `钅` `钅` `钌` `错` `错` `错` `错`
咸	戈 gē spear	`一` `厂` `厂` `厂` `后` `后` `咸` `咸` `咸`
味	口 kǒu mouth	`丨` `丨` `口` `口` `叮` `呋` `味` `味`
道	辶 chuò walk	`、` `丷` `丷` `丷` `丷` `首` `首` `首` `首` `道` `道`
怎	心 xīn heart	`丿` `𠂉` `个` `乍` `乍` `作` `怎` `怎` `怎`
太	大 dà big	`一` `丆` `大` `太`
要	西 yà cover	`一` `𠃍` `𠃊` `西` `西` `西` `要` `要` `要`
因	囗 wéi enclosure	`丨` `冂` `冂` `冈` `因` `因`
为	、 diǎn dot	`、` `丷` `为` `为`
肉	肉 ròu meat	`丨` `冂` `内` `内` `肉` `肉`
素	糸 sī silk	`一` `二` `𡗗` `𡗗` `𡗗` `素` `素` `素` `素` `素`
用	冂 jiōng countryside	`丿` `刀` `月` `月` `用`

💬 PRACTICE 4.17

🎤 Make an audio recording and send it to your teacher. In the recording, talk about a trip to a restaurant. State who you will go with and what you would like to order.

PRACTICE 4.18

Type the following sentences on your computer and provide answers to the questions.

1. 你喜欢不喜欢吃米饭？
2. 烧鸡的味道怎么样？
3. 我要一碗米饭和一盘青菜。
4. 你不会用筷子吗？
5. 今天晚饭我请客！

PRACTICE 4.19

李中平：你喜欢吃中国菜吗？
张安娜：我只吃美国菜！
李中平：试一下中国菜吧！
张安娜：我不会用筷子。
李中平：用筷子很简单！我教你。
张安娜：哦！中国菜很好吃！

Read the dialogue and answer the following questions.
1. Why does Zhang Anna have difficulties with Chinese food?
2. What does Zhang Anna say is the only kind of food she eats?

PRACTICE 4.20

张丽丽是加拿大人，她只会用刀子叉子，不会用筷子。
黄东平是中国人，他喜欢吃烧鸡和米饭，他不吃素。
孙美安是美国人，她喜欢吃中国菜，也喜欢吃辣的。

Read the passage and answer the following questions.
1. What does Huang Dongping like to eat?
2. What kind of things does Sun Mei'an like to eat?

PRACTICE 4.21

明天是王小美的生日，我们想去饭馆。因为小美喜欢吃烧鸡，我会点一只烧鸡。因为小美不喜欢吃辣的，我不会点酸辣汤。因为小美和中平都喜欢吃咸的，我会点饺子。明天的晚饭我会请客。

Read Chen Dadong's diary and answer the following questions.
1. What does Wang Xiaomei not like to eat?
2. Who will pay the bill?

Chinese Dining Etiquette

The use of 筷子 (kuàizi: "chopsticks") is probably the most striking difference between Chinese and Western dining customs, but there are a number of other habits that distinguish Chinese table manners from Western table manners. Below is a short guide on what to do and what not to do when eating in a formal setting in China.

What to Do

• In China it is acceptable to raise a bowl of rice to one's mouth, just as it is common to lift a bowl of soup from the table and directly drink the remainder.
• It is polite to sample at least a bit of every dish.
• In a family setting, let the elders begin to eat before taking food for oneself.

What Not to Do

• Don't leave chopsticks pointing vertically out of your bowl, as this resembles the incense sticks used in ceremonies for the deceased.
• Avoid taking the last portion of anything from the communal plate or bowl.

The Art of Tea

Records of tea-drinking in China can be traced back to the first millennium B.C., and legend has it that the Emperor Shennong discovered it a thousand years before that, when a tea leaf dropped unnoticed into his boiling water. Today, the Chinese drink tea both for its physical benefits, believing it aids in digestion and alertness, and the social pleasures it provides. Teahouses are enormously popular throughout the country, providing people with a place to socialize and to enjoy China's many varieties of tea.

While serving and drinking tea, there are also certain customs to follow. In Chinese society, the younger generation serves tea to the older generation as a form of respect. It is also customary to pour tea for others before filling one's own cup. In restaurants, another popular practice is to remove the lid of a teapot to alert the waiter that it needs refilling.

In a teahouse, one may find 绿茶 (lǜ chá: "green tea"), 红茶 (hóng chá: "black tea"), 乌龙茶 (wūlóng chá: "Oolong tea"), and 白茶 (báichá: "white tea"). Another popular drink in tea shops today is 珍珠奶茶 (zhēnzhū nǎichá: "pearl milk tea"). Originating from Taiwan, this drink contains chewy tapioca balls, a modern twist on an old tradition. Today, whether it is the traditional loose-leaf teas or milk tea with sweet delicacies inside, tea drinking still appeals to people of all ages and cultures.

陈大东：	酸辣汤真好喝！我喜欢酸辣的味道。	The Hot and Sour Soup is really good! I like the taste of hot and sour dishes.
孙玛丽：	烧鸡也不错。中平，青菜的味道怎么样？	The roast chicken is pretty good. Zhongping, how do the vegetables taste?
李中平：	太咸了。我要叫一碗米饭。	Too salty. I want to order a bowl of rice.
陈大东：	中平，你为什么不吃肉？	Zhongping, why don't you eat meat?
李中平：	因为我吃素。	Because I am a vegetarian.

孙玛丽：	安娜，你不会用筷子吗？	Anna, don't you know how to use chopsticks?
张安娜：	不会。我只会用刀子，叉子……	No. I only know how to use knives and forks. . .
李中平：	试一下吧！我教你。	Give it a try! I'll teach you.
张安娜：	哦，用筷子很简单啊！	Oh, using chopsticks is simple!
陈大东：	大家吃饱了吗？今天晚饭我请客！	Is everyone full? Tonight it's my treat!

What Can You Do?

INTERPRETIVE
- I can understand different terms for flavors and utensils in Chinese.

INTERPERSONAL
- I can offer assistance to others and receive it in return.
- I can offer to treat others and accept invitations to a meal.
- I can ask and answer "why" questions.
- I can exchange opinions about food with others.

PRESENTATIONAL
- I can present the basic flavors of foods to others.

ACT IT OUT

Working in groups, compose an original three-minute skit that utilizes the vocabulary and structures introduced in Unit 4. Each of you should assume a role and have a roughly equal number of lines in the skit. Be prepared to perform your skit in class. You can either come up with your own story or choose from one of the following situations:

a) You work at a Chinese restaurant and take the orders from a group of customers.

b) You and your friends want to go out to dinner, but no one likes the same dishes.

c) You are a food critic and you ask the chef to explain the flavors of each of your dishes.

CHECK WHAT YOU CAN DO

RECOGNIZE

Adjectives
- 新
- 好吃
- 饿
- 好喝
- 酸
- 辣
- 不错
- 咸
- 渴
- 甜
- 苦

Adverb
- 太

Auxiliary Verbs
- 想
- 要

Conjunctions
- 因为
- 那(么)

Idiomatic Expression
- 欢迎光临

Measure Words
- 杯
- 盘
- 份
- 碗
- 家
- 一下

Name
- 张安娜

Nouns
- 茶
- 菜单
- 中国菜
- 饺子
- 烧鸡
- 青菜
- 酸辣汤
- 饭馆
- 味道
- 米饭
- 肉
- 筷子
- 叉子

- 刀子
- 晚饭
- 水
- 早饭
- 午饭

Particles
- 哦
- 啊

Question Words
- 几位
- 怎么样
- 为什么

Verbs
- 坐
- 喝
- 给
- 点(菜)
- 叫
- 吃素
- 用
- 试
- 教
- 吃饱
- 请客
- 吃饭
- 做饭

WRITE

- 国
- 杯
- 饿
- 光
- 位
- 坐
- 想
- 喝
- 给
- 新
- 份
- 青
- 菜
- 饭
- 馆

- 请
- 晚
- 不错
- 咸
- 味
- 道
- 怎
- 太
- 要
- 因
- 为
- 肉
- 素
- 用

USE

- 想 to indicate a desired action
- 给 to mean "to give"
- 喜欢 to express liking something or someone
- Verb + 不 + Verb with two-character verbs to form affirmative-negative questions
- 那(么) to mean "Well then" or "In that case"
- 好 + Verb to form a compound adjective

- 怎么样 to ask for an opinion of something
- 太……了 to describe an exaggerated attribute
- 要 to indicate desire
- 为什么 and 因为 to ask questions and give explanations respectively
- 一下 to express the brevity of an action

住

Daily Lives

Communication Goals

Lesson 1: 校园生活 **Campus Life**
- Make simple introductions of others
- Be able to state where you or others live
- Name buildings and facilities on campus
- Be able to describe relative locations

Lesson 2: 在哪里？ **Where Is It?**
- Name furniture and rooms in a house
- Use the appropriate expressions on the telephone
- Ask and answer questions about relative locations

你们现在去哪儿？

我去健身房运动，大东去图书馆。

哦，我也要去图书馆看书。

可不可以跟你一起去？

当然可以。

中平，回头见！

LESSON TEXT 5.1

Campus Life 校园生活

Wang Xiaomei runs into Li Zhongping and Chen Dadong in the quad. Li Zhongping introduces Chen Dadong to her. After chatting, Wang Xiaomei and Chen Dadong leave for the library together.

李中平：	小美，我介绍一下，这是陈大东，祥安的室友。	Xiǎoměi, wǒ jièshào yí xià. Zhè shì Chén Dàdōng, Xiáng'ān de shìyǒu.
陈大东：	你好，很高兴认识你。	Nǐ hǎo, hěn gāoxìng rènshi nǐ.
王小美：	你好，大东。你住在哪儿？	Nǐ hǎo, Dàdōng. Nǐ zhù zài nǎr?
陈大东：	我住在校内。我的公寓在餐厅对面。	Wǒ zhù zài xiào nèi. Wǒ de gōngyù zài cāntīng duìmiàn.

―――――――――

王小美：	你们现在去哪儿？	Nǐmen xiànzài qù nǎr?
李中平：	我去健身房运动，大东去图书馆。	Wǒ qù jiànshēnfáng yùndòng, Dàdōng qù túshūguǎn.
王小美：	哦，我也要去图书馆看书。可以不可以跟你一起去？	Ò, wǒ yě yào qù túshūguǎn kàn shū. Kěyǐ bu kěyǐ gēn nǐ yìqǐ qù?
陈大东：	当然可以。中平，回头见！	Dāngrán kěyǐ. Zhōngpíng, huítóu jiàn!

字 词 VOCABULARY

LESSON VOCABULARY 5.1

	SIMPLIFIED	TRADITIONAL	PINYIN	WORD CATEGORY	DEFINITION
1.	介绍	介紹	jièshào	v, n	to introduce; introduction
2.	室友		shìyǒu	n	roommate
3.	很高兴认识你	很高興認識你	hěn gāoxìng rènshi nǐ	ie	pleased to meet you
	认识	認識	rènshi	v, n	to know (someone); knowledge
4.	住		zhù	v	to live (somewhere)
5.	在		zài	prep	at, in, on
6.	哪儿 / 哪里	哪兒 / 哪裏	nǎr / nǎlǐ	pr	where (regional usage in Northern China) / where
7.	校内		xiào nèi	n	on-campus
8.	公寓		gōngyù	n	apartment
9	餐厅	餐廳	cāntīng	n	dining hall
10.	对面	對面	duìmiàn	n	across; facing
	对	對	duì	adj	opposite; correct, right
	面		miàn	n	surface; face
11.	健身房		jiànshēnfáng	n	fitness room
	健身		jiànshēn	v	to work out, to exercise
12.	运动	運動	yùndòng	v	to work out, to exercise
13.	图书馆	圖書館	túshūguǎn	n	library
14.	看书	看書	kàn shū	vo	to read (books)
	书	書	shū	n	book
15.	可以		kěyǐ	av	can; may
16.	跟		gēn	cj	with
17.	一起		yìqǐ	adv	together
18.	当然	當然	dāngrán	adv	of course
19.	回头见	回頭見	huítóu jiàn	ie	see you later
	回头	回頭	huítóu	adv	in a moment; later

REQUIRED VOCABULARY 5.1

	SIMPLIFIED	TRADITIONAL	PINYIN	WORD CATEGORY	DEFINITION
RELATIVE LOCATIONS					
20.	边	邊	biān	*n*	side
21.	前面		qiánmiàn	*n*	in front of
22.	后面	後面	hòumiàn	*n*	behind
23.	校园		xiàoyuán	*n*	campus
CAMPUS LIFE					
24.	同屋		tóngwū	*n*	roommate
25.	教室		jiàoshì	*n*	classroom
26.	校外		xiào wài	*n*	off-campus

OPTIONAL VOCABULARY 5.1

CAMPUS BUILDINGS					
27.	体育馆	體育館	tǐyùguǎn	*n*	gymnasium
28.	活动中心	活動中心	huódòng zhōngxīn	*n*	activity center
29.	博物馆	博物館	bówùguǎn	*n*	museum
30.	办公室	辦公室	bàngōngshì	*n*	office
31.	礼堂	禮堂	lǐtáng	*n*	auditorium
MEASURE WORD					
32.	本		běn	*mw*	(used for books and bound volumes)
RELATIVE LOCATIONS					
33.	旁		páng	*n*	side
34.	旁边	旁邊	pángbiān	*n*	(by) the side of; next to

ONLINE RESOURCES

Visit *http://college.betterchinese.com* for a list of other campus buildings and facilities.

语言注释 LANGUAGE NOTES

Introductions in Chinese

When introduced to a new person, the most common way to greet them is with 你好 (nǐ hǎo). You may also say 很高兴认识你 (hěn gāoxìng rènshi nǐ), which means "pleased to meet you" (you may occasionally also hear 认识你很高兴), when you meet someone for the first time.

If you meet someone famous, you can greet them with the phrase 久闻大名 (jiǔ wén dà míng): an extremely polite phrase, it means "I've heard a lot about you and have long wanted to make your acquaintance." If someone greets you with this phrase, you may reply 彼此，彼此 (bǐcǐ, bǐcǐ) if they are a person of equal celebrity, meaning "likewise."

Verb-Object Compounds

Chinese contains one-character verbs, such as 看 (kàn: "to look"), and two-character verbs such as 介绍 (jièshào: "to introduce"). Some expressions in Chinese may be mistaken for two-character verbs but are actually compound expressions of a transitive verb and an object, for example 看书 (kàn shū: "to read") 吃饭 (chī fàn: "to eat"). These expressions are marked as "vo" in the vocabulary list.

看	+	书	=	看书
kàn		shū		kàn shū
v		o		vo
to look		book		to read

吃	+	饭	=	吃饭
chī		fàn		chī fàn
v		o		vo
to eat		meal		to eat

It is important to remember which verb phrases are verb-object compounds so as not to insert an additional object after the verb-object compound. For example, although we would translate 吃饭 as "to eat," its literal meaning is "to eat a meal," with "meal" functioning as the object. It would therefore be ungrammatical to say *吃饭中国菜.

Understanding the distinction between two-character verbs and verb-object constructions will also come in handy when studying certain grammar patterns in Chinese, as there are a few structures that change depending on which of these kinds of verbs you are using. So, when learning new vocabulary, it can help to check the word category column and try to remember whether a word is a two-character verb or a verb-object compound.

STRUCTURE NOTE 5.1
Use 在 to indicate location

在 (zài) *is a preposition meaning "at," "in," or "on." It also serves as a verb in sentences that state where something is, in which case its meaning is "to be at (a location)." To negate the statement, simply place* 不 *in front of* 在.

Subject (+ 不) + 在 + Location

In statements that describe where something is in relation to somewhere else, a relative place word is added after the above pattern, often preceded by 的. *Relative place words, such as "to the left of" or "in front of," are created by adding the suffixes* 面 *(miàn), meaning "surface",* 边 *(biān), meaning "side", or* 头 *(tóu), meaning "head" to the place word. With the notable exceptions of* 对面 *(duìmian) and* 旁边 *(pángbian), meaning "opposite" and "next to," these suffixes are largely interchangeable, so "in front of" could be* 前面, 前边, *or* 前头. *See Language Note 5.2 for more details.*

Subject + 在 + Location (+ 的) + Place Word

From the Lesson Text:
我的公寓在餐厅对面。
Wǒ de gōngyù zài cāntīng duìmiàn.
My apartment is across from the cafeteria.

Other examples:
图书馆在健身房前边。
Túshūguǎn zài jiànshēnfáng qiánbian.
The library is in front of the gym.

咖啡店在饭馆后面。
Kāfēi diàn zài fànguǎn hòumiàn.
The coffee shop is behind the restaurant.

NOTE: *Certain place words such as* 里 *(lǐ), meaning "in, inside," and* 外 *(wài), meaning "out, outside," are often shortened into more concise and simple forms.* 校园外面 *(xiàoyuán wàimiàn) , for example, becomes* 校外 *(xiào wài), meaning "off campus," while* 餐厅里 *(cāntīng lǐ), "in the dining hall," would be preferred to something more cumbersome like* 餐厅里头.

Practice: Use 在 in conjunction with relative place words to describe the locations of the given subjects, following the prompts in parentheses.

Example: 我的狗 (behind the library) → 我的狗在图书馆的后边。

1.   他们的公寓 (behind our apartment)   _____

2.   她妈妈 (not inside the restaurant)   _____

3.   老师 (outside the classroom)   _____

4.   你的书 (not inside the cafeteria)   _____

5.   李中平 (across from the coffee shop)   _____

STRUCTURE NOTE 5.2
Use 在 as a verb complement

In addition to its role as a verb, 在 may also function as a verb complement. In this lesson, this structure is used to describe where one lives, but it is also commonly seen with verbs such as "to put" or "to sit." When 在 follows a verb, it serves to specify where something takes place. As 在 does not function as a verb in this pattern, 不 must be placed before the verb to negate the sentence.

Subject (+ 不) + Verb + 在 + Location

From the Lesson Text:

你住在哪儿?
Nǐ zhù zài nǎr?
Where do you live?

Other examples:

我坐在你前边吧。
Wǒ zuò zài nǐ qiánbian ba.
I'll sit in front of you.

他们不住在一起。
Tāmen bú zhù zài yìqǐ.
They don't live together.

Practice: Rewrite the following sentences in Chinese, following the example provided.

Example: My older brother lives in China. → 我哥哥住在中国。

1. Chen Dadong and Huang Xiang'an live together.

   _____

2. My classmate lives in America.

   _____

3. We don't live on campus.

   _____

4. Let's sit together.

   _____

5. He doesn't live in Canada.

   _____

STRUCTURE NOTE 5.3
Use 哪儿/哪里 to ask "where"

In order to inquire about the location of something or someone, simply state the subject followed by 在哪儿/在哪里 (zài nǎr/zài nǎlǐ). 哪儿/哪里, meaning "where," takes the place of the location in the sentence. This pattern can also be used with a verb (e.g., 你去哪儿) or when 在 acts as a verb complement. In Northern China, 哪儿 is usually used rather than 哪里.

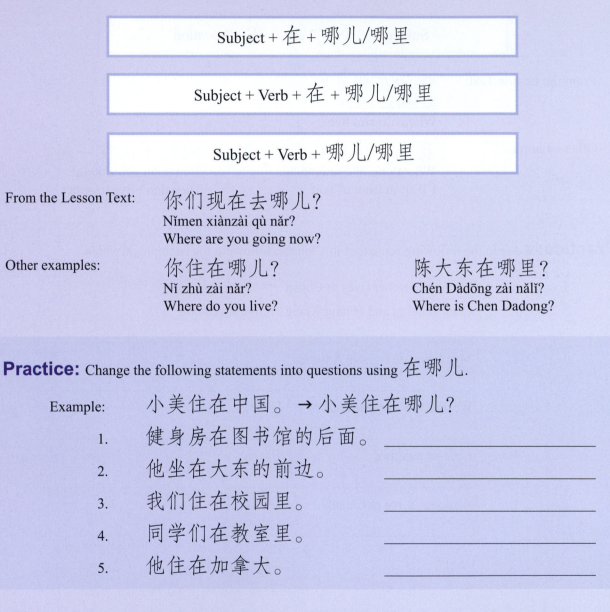

Subject + 在 + 哪儿/哪里

Subject + Verb + 在 + 哪儿/哪里

Subject + Verb + 哪儿/哪里

From the Lesson Text:　你们现在去哪儿?
Nǐmen xiànzài qù nǎr?
Where are you going now?

Other examples:　　你住在哪儿?　　　　　陈大东在哪里?
Nǐ zhù zài nǎr?　　　　　Chén Dàdōng zài nǎlǐ?
Where do you live?　　　　Where is Chen Dadong?

Practice: Change the following statements into questions using 在哪儿.

Example:　　小美住在中国。 → 小美住在哪儿?

1.　健身房在图书馆的后面。 _____
2.　他坐在大东的前边。 _____
3.　我们住在校园里。 _____
4.　同学们在教室里。 _____
5.　他住在加拿大。 _____

STRUCTURE NOTE 5.4
Use 要 to talk about future events

In Structure Note 4.9, 要 *(yào) was introduced as "to want," but in this lesson,* 要 *is also used to talk about an action that one plans to perform in the future, similar to* 会 *in Structure Note 3.1. Context is important when determining whether* 要 *is used in a particular sentence to mean "desire" or to mark a future event.*

> Subject + 要 + Verb Phrase

From the Lesson Text:

我也要去图书馆看书。
Wǒ yě yào qù túshūguǎn kàn shū.
I'm also going to the library.

Other examples:

你今年要去中国吗？ 我们要去看足球比赛。
Nǐ jīnnián yào qù Zhōngguó ma? Wǒmen yào qù kàn zúqiú bǐsài.
Are you going to China this year? We are going to watch the soccer match.

NOTE: *When* 要 *(yào) is negated using* 不 *as in* 不要, *this expresses a negative imperative, and therefore shouldn't be used to talk about future events not happening. To talk about events that will not happen in the future, replace* 要 *with* 不, *or use* 不会.

Examples:

我今天不去学校。
Wǒ jīntiān bú qù xuéxiào.
or
我今天不会去学校。
Wǒ jīntiān bú huì qù xuéxiào.
I will not go to school today.

Practice: Create complete sentences using 要 and the the appropriate verb with the information provided below.

他四点		中国	Example: 她明天要做什么？
你今晚		图书馆	_____
我今年	要 + (Verb)	美国	_____
我明年		咖啡店	_____
她明天		什么	_____

STRUCTURE NOTE 5.5

Use 跟……一起 to express doing things together

跟 (gēn) means "with" and 一起 (yìqǐ) means "together." In Chinese, these two terms are often used in conjunction to describe people doing things together. Time phrases and auxiliary verbs generally come before this expression. To negate this pattern, place 不 before 跟.

> Subject 1 + 跟 + Subject 2 (+ 一起) + Verb Phrase

From the Lesson Text:

可以不可以跟你一起去？
Kěyǐ bu kěyǐ gēn nǐ yìqǐ qù?
Can (I) go with you?

Other examples:

我今天跟她一起去饭馆。
Wǒ jīntiān gēn tā yìqǐ qù fànguǎn.
Today I'm going to a restaurant with her.

我不跟他一起住。
Wǒ bù gēn tā yìqǐ zhù.
I don't live with him.

Practice: Answer the questions below using complete sentences in Chinese.

Example: Who did you eat with? → 我跟我弟弟一起吃晚饭。

1.   Who did you go to the soccer match with?

    _____

2.   Who did he have Chinese food with?

    _____

3.   Who are you living with?

    _____

4.   Who will not go with you to the cafe today?

    _____

5.   Who are you having dinner with on Friday?

    _____

STRUCTURE NOTE 5.6
Use 可以 to express permission

可以 (kěyǐ) *is equivalent to "may," as in, "May I go with you?" and is used to express or request permission to do something. To negate this pattern, place* 不 *before* 可以*, which indicates that the subject is not allowed to do something.*

> Subject + 可以 + Verb Phrase

From the Lesson Text:

可以不可以跟你一起去？
Kěyǐ bu kěyǐ gēn nǐ yìqǐ qù?
Can (I) go with you?

Other examples:

你现在可以来吗？
Nǐ xiànzài kěyǐ lái ma?
Can you come now?

在图书馆不可以喝咖啡。
Zài túshūguǎn bù kěyǐ hē kāfēi.
You may not drink coffee in the library.

Practice: Ask permission to do the following things using 可以.

Example: 跟你去健身房 → 我可以跟你去健身房吗？

1. 跟你去餐厅吃饭 _____
2. 跟你一起看足球 _____
3. 今年去中国 _____
4. 不送她礼物 _____
5. 不去生日派对 _____

PRACTICE 5.1

Working in a group of three, compose and act out a dialogue based on the following scenario: your pen pal comes to visit you on campus. You run into your classmate in the cafeteria, and introduce your pen pal to your classmate. Working with a partner, ask if he or she lives on campus and if he or she has a roommate or not. Use the vocabulary you have learned in the lesson when writing your dialogue.

Example:

A: 我介绍一下我的同学，玛丽。
B: 玛丽，你好。我叫陈大东。
C: 很高兴认识你！你住在哪儿？
B: 我住在校外。你呢？
A: 我住在校内。我的公寓在餐厅后面。
A: 你有没有室友？
B: 有。他是我的好朋友。

PRACTICE 5.2

Draw a simple map of your school campus, including the main buildings and facilities. Present it to the class using the vocabulary you have learned.

PRACTICE 5.3

Identify the locations in the pictures below and note down their Chinese names in the spaces provided. Using these locations, ask a friend where he or she is going and ask if you can go with him or her.

Example:

A: 你现在去哪儿？
B: 我要去图书馆。
A: 我也想去图书馆，可以不可以跟你一起去？
B: 当然可以。

图书馆

💬 PRACTICE 5.4

Do a survey of the class to find out which school facility students use. Record your answers in the table below.

School Facility	Number of Students

PRACTICE 5.5

	Radical	Stroke Order
高	高 gāo tall	亠 亠 亠 亠 亠 亠 高 高 高 高
兴	八 bā eight	丶 丷 丷 丷 兴 兴
认	讠(言) yán speech	丶 讠 讠 认
识	讠(言) yán speech	丶 讠 讠 识 识 识 识
住	亻(人) rén person	丿 亻 亻 住 住 住 住
校	木 mù wood	一 十 才 木 杧 杧 柠 柠 柠 校
园	囗 wéi enclosure	丨 冂 冂 囚 囩 园 园
里	里 lǐ village	丨 口 曰 曰 甲 里 里
面	面 miàn surface	一 丆 丆 而 而 而 面 面
运	辶 chuò walk	一 二 云 云 运 运 运
看	目 mù eye	一 二 三 手 看 看 看 看 看
书	乛 zhé bent	乛 乛 书 书
跟	足 zú foot	丶 口 口 卫 卫 足 趵 趵 趵 跟 跟 跟
当	彐 jì snout	丨 丬 丬 当 当 当
然	灬(火) huǒ fire	丿 勹 夕 夕 夕 タ 外 然 然 然 然 然

PRACTICE 5.6

Make an audio recording and send it to your teacher. In the recording, state whether or not you live on campus and what major buildings are located near you.

PRACTICE 5.7

Type the following sentences on your computer and provide answers to the questions.

1. 我介绍一下我的朋友。
2. 你住在校内吗？
3. 你们现在要去哪儿呢？
4. 我也要去健身房健身。
5. 可不可以跟你一起去？

PRACTICE 5.8

陈大东：你好，我叫陈大东。
　　　　请问你叫什么名字？
王小美：你好，我叫王小美。
陈大东：你是这个学校的学生吗？
王小美：是。你呢？
陈大东：我也是这个学校的学生，
　　　　我学汉语。

Read the dialogue and answer the following questions.
1. Are Chen Dadong and Wang Xiaomei schoolmates?
2. What language does Chen Dadong study at school?

PRACTICE 5.9

中平：
今天很高兴认识你。
我们现在要去图书馆
前面的餐厅吃饭。你
想跟我们一起去吗？
我想介绍一下我的
好朋友王小美给你认
识。

玛丽

Read the note and answer the following questions.
1. Where is Sun Mali going?
2. Whom does Sun Mali want to introduce to Li Zhongping?

PRACTICE 5.10

刘丽是美国人，她学中文，她住在
校外。她早上去图书馆看书，中午
跟同学们一起吃饭，晚上去健身房
健身。

Read the passage and answer the following questions.
1. Where does Miss Liu live?
2. What does she do in the evenings?

Si He Yuan

The 四合院 (sìhéyuàn: "courtyard compound") is a classic style of Beijing residential architecture dating back to the 10th century BC. Consisting of a central courtyard surrounded by four houses and protected by high walls, these compounds enabled families to realize the traditional aspiration of having four generations under one roof. The main house, situated at the north side, was for the head of the family, and the east and west houses were reserved for the family's sons. The guesthouse or study was located on the south side, while daughters had their quarters at the back of the main houses.

Today, though 四合院 are still the residences of many Beijing families, a great number are being demolished as Beijing's expanding population demands more modern housing. Fortunately, some 四合院 are being marked as sites of cultural heritage. Among the 四合院 preserved in their original states as tourist attractions are the former residences of the famous writers 鲁迅 (Lǔ Xùn), 老舍 (Lǎo Shě), and 茅盾 (Máo Dùn).

Study Abroad Programs

Many universities in mainland China and Taiwan offer study abroad opportunities. In Beijing, Peking University (北京大学 Běijīng Dàxué, or 北大 Běidà), Tsinghua University (清华大学 Qīnghuá Dàxué), and Beijing Normal University (北京师范大学 Běijīng Shīfàn Dàxué or 北师大 Běishīdà) are three prestigious universities that offer rich academic and cultural experiences. Further south, Shanghai Fudan University (上海复旦大学 Shànghǎi Fùdàn Dàxué) and Nanjing University (南京大学 Nánjīng Dàxué) are both excellent places to improve one's Chinese. In Taiwan, also, there are a number of long-standing study abroad

programs that offer students the chance to learn Mandarin with traditional characters. National Taiwan University (国立台湾大学 Guólì Táiwān Dàxué) and the Mandarin Training Center at National Taiwan Normal University (国立台湾师范大学 Guólì Táiwān Shīfàn Dàxué) are both popular destinations for international students.

A number of universities in the West have well-established exchange programs with these institutions, providing international students with the opportunity to attend their Chinese language courses. The programs on offer are highly varied and flexible, ranging from short summer courses to programs spanning a full degree length. The whole spectrum of language learning is covered: listening, reading, writing, and speaking, as well as a number of courses on various aspects of Chinese culture. Usually, Chinese language programs are run at a separate college for foreign students within the university, although it is often still possible to audit other classes that you are interested in. Regardless of where you go, there is no doubt that the study abroad experience provides a great opportunity for the student of Chinese to gain a deeper understanding of Chinese language and culture, all while experiencing it first-hand.

李中平：	小美，我介绍一下。这是陈大东，祥安的室友。	Xiaomei, let me introduce you. This is Chen Dadong, Xiang'an's roommate.
陈大东：	你好，很高兴认识你。	Hello, nice to meet you.
王小美：	你好，大东。你住在哪儿？	Hello, Dadong. Where do you live?
陈大东：	我住在校内。我的公寓在餐厅对面。	I live on-campus. My apartment is across from the cafeteria.

王小美：	你们现在去哪儿？	Where are you going now?
李中平：	我去健身房运动，大东去图书馆。	I'm going to the fitness room to exercise; Dadong's going to the library.
王小美：	哦，我也要去图书馆看书。可以不可以跟你一起去？	Oh, I'm also going to the library. May I go with you?
陈大东：	当然可以。中平，回头见！	Of course you can. See you later, Zhongping!

What Can You Do?

INTERPRETIVE
- I can identify locations and buildings on a college campus.
- I can understand positions in relation to other locations.

INTERPERSONAL
- I can make and respond to the proper introductions and greetings when meeting new people.
- I can ask others where they are going and if I may join them after they reply.

PRESENTATIONAL
- I can give a presentation about my campus or another area which describes the main locations and where they are in relation to each other.

LESSON TEXT 5.2

Where Is It? 在哪儿？

Chen Dadong calls Huang Xiang'an to help him find his textbook. When Huang Xiang'an finally finds the textbook under the sofa in his dorm's living room, Chen Dadong decides to come right back to the dorm to get it.

黄祥安：	喂？你好。	Wéi? Nǐ hǎo.
陈大东：	祥安，我是大东。你在哪儿？	Xiáng'ān, wǒ shì Dàdōng. Nǐ zài nǎr?
黄祥安：	我在宿舍看电视。有事吗？	Wǒ zài sùshè kàn diànshì. Yǒu shì ma?
陈大东：	我找不到我的课本了。帮我找一下，好吗？	Wǒ zhǎo bu dào wǒ de kèběn le. Bāng wǒ zhǎo yí xià, hǎo ma?
黄祥安：	好吧。你的课本在卧室里面吗？	Hǎo ba. Nǐ de kèběn zài wòshì lǐmiàn ma?

陈大东：	可能在我的床上。	Kěnéng zài wǒ de chuáng shàng.
黄祥安：	不在那儿，也不在书桌上。	Bú zài nàr, yě bú zài shūzhuō shàng.
陈大东：	……那会在哪儿呢？	. . . Nà huì zài nǎr ne?
黄祥安：	哦，我找到了！课本就在客厅的沙发下面！	Ò, wǒ zhǎodào le! Kèběn jiù zài kètīng de shāfā xiàmiàn!
陈大东：	太好了！我现在马上回去拿。	Tài hǎo le! Wǒ xiànzài mǎshàng huíqù ná.

LESSON VOCABULARY 5.2

	SIMPLIFIED	TRADITIONAL	PINYIN	WORD CATEGORY	DEFINITION
1.	喂		wéi, wèi	*interj*	hello? (for answering telephones only)
2.	宿舍		sùshè	*n*	dormitory
3.	电视	電視	diànshì	*n*	television
4.	有事吗？	有事嗎？	yǒu shì ma?	*ie*	what's up?
	事		shì	*n*	thing; matter
5.	找到		zhǎo dào	*rv*	to find
	找		zhǎo	*v*	to look for
	到		dào	*rc*	(indicates completion or arrival at a goal)
6.	课本	課本	kèběn	*n*	textbook
7.	帮	幫	bāng	*v*	to help
8.	卧室		wòshì	*n*	bedroom
9.	里面	裏面	lǐmiàn	*n*	inside, within
	里	裏，裡	lǐ	*n*	in
10.	可能		kěnéng	*adv, adj*	maybe, possibly; possible
11.	床		chuáng	*n*	bed
12.	那儿 / 那里	那兒 / 那裏	nàr / nàlǐ	*pr*	there (regional usage in Northern China) / there
13.	书桌	書桌	shūzhuō	*n*	desk
14.	上(面)		shàng	*n*	up; on
15.	就		jiù	*adv*	(indicates precision or earliness of action)
16.	客厅	客廳	kètīng	*n*	living room
17.	沙发	沙發	shāfā	*n*	sofa
18.	下面		xiàmiàn	*n*	under; below
	下		xià	*n*	under; below; down
19.	马上	馬上	mǎshàng	*adv*	immediately, right away
20.	回去		huíqù	*v*	to return

LESSON VOCABULARY 5.2 (continued)

SIMPLIFIED	TRADITIONAL	PINYIN	WORD CATEGORY	DEFINITION
回		huí	*v*	to return
21. 拿		ná	*v*	to hold; to get; to take

REQUIRED VOCABULARY 5.2

PRONOUNS

22. 这儿 / 这里	這兒 / 這裏	zhèr / zhèlǐ	*pr*	here (regional usage in Northern China) / here

PARTICLES

23. 得		de	*p*	(indicates the potential to achieve an action or goal)

ROOMS AND FURNITURE

24. 房间	房間	fángjiān	*n*	room
25. 厕所	厕所	cèsuǒ	*n*	toilet; bathroom
26. 桌子		zhuōzi	*n*	table
27. 张	張	zhāng	*mw*	(used for tables, desks, and other flat surfaces)

ONLINE RESOURCES

Visit *http://college.betterchinese.com* for a list of words related to other household items.

OPTIONAL VOCABULARY 5.2

ROOMS AND FURNITURE

28. 洗手间	洗手間	xǐshǒujiān	*n*	restroom
29. 厨房	廚房	chúfáng	*n*	kitchen
30. 间	間	jiān	*mw*	(used for rooms)
31. 椅子		yǐzi	*n*	chair
32. 书架	書架	shūjià	*n*	bookshelf
33. 衣柜	衣櫃	yīguì	*n*	wardrobe
34. 窗户		chuānghu	*n*	window

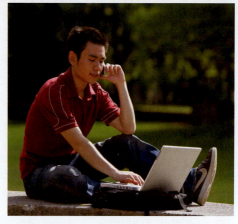

On the Telephone

One hears "你好" (nǐ hǎo) in a manner mostly equivalent to the English "Hello!" When on the telephone, however, one does not answer directly with "你好" but with the greeting "喂" (wéi)? In many mainland Chinese cities, people now answer phones with "喂?" quickly followed by "你好!", "喂?" can be spoken in either the second or the fourth tone, but the second tone inflection has a slightly more polite and questioning sound.

Spatial Location Review

To indicate position, Mandarin combines location specifiers, such as 对 (duì) or 后 (hòu), with the suffixes 面 (miàn), 边 (biān), or 头 (tóu) to create relative place words. With the exceptions of 对面 and 旁边, relative place words in Mandarin can generally be freely combined with either 面, 边, or 头. Remember that location phrases involving 里 and 外 are often shortened; for example, one might more naturally say 教室外 and 咖啡店里 instead of 教室的外边 or 咖啡店的里面.

Below is a review of the relative place words covered in this unit.

Location Term	Pinyin	Meaning
后面 / 边	hòumiàn / bian	behind
前面 / 边	qiánmiàn / bian	in front
外面 / 边	wàimiàn / bian	outside
里面 / 边	lǐmiàn / bian	inside
上面 / 边	shàngmiàn / bian	on top
下面 / 边	xiàmiàn / bian	underneath
旁边	pángbiān	(by) the side of, next to
对面	duìmiàn	opposite

STRUCTURE NOTE 5.7

Use 在 *with an action verb to indicate the location of an activity*

As introduced in Structure Note 5.2, certain verbs can precede 在 *when it acts as a complement. In this lesson we encounter verb phrases that follow* 在 *location phrases. This is the most common structure used to express what action is occurring in some location.*

> Subject + 在 + Location + Verb Phrase

From the Lesson Text:

我在宿舍看电视。
Wǒ zài sùshè kàn diànshì.
I'm watching television in the dorm.

Other examples:

她在餐厅吃饭。
Tā zài cāntīng chī fàn.
She is eating in the cafeteria.

他在图书馆看书。
Tā zài túshūguǎn kàn shū.
He is reading in the library.

Practice: Create sentences in Chinese by inserting 在 and the appropriate verb, using the information provided below.

Example:　　He / Restaurant / Dumplings → 他在餐厅吃饺子。

1. Teacher / Classroom / Book _____
2. Dadong / Coffee shop / Coffee _____
3. She / Living room / Television _____
4. Xiaomei / Bedroom / Textbook _____
5. They / Campus / Soccer match _____

STRUCTURE NOTE 5.8

Use 到 *as a resultative complement to indicate completion of an action*

到 *is an example of a resultative complement, meaning that it follows a verb to indicate the outcome of an activity. English distinguishes between the verbs "look for" and "find," where one is an activity and the other is the result of an activity. In Chinese, the verb* 找 *(zhǎo) is used in isolation when describing the action of searching while* 到 *(dào) literally means "to reach." Thus, Verb +* 到 *indicates an action has been carried to completion, such as with* 找到, *which means to have found something successfully. Note that verbs with resultative complements such as* 找到 *are often paired with the completed action* 了 *(see Structure Note 5.11).*

> Subject + Verb + 到 (+ Object)

From the Lesson Text:

我找到了！
Wǒ zhǎo dào le!
I found it!

Other examples:

我看到你的老师了。
Wǒ kàn dào nǐ de lǎoshī le.
I saw your teacher.

她找到她的狗了。
Tā zhǎo dào tā de gǒu le.
She found her dog.

Practice: Create resultative verb pattern sentences using the elements given.

Example: 找 / 你的同学 → 我找到你的同学了。

1. 看 / 你的朋友 _____
2. 找 / 妹妹的生日礼物 _____
3. 看 / 三只猫 _____
4. 吃 / 妈妈做的菜 _____
5. 看 / 刘老师 _____

STRUCTURE NOTE 5.9

Use 得 or 不 and a resultative complement to indicate whether it is possible or not possible to reach a result

To indicate that someone is engaged in an action, but cannot successfully achieve or complete it, insert 不 before a resultative complement such as 到.

> Subject + Verb + 不 + Resultative Complement (+ Object)

From the Lesson Text:
我找不到我的课本了。
Wǒ zhǎo bu dào wǒ de kèběn le.
I can't find my textbook.

Other examples:
他在美国饭馆吃不到饺子。
Tā zài Měiguó fànguǎn chī bu dào jiǎozi.
In American restaurants, he doesn't get the chance to eat dumplings.

对不起，我做不到！
Duìbuqǐ, wǒ zuò bu dào!
Sorry, I can't do it!

To express that someone is capable of achieving or completing the goal at hand, use the particle 得 (de), instead of 不 (bù) in the structure pattern.

> Subject + Verb + 得 + Resultative Complement (+ Object)

Examples:
他在中国饭馆吃得到饺子。
Tā zài Zhōngguó fànguǎn chī de dào jiǎozi
He can eat dumplings at Chinese restaurants.

我当然找得到你家！
Wǒ dāngrán zhǎo de dào nǐ jiā!
Of course I can find your house!

Practice: Create sentences with 得 or 不 using the information provided below.

Example: 找 / 我的课本 / (negative) → 我找不到我的课本。

1. 看 / 老师 / (affirmative) _____
2. 找 / 妹妹 / (affirmative) _____
3. 看 / 他写的字 / (negative) _____
4. 吃 / 妈妈做的菜 / (negative) _____
5. 找 / 工作 / (negative) _____

STRUCTURE NOTE 5.10

Use 可能 to express likelihood

可能 (kěnéng), *meaning "possibly," "maybe," or "might," addresses the likelihood of some event or situation. In contrast,* 会 *denotes with implied certainty an action that will occur in the future.* 可能 *and* 会 *are sometimes used in conjunction to express the possibility of something happening in the future.*

> Subject + 可能 (+ 会) + Verb Phrase

From the Lesson Text: 可能在我的床上。
Kěnéng zài wǒ de chuáng shàng.
Might be on top of my bed.

Other examples: 她可能不想来。   我可能会去北京。
Tā kěnéng bù xiǎng lái.   Wǒ kěnéng huì qù Běijīng.
Maybe she does not wish to come.   I might go to Beijing.

Practice: Transform these sentences using 可能 or 可能会.

Example: Your textbook might be on the bed → 你的课本可能在床上。

1. He might go to Canada on Wednesday. _____
2. She might return to China tomorrow. _____
3. Maybe Dadong is reading in the café. _____
4. The library might have that book. _____
5. Maybe I will eat at a restaurant tonight. _____

STRUCTURE NOTE 5.11

Use completion 了 *to describe completed actions*

In Structure Note 3.10, the aspect marker 了 was used to express a change of state or a new situation, as in, 她没有工作了, "she doesn't have a job anymore." The 了 particle is also used to indicate that something has taken place (and is finished) or that an action has been completed. Although Chinese does not mark the past tense in the same way that English does, the completion marker 了 is frequently used to describe events in the past. This completion 了 is placed at the end of the sentence (in the same way as the change of state 了), and it is usually used with generalized, non-specific situations and objects.

> Subject + Verb (+ Object) + 了

From the Lesson Text:

哦，我找到了！
Ò, wǒ zhǎodào le!
Oh, I found it!

Other examples:

他昨天吃中国菜了。
Tā zuótiān chī Zhōngguó cài le.
He ate Chinese food yesterday.

我在图书馆看到你的朋友了。
Wǒ zài túshūguǎn kàndào nǐ de péngyou le.
I spotted your friend at the library.

When describing an event or action that did not take place in the past, it is incorrect to use 了. Negation is achieved instead by placing 没有 or 没 before the verb.

> Subject + 没 (有) + Verb (+ Object)

Examples:

我昨天没有去健身房。
Wǒ zuótiān méiyǒu qù jiànshēnfáng.
I didn't go to the gym yesterday.

我今天没吃早饭。
Wǒ jīntiān méi chī zǎofàn.
I didn't eat breakfast today.

There are several patterns that can be used to ask about whether an action has been completed or not.

> Subject + Verb (+ Object) + 了 + 吗？

Example:

你吃饭了吗？
Nǐ chī fàn le ma?
Have you eaten yet?

> Subject + Verb (+ Object) + 了 + 没 (有)？

Example:

你吃饭了没有？
Nǐ chī fàn le méiyǒu?
Have you eaten yet?

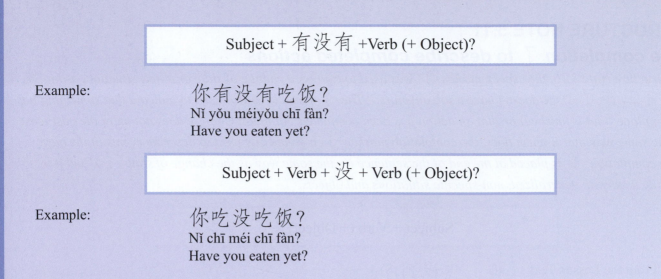

| Subject + 有没有 + Verb (+ Object)? |

Example:　你有没有吃饭？
Nǐ yǒu méiyǒu chī fàn?
Have you eaten yet?

| Subject + Verb + 没 + Verb (+ Object)? |

Example:　你吃没吃饭？
Nǐ chī méi chī fàn?
Have you eaten yet?

Practice: Using the patterns above, transform the following phrases into affirmative or negative statements, as directed.

Example:　她去健身房 / (negative) → 她没去健身房。

1. 他吃晚饭 / (negative)　_____
2. 妈妈早上去图书馆 / (affirmative)　_____
3. 他去年去中国 / (negative)　_____
4. 我今天下午去上课 / (affirmative)　_____
5. 我昨天看电视 / (affirmative)　_____

STRUCTURE NOTE 5.12

Use 就 to indicate "right" or "precisely"

就 (jiù) *has several uses and can be translated into English in a number of ways. In this lesson,* 就 *precedes a location phrase, in which case its meaning is "right" or "precisely," as in "he's right over there." In certain other contexts,* 就 *precedes a noun phrase in order to emphasize or precisely identify the noun. In such cases, there is not always a direct English translation of* 就.

| Subject + 就 + Verb (+ Object) |

From the Lesson Text:　课本就在客厅的沙发下面！
Kèběn jiù zài kètīng de shāfā xiàmian!
The textbook's right underneath the living room sofa!

Other examples:　那就是他的狗。　　　　　她就在那边看书。
Nà jiù shì tā de gǒu.　　　　　Tā jiù zài nà bian kàn shū.
That's his dog.　　　　　　　She's reading right over there.

Practice: Rewrite each sentence using 就, following the example given.

Example: 那是我弟弟。→ 那就是我弟弟。

1.   你的猫在床上。   _____

2.   那是我。   _____

3.   这是我的朋友。   _____

4.   我们在这儿见吧。 _____

5.   那是刘老师的妹妹。 _____

PRACTICE 5.11

Work in groups of three or four to play a game of charades. One of your friends has lost his or her dog; use one of the following pictures as a prompt and act out where the dog is. Your classmates must call out the location in Chinese. Refer to the Optional Vocabulary if necessary.

1.

2.

3.   4.   5.

PRACTICE 5.12

Bring a picture of your room to class. Present the picture to your classmates and describe the layout of your room. Be sure to use the lesson vocabulary to describe your furniture.

Example:
我的卧室里有一张桌子。
卧室里也有一张床。我喜
欢坐在床上看电视。

PRACTICE 5.13

Working with a partner, create and act out a dialogue based on the following situation. Student A and Student B are roommates. A calls B to ask for help finding his or her Chinese book in his or her dorm room. Look at the picture below to describe a possible location for the book.

PRACTICE 5.14

Draw a floor plan of your house using the vocabulary provided below. Refer to the Optional Vocabulary if necessary.

卧室　客厅　房间　厕所　厨房　桌子　椅子　书架　衣柜

	Radical	Stroke Order
吗	口 kǒu mouth	丿 丨冂 口 叮 吗 吗
回	囗 wéi enclosure	丨 冂 冂 同 回 回
电	田 tián field	丨 冂 曰 曰 电
视	见 jiàn see	丶 丿 礻 礻 礻 初 初 视
事	一 yī one	一 一 一 一 亘 写 写 事
找	扌(手) shǒu hand	一 十 才 扩 找 找 找
到	刂(刀) dāo knife	一 乙 云 丞 至 至 到 到
课	讠(言) yán speech	丶 讠 讠 识 识 识 识 课 课
本	木 mù wood	一 十 才 木 本
桌	木 mù wood	丿 丨 卜 占 占 卣 卓 卓 桌
能	肉 ròu meat	厶 厶 育 育 育 育 育 能 能 能
就	尢 wāng lame	丶 二 亠 亠 古 亨 京 京 京 就 就 就
沙	氵(水) shuǐ water	丶 冫 氵 沙 沙 沙 沙
发	又 yòu again	乀 乄 发 发 发
马	马 mǎ horse	乛 马 马

🖥️ **PRACTICE 5.16**

Type the following sentences on your computer and provide an answer to the question.

1. 你住在宿舍吗？
2. 我找不到我的法文课本。
3. 我的课本可能在客厅的沙发上。
4. 你马上去图书馆找刘老师。
5. 玛丽不在健身房，也不在宿舍。

PRACTICE 5.17

Make an audio recording and send it to your teacher. In the recording, describe your bedroom, paying particular attention to the furniture and where things are in relation to each other.

PRACTICE 5.18

李中平：玛丽，你住在宿舍吗？

孙玛丽：对。我住在健身房后面的宿舍。你呢？

李中平：我住在餐厅前面的宿舍。

孙玛丽：我今天在那个餐厅吃饭。

李中平：哦，我们一起去吃饭，好吗？

孙玛丽：好啊！我们六点半在餐厅前面见吧！

李中平：回头见！

Read the dialogue and answer the following questions.
1. Where is Sun Mali's dorm?
2. Where and when do Sun Mali and Li Zhongping arrange to meet?

PRACTICE 5.19

Sender	大东
Subject	生日派对

安娜：

星期五晚上你有事吗？我想请你来我的生日派对。生日派对晚上七点半开始。祥安、中平和小美也会来。

Sender	安娜
Subject	Re:生日派对

大东：

对不起！星期五晚上我有事。我要跟玛丽去图书馆看书。我们八点要跟朋友去饭馆吃饭。

Read the e-mails and answer the following questions.
1. What does Chen Dadong invite Zhang Anna to?
2. Why can't Zhang Anna go?

PRACTICE 5.20

我的宿舍很大，有三间卧室，一间厕所和一间厨房。我跟三个同学一起住。我的卧室里面有一张床，还有沙发和电视。餐厅就在宿舍的下面，健身房就在宿舍的后面，图书馆就在健身房的对面。

Read the passage and answer the following questions.
1. How many bedrooms are there in the dorm?
2. Where is the library?

Text Talk

Cell phones and text messaging are just as popular in China as they are elsewhere in the world, and just like in the West, young people are fond of using quick and easy text slang when they message one another. Romantic partners may text each other the numbers "520" or "520 1314," because 五 (wǔ), 二 (èr), and 零 (líng) sound roughly like "我爱你" (wǒ ài nǐ), "I love you," and 一三一四 (yī sān yī sì) sounds like "一生一世" (yìshēngyíshì), meaning "for a lifetime" or "all one's life."

If you are thinking of someone, you could text "530," which sounds like "我想你" (wǒ xiǎng nǐ), "I miss you." A cute, brief "thank you" can be written as "3Q": 三 (sān) and "Q" together sound very much like the English phrase. For a quick sign-off, you might text a Chinese friend "881" (bā bā yī) – "Bye bye!"

Living in Harmony: Feng Shui

Living in harmony with one's surroundings and improving one's life by gathering positive 气 (qì: "life force" or "energy") is a traditional Chinese belief that many people still follow today. This system is known as feng shui (风 fēng: "wind"; 水 shuǐ: "water").

Feng shui was first used to determine the best way to locate and arrange buildings, and many of the major cities of China were originally designed according to its rules. To maximize *qi*, the location, environment, and even quality of the earth would be considered in the planning of a building.

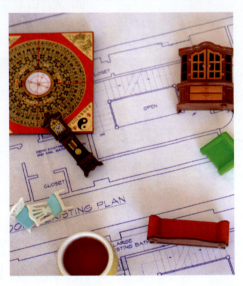

Contemporary buildings are still designed with feng shui principles in mind. During the design and construction of the Taipei 101 skyscraper in Taiwan, for example, feng shui masters were consulted throughout the process. Most strikingly, the entire exterior of the building is designed to look like a stalk of bamboo, a plant believed to attract prosperity and abundance. The building is also segmented into eight sections, eight being a lucky number in Chinese culture, and a fountain placed at one of the entrances creates positive *qi* with its flowing water.

In the West, feng shui has become popular as a style of interior decorating. In this modern take on the ancient art form, people arrange their furniture and decorations to maximize the flow of *qi*. For instance, it is believed a bed should not be placed across from a door, as the life force will flow out of the room. Mirrors placed across from the front door are thought to repel negative energy, while an indoor bamboo plant and goldfish are considered good luck.

黄祥安：	喂？你好。	Hello?
陈大东：	祥安，我是大东。你在哪儿？	Xiang'an, it's Dadong. Where are you?
黄祥安：	我在宿舍看电视。有事吗？	I'm watching television in the dorm. What's up?
陈大东：	我找不到我的课本了。帮我找一下，好吗？	I can't find my textbook. Can you help me look for it?
黄祥安：	好吧。你的课本在卧室里面吗？	Sure. Is your textbook in the bedroom?

陈大东：	可能在我的床上。	Might be on top of my bed.
黄祥安：	不在那儿，也不在书桌上。	It's not there; it's not on the desk either.
陈大东：	……那会在哪儿呢？	. . . So where could it be?
黄祥安：	哦，我找到了！课本就在客厅的沙发下面！	Oh, I found it! The textbook's right underneath the living room sofa!
陈大东：	太好了！我现在马上回去拿。	Great! I'll come back to the dorm rightaway to get it.

What Can You Do?

INTERPRETIVE
- I can understand different terms for furniture and rooms.
- I can understand telephone expressions.

INTERPERSONAL
- I can exchange information about locations with others.
- I can tell someone where I am and what I am doing there when I am asked.
- I can ask someone for help and respond when someone asks me for a favor.

PRESENTATIONAL
- I can present the location of an item to others and tell them where to find it.

ACT IT OUT

Working in groups, compose an original three-minute skit that utilizes the vocabulary and structures introduced in Unit 5. Each of you should assume a role and have a roughly equal number of lines in the skit. Be prepared to perform your skit in class. You can either come up with your own story or choose from one of the following situations:

a) You welcome a new student to school and show them around campus.

b) Your dog is hiding somewhere in the apartment. Ask your friend to help you find him.

c) You and your roommates are moving in together. Decide what furniture you will need.

CHECK WHAT YOU CAN DO

RECOGNIZE

Adverbs
- □ 一起
- □ 当然
- □ 可能
- □ 就
- □ 马上

Auxiliary Verb
- □ 可以

Conjunction
- □ 跟

Idiomatic Expressions
- □ 很高兴认识你
- □ 回头见
- □ 有事吗？

Interjection
- □ 喂

Measure Word
- □ 张

Nouns
- □ 室友
- □ 校内
- □ 公寓
- □ 餐厅
- □ 对面
- □ 健身房
- □ 图书馆
- □ 边
- □ 前面
- □ 后面
- □ 校园
- □ 同屋
- □ 教室
- □ 校外
- □ 宿舍
- □ 电视
- □ 课本
- □ 卧室
- □ 里面
- □ 床
- □ 书桌
- □ 上(面)
- □ 客厅
- □ 沙发
- □ 下面
- □ 房间
- □ 厕所
- □ 桌子

Particle
- □ 得

Prepositions
- □ 在

Pronouns
- □ 哪儿/哪里
- □ 那儿/那里
- □ 这儿/这里

Verbs
- □ 介绍
- □ 住
- □ 运动
- □ 看书
- □ 找到
- □ 帮
- □ 回去
- □ 拿

WRITE

- □ 高兴
- □ 认识
- □ 住校园里面
- □ 运
- □ 看书跟
- □ 当然
- □ 吗
- □ 回电视
- □ 事找到
- □ 课本桌能就沙发
- □ 马

USE

- □ 在 to indicate location
- □ 在 as a verb complement
- □ 哪儿/哪里 to ask "where"
- □ 要 to talk about future events
- □ 跟⋯⋯一起 to express doing things together
- □ 可以 to express permission

- □ 在 with an action verb to indicate the location of an activity
- □ 到 as a resultative complement to indicate completion of an action
- □ 得 or 不 and a resultative complement to indicate whether it is possible or not possible to reach a result
- □ 可能 to express likelihood
- □ Completion 了 to describe completed actions
- □ 就 to indicate "right" or "precisely"

Shopping

第六单元
UNIT 6

Communication Goals

Lesson 1: 买东西 **Shopping**
- Ask about the availability and cost of different items or products in a store
- Understand and use different denominations and amounts of money
- Negotiate prices

Lesson 2: 付现金还是刷卡? **Cash or Credit Card?**
- Indicate that you wish to pay for an item with either cash or credit card
- Use the correct expressions when paying with cash and receiving change

LESSON TEXT 6.1

Shopping 买东西

Zhang Anna and Sun Mali go shopping together. Anna tries to bargain for a cell phone with which she could call her parents.

张安娜：	这家商店卖什么东西？	Zhèi jiā shāngdiàn mài shénme dōngxi?
孙玛丽：	这儿卖的东西很多。你看，有衣服，有文具，还有电子用品。	Zhèr mài de dōngxi hěn duō. Nǐ kàn, yǒu yīfu, yǒu wénjù, háiyǒu diànzǐ yòngpǐn.
张安娜：	我得买一个手机。我很想我爸妈，要给他们打电话。小姐，请问，这个手机多少钱？	Wǒ děi mǎi yí gè shǒujī. Wǒ hěn xiǎng wǒ bà mā, yào gěi tāmen dǎ diànhuà. Xiǎojiě, qǐngwèn, zhèige shǒujī duōshao qián?
售货员：	两百九十块九毛九。	Liǎngbǎi jiǔshí kuài jiǔ máo jiǔ.
张安娜：	太贵了！一百块卖不卖？	Tài guì le! Yì bǎi kuài mài bu mài?

售货员：	不好意思，这个手机的价钱是两百九十块九毛九。	Bù hǎoyìsi, zhèige shǒujī de jiàqián shì liǎngbǎi jiǔshí kuài jiǔ máo jiǔ.
张安娜：	这样吧，我给你一百五十块，怎么样？	Zhèyàng ba, wǒ gěi nǐ yìbǎi wǔshí kuài, zěnmeyàng?
孙玛丽：	安娜，他们这儿不讲价！小姐，有没有便宜一点儿的？	Ānnà, tāmen zhèr bù jiǎngjià! Xiǎojiě, yǒu méiyǒu piányi yìdiǎnr de?
张安娜：	我不要便宜的！算了，我们还是去别的商店看一下吧。	Wǒ bú yào piányi de! Suàn le, wǒmen háishi qù bié de shāngdiàn kàn yí xià ba.

LESSON VOCABULARY 6.1

	SIMPLIFIED	TRADITIONAL	PINYIN	WORD CATEGORY	DEFINITION
1.	商店		shāngdiàn	n	store; shop
2.	卖	賣	mài	v	to sell
3.	东西	東西	dōngxi	n	thing
4.	衣服		yīfu	n	clothing
5.	文具		wénjù	n	stationary
6.	电子用品	電子用品	diànzǐ yòngpǐn	n	electronic device
	用品		yòngpǐn	n	product; goods
7.	得		děi	av	must
8.	买	買	mǎi	v	to buy
9.	手机	手機	shǒujī	n	cellular phone
10.	想		xiǎng	v	to miss (someone or something)
11.	打电话	打電話	dǎ diànhuà	vo	to make a phone call
	打		dǎ	v	to hit; strike
	电话	電話	diànhuà	n	telephone
12.	多少钱	多少錢	duōshao qián	qw	how much is it
	多少		duōshao	qw	how much; how many
	钱	錢	qián	n	money
13.	百		bǎi	nu	hundred
14.	块	塊	kuài	mw	Chinese dollar (colloquial)
15.	毛		máo	mw	1/10 of a kuai
16.	贵	貴	guì	adj	expensive
17.	不好意思		bù hǎoyìsi	ie	sorry for the inconvenience
18.	价钱	價錢	jiàqián	n	price
19.	这样吧	這樣吧	zhèyàng ba	ie	how about this
20.	讲价	講價	jiǎng jià	vo	to haggle; to bargain
	讲	講	jiǎng	v	to speak, to say
21.	便宜		piányi	adj	cheap
22.	算了		suàn le	ie	forget it
23.	还是	還是	háishi	adv	had better; should

SIMPLIFIED	TRADITIONAL	PINYIN	WORD CATEGORY	DEFINITION
24. 别的		bié de	*pr*	other

REQUIRED VOCABULARY 6.1

CURRENCY

SIMPLIFIED	TRADITIONAL	PINYIN	WORD CATEGORY	DEFINITION
25. 千		qiān	*nu*	thousand
26. 万	萬	wàn	*nu*	ten thousand
27. 元		yuán	*mw*	the Chinese dollar (formal)
28. 分		fēn	*mw*	1/100 of a kuai
29. 人民币	人民幣	Rénmínbì	*n*	RMB (currency of the PRC)

MAKING PURCHASES

SIMPLIFIED	TRADITIONAL	PINYIN	WORD CATEGORY	DEFINITION
30. 售货员	售貨員	shòuhuòyuán	*n*	salesperson
31. 一共		yígòng	*adv*	altogether
32. 付钱	付錢	fù qián	*vo*	to pay (money)

OTHER

SIMPLIFIED	TRADITIONAL	PINYIN	WORD CATEGORY	DEFINITION
33. 写信	寫信	xiě xìn	*vo*	to write a letter

OPTIONAL VOCABULARY 6.1

SHOPPING

SIMPLIFIED	TRADITIONAL	PINYIN	WORD CATEGORY	DEFINITION
34. 怎么卖	怎麼賣	zěnme mài	*ie*	how much does it cost? (colloquial)
35. 购物中心	購物中心	gòuwù zhōngxīn	*n*	shopping center
36. 百货公司	百貨公司	bǎihuò gōngsī	*n*	department store
37. 美元		Měiyuán	*n*	the American dollar

Chinese Currency

The official currency in mainland China is called 人民币 Rénmínbì (RMB), meaning the "the people's currency." The basic unit of RMB is the 元 yuán (just as the dollar is the basic unit of US currency). The symbol for 元 is ¥. In Chinese, there are formal and informal ways of referring to the various units of currency, just as in America, one refers to bucks or dollars. The informal variants are used more frequently in everyday speech:

Units of Currency:	Formal	Informal	Monetary Value
	元 yuán	块 kuài	1 RMB
	角 jiǎo	毛 máo	1/10 of a 块 (a "dime")
	分 fēn	---	1/100 of a 块 (a "cent")

While in English, amounts less than a dollar are expressed in terms of cents ("three dollars and thirty-five cents"), in Chinese, these amounts are expressed using both dime and cent units, so "thirty-five cents" would be expressed as three 毛 máo and five 分 fēn.

In Chinese, money expressions are constructed with units of currency (块, 毛) serving as measure words, and 钱 serving as the noun. Just as we use "一个人" to say "one person," we say "一块钱" (literally, "1 块 of money"). In money expressions, however, the noun "钱" at the end of the sentence is optional. If there is more than one monetary unit required in the expression, the final unit may also be omitted.

Examples:
一元三角六分钱 (Formal) (¥ 1.36)
十一块（钱）(¥ 11)
五毛（钱）(¥ 0.5)
三分（钱）(¥ 0.03)
十块八（毛）（钱）(¥ 10.8)
八十二块四毛五（分）（钱）(¥ 82.45)
十七块零五分（钱）(¥ 17.05)

Note that in the last example, because the dime unit is empty, a 零 líng or 0 is placed before the cent value, and the noun 分 fēn is mandatory.

Counting

Numbers 100 – 999: As explained in the Language Notes in Unit 1, Lesson 2, the numbers from 11 to 19 and the numbers from 20 to 99 each follow a regular pattern. The numbers from 100 to 999 also follow regular patterns. Multiples of 100, such as the number 200 (二百: èrbǎi), are composed of the first number, two (二), followed by the number hundred (百: bǎi). With this forumla, we can create most of the numbers between 100 and 1,000 by adding the numbers 11 – 19 or 20 – 99 after a multiple of 100. For example, 121 is 一百二十一 (yìbǎi èrshíyī). One exception is the number 11, which becomes yī shí yī in numbers after 100. For numbers with a zero in the tens place, such as 101, we say the number 100 (一百: yìbǎi), then the number zero (零), and lastly the number one (一).

Numbers 1,000 – 9,999 and above: The numbers 1,000 – 9,999 also follow regular patterns. In general, we say the first number, then the number thousand (千: qiān), and lastly the number represented by the last three digits. If there is a zero in the hundreds place, it is also expressed. For example, the number 1,229 is 一千两百二十九 (yìqiān liǎngbǎi èrshíjiǔ) and the number 1,011 is 一千零一十一 (yìqiān líng yīshíyī). If there are zeros in the hundreds and tens places, they are replaced by a single zero. The number 1,001, for example, is 一千零一 (yìqiān líng yī). For numbers 10,000 and above, the Chinese system counts by factors of 10,000 (万: wàn). The number 30,000, for example, is 三万 (sānwàn).

STRUCTURE NOTE 6.1

Use 有 to express existence rather than possession

In Structure Note 2.1, 有 was used to express possession. In this lesson, 有 expresses the existence of something, as in "there are clothes in the shop." When the context is clear, the specific location can be omitted.

> (Location +) 有 + Noun Phrase

As in Structure Note 2.2, 没 can also be inserted before 有 to express an absence of something.

From the Lesson Text:

有衣服，有文具，还有电子用品。
Yǒu yīfu, yǒu wénjù, háiyǒu diànzǐ yòngpǐn.
They have clothes, stationery, as well as electronics.

Other examples:

这儿有中国菜吗？
Zhèr yǒu Zhōngguó cài ma?
Is there Chinese food here?

书店没有你要的书。
Shūdiàn méiyǒu nǐ yào de shū.
The bookstore does not have the book you want.

Practice: Construct Chinese questions and sentences using 有 and the information provided below.

你们大学	→	美国学生	Example: 你们大学有美国学生吗？
中国		好吃的菜	
这儿	有	猫	_____
你的房间		桌子	_____
书店		文具	_____
那儿		筷子	_____

STRUCTURE NOTE 6.2

Use 得 to express "must"

The character 得 can be pronounced in two ways: de and děi. When 得 is used as the auxiliary verb meaning "must" or "have to," it is pronounced děi. 得 (děi) can only be used in the affirmative to express that something must be done and cannot be directly transformed into a negative form.

> Subject + 得 + Verb Phrase

From the Lesson Text: 我得买一个手机。
Wǒ děi mǎi yí gè shǒujī.
I have to buy a cell phone.

Other examples: 你得做什么？
Nǐ děi zuò shénme?
What do you have to do?

她今天得去学校。
Tā jīntiān děi qù xuéxiào.
She must go to school today.

Practice: Create 得 sentences by adding the appropriate verb and using the information provided below.

Example: 早饭 → 你得吃早饭。

1. 商店 _____

2. 晚饭 _____

3. 生日礼物 _____

4. 汉语 _____

5. 咖啡店 _____

STRUCTURE NOTE 6.3
Use 给 as the preposition "to"

In Structure Note 4.2, 给 was used as a verb associated with the giving of an object. In this lesson, 给 is introduced as a preposition, similar in meaning to "to." It can be used, among other things, to indicate to whom one makes a phone call, writes a letter, or gives a present.

Subject + 给 + Object + Verb Phrase

From the Lesson Text: 我很想我爸妈，要给他们打电话。
Wǒ hěn xiǎng wǒ bà mā, yào gěi tāmen dǎ diànhuà.
I miss my parents, and I want togive them a call.

Other examples: 你明天给他打电话吧。
Nǐ míngtiān gěi tā dǎ diànhuà ba.
Why don't you call him tomorrow.

我要给玛丽买个生日礼物。
Wǒ yào gěi Mǎlì mǎi gè shēngrì lǐwù.
I want to buy Mali a birthday present.

Practice: Create sentences using 给, applying the specified recipients and actions.

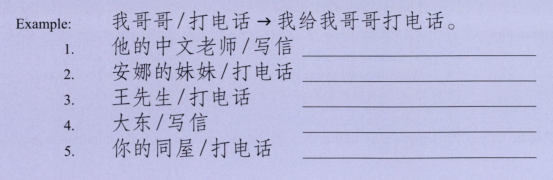

Example:　我哥哥／打电话 → 我给我哥哥打电话。
1.　他的中文老师／写信 _____
2.　安娜的妹妹／打电话 _____
3.　王先生／打电话 _____
4.　大东／写信 _____
5.　你的同屋／打电话 _____

STRUCTURE NOTE 6.4
Use 多少 to ask "how many" or "how much"

多少 (duōshao) *is used to ask about quantities. In this lesson,* 多少 *is used to ask about price. When asking for prices,* 多少 *is followed by the noun* 钱 (qián, *"money"*).

> Subject (+ Verb) + 多少 + Noun

From the Lesson Text:　这个手机多少钱？
Zhèige shǒujī duōshao qián?
How much is this cell phone?

Other examples:　你们学校有多少学生？　你有多少钱？
Nǐmen xuéxiào yǒu duōshao xuéshēng?　Nǐ yǒu duōshao qián?
How many students are at your school?　How much money do you have?

As mentioned previously, the term 几 *is used to ask about quantities expected to be 10 or less.* 多少 *is therefore used to ask about quantities expected to be greater than 10. In the* 几 *pattern, measure words are always included between* 几 *and the item in question. In* 多少 *questions, the measure word is usually omitted.*

Examples:　你有几本书？　你有多少书？
Nǐ yǒu jǐ běn shū?　Nǐ yǒu duōshao shū?
How many books do you have?　How many books do you have?
(expected quantity less than 10)　(expected quantity greater than 10)

Practice: Create questions using 多少 using the information provided below.

Example: How many waiters are at the restaurant? → 这家饭馆有多少服务员？

1.   How many Chinese books does this library have?

_____

2.   How many tables does the restaurant have?

_____

3.   How many Chinese people are there in America?

_____

4.   How many textbooks does the bookstore carry?

_____

5.   How much is this plate of dumplings?

_____

STRUCTURE NOTE 6.5
Use Adjectives with (一)点(儿) to express "a little more"

In English, the expressions "a little hot" and "a little hotter" are distinguished by modification of the adjective. In Chinese, the difference in these meanings is expressed by the placement of (一)点 (儿)(yìdiǎnr) *before or after the adjective. When* (一)点 (儿) *precedes the adjective, it means "a bit (adjective)." When it follows the adjective, it means "a bit more (adjective)." This lesson practices the second pattern.*

> Subject + Adjective + (一)点(儿)

From the Lesson Text:

小姐，有没有便宜一点儿的？
Xiǎojiě, yǒu méiyǒu piányi yìdiǎnr de?
Miss, is there one that's a bit cheaper?

Other examples:

这个手机好一点儿。
Zhège shǒujī hǎo yìdiǎnr.
This cell phone is a bit better.

那个沙发贵一点。
Nèige shāfā guì yìdiǎn.
That sofa is a little more expensive.

Practice: Create complete sentences in Chinese by adding（一）点（儿）and using the provided information.

Example:　　　这盘饺子／好吃 → 这盘饺子好吃一点。

1.　那本书／便宜　　　_____

2.　这张书桌／贵　　　_____

3.　我们的家／小　　　_____

4.　那个蛋糕／甜　　　_____

5.　这杯咖啡／好喝　　_____

STRUCTURE NOTE 6.6
Use 还是······吧 *to express a suggested alternative*

The expression 还是 *(háishì) usually means "or" in an alternative question, as in "either this or that." In this lesson, it is used to introduce a suggestion that the speaker thinks is a better alternative. The location of* 还是 *in relation to the rest of the sentence determines which aspect of the suggestion is being emphasized, but most frequently it is placed between the subject and the verb phrase. Usually, these sentences end in the suggestion particle* 吧.

Subject + 还是 + Verb Phrase + 吧

From the Lesson Text:　　我们还是去别的商店看一下吧。
Wǒmen háishi qù bié de shāngdiàn kàn yí xià ba.
Let's go to another store to take a look.

Other examples:　　你还是明天去吧。　　　我不会用筷子，还是给
Nǐ háishi míngtiān qù ba.　　我叉子吧。
It would be better for you to go tomor-　Wǒ bú huì yòng kuàizi, háishi gěi wǒ
row.　　　　　　　　　　　chāzi ba.
　　　　　　　　　　　　　I don't know how to use chopsticks.
　　　　　　　　　　　　　Please give me a fork.

Practice: Create suggestions using the 还是……吧 pattern with the given words.

Example:　你／去中国 → 你还是去中国吧。

1.　你／早一点儿吃晚饭

　　　_____

2.　你们／去看弟弟的比赛

　　　_____

3.　我／给他打个电话

　　　_____

4.　我们／在宿舍见

　　　_____

5.　我们／去健身房

　　　_____

PRACTICE 6.1

Write the name of the products shown below on the corresponding price tags. Then, working with a partner, create a script where you roleplay a customer and a store clerk. The customer should ask for the cost of the various items listed below and bargain over the price.

给　　有，有，还有　　多少钱　　卖不卖？　　一点儿　　还是……吧

Example:

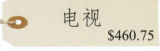

电视
$460.75

A: 请问，这里卖电子用品吗？
B: 卖。
A: 这个电视多少钱？
B: 四百六十块七毛五。
A: 太贵了！三百块卖不卖？
B: 好啊。三百块卖给你。
　　/ 不卖，这个很便宜了。
A: 好，谢谢。
　　/ 算了，不买了。

1. $7.50

2. $10.80

3. $485.99

4. $230.75

5. $84.00

6. $149.50

	Radical	Stroke Order
写	冖 mì cover	⺀ 冖 写 写 写
买	乛 zhé bent	乛 乛 ⺕ 三 买 买
卖	十 shí ten	一 十 土 古 吉 吉 卖 卖
东	一 yī one	一 七 车 车 东
西	西 yà cover	一 丆 丆 丙 西 西
手	手 shǒu hand	一 二 三 手
得	彳 chì step	丿 彳 彳 彳 彳 彳 彳 得 得 得
少	小 xiǎo small	丨 小 小 少
钱	钅(金) jīn gold	丿 𠂉 钅 钅 钅 钅 钅 钱 钱 钱
百	白 bái white	一 丆 丆 百 百 百
块	土 tǔ earth	一 十 土 圹 圹 块 块
意	心 xīn heart	丶 丶 亠 立 音 音 音 音 意 意 意
思	心 xīn heart	丶 口 口 田 田 思 思 思
价	亻(人) rén person	丿 亻 亻 价 价 价
信	亻(人) rén person	丿 亻 亻 信 信 信 信 信 信

PRACTICE 6.3

Make an audio recording and send it to your teacher. In the recording, describe a shopping experience. You should answer the following questions: What items were sold at the store? What did you buy? How much did it cost? Use as many of the sentence structures that you have learned as you can.

PRACTICE 6.4

Type the following sentences on your computer and provide answers to the questions.

1. 这家商店卖什么东西？
2. 请问这个手机多少钱？
3. 太贵了！一百块卖不卖？
4. 这个手机的价钱是两百九十块九毛九。
5. 不好意思，我们这儿不讲价！

PRACTICE 6.5

Write down the Chinese characters for the following prices.

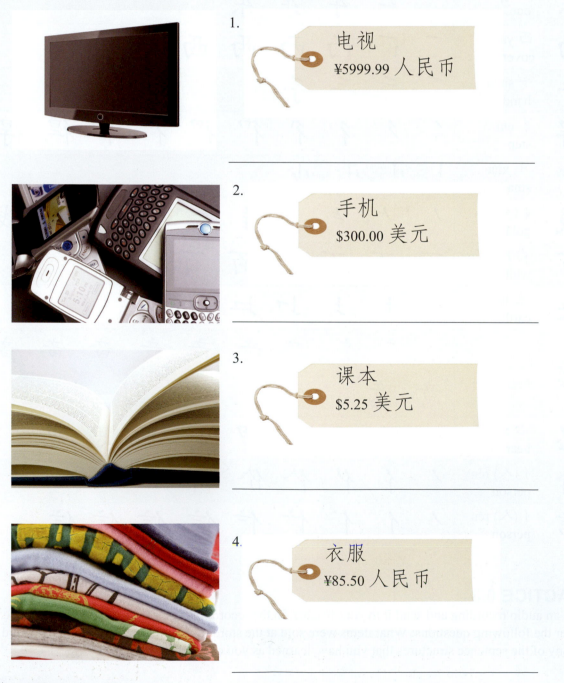

1.

电视
¥5999.99 人民币

2.

手机
$300.00 美元

3.

课本
$5.25 美元

4.

衣服
¥85.50 人民币

PRACTICE 6.6

玛丽和她的朋友安娜去学校对面的商店买东西。
玛丽：安娜，你想买什么？
安娜：我想买一个手机给妈妈打电话。
玛丽：可是这里卖的手机太贵了！
安娜：算了，我们还是去别的商店看一下吧。

Read the dialogue and answer the following questions.
1. What does Zhang Anna want to buy?
2. What does she decide to do in the end?

PRACTICE 6.7

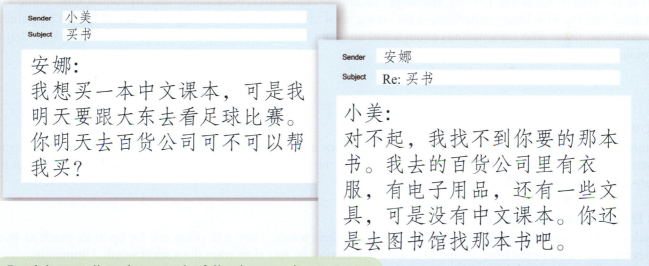

Sender	小美
Subject	买书

安娜：
我想买一本中文课本，可是我明天要跟大东去看足球比赛。你明天去百货公司可不可以帮我买？

Sender	安娜
Subject	Re: 买书

小美：
对不起，我找不到你要的那本书。我去的百货公司里有衣服，有电子用品，还有一些文具，可是没有中文课本。你还是去图书馆找那本书吧。

Read the e-mails and answer the following questions.
1. What did Wang Xiaomei ask Zhang Anna to buy for her?
2. Did Zhang Anna buy it for her?

PRACTICE 6.8

昨天我去商店了，我想买一件新衣服，可是价钱不便宜。我问售货员有没有便宜一点儿的，售货员给我看便宜点儿的，可是我还是不喜欢。我没有买衣服就回家了。

Read Wang Xiaomei's diary and answer the following questions.
1. What did the salesperson show to Wang Xiaomei?
2. What did Wang Xiaomei do in the end?

Shopping in Beijing: Silk Street

With over seven floors and more than 1,500 stalls, Beijing's Silk Street shopping mall (秀水街 Xiùshuǐ Jiē) is a favorite destination for tourists and locals alike. In the past, Silk Street was an outdoor market consisting of approximately 400 stalls. Strolling down the alleys around Silk Street, one could find goods ranging from tapestries, jade, and fine silk to a wide range of knock-off brand-name goods.

In 2005, the original Silk Street market was closed due to fire safety concerns and land permit issues. The new Silk Street market, a multistorey indoor shopping mall, opened in January 2005. This new market has around 1,500 stalls, over twice the amount of the original street. Aside from the brand-name products of dubious origin, there are many other things to find at the market, including jewelry, paintings, traditional crafts, toys, electronics, and, of course, silk. Some visitors may find the Silk Street experience a bit taxing, as it invariably involves large crowds and heated bargaining. Nevertheless, those who are tenacious enough will no doubt be able to pick up a bargain at this landmark of Beijing shopping.

How to Bargain in China

In modern China, one would not expect to negotiate prices in department stores and supermarkets, but it is expected at street shops and stalls, like the ones at Silk Street. So, the next time you have a chance to go to China, try out this four-step bargaining technique:

1. Drive a hard bargain

Vendors will commonly wildly overstate the prices of their wares. They will often ask for up to as much as thirty times the real value of the item. Respond in kind by offering far less than what the item is worth. Ultimately, expect to reach a deal somewhere between the two extremes.

2. Hide your feelings

Some shoppers cannot help but show that they really like something, but experienced sellers will notice this and raise the price of the item. Therefore, it is best to pretend one is browsing and somewhat uninterested.

3. Point out defects in the goods

No item will be perfect. Just as the seller boasts about his goods, go tit-for-tat and point out inadequacies to try and bring the price lower.

4. Walk away

The vendor will feel frustrated if he or she does not manage to sell any item after all the time spent with you and will often compromise if you wear him or her down. If the seller will not accept your final offer, then turn and begin to walk away. It may not always work, but this last-ditch tactic might just break their resistance and land you your desired bargain.

张安娜： 这家商店卖什么东西？

What sorts of things does this store sell?

孙玛丽： 这儿卖的东西很多。你看，有衣服，有文具，还有电子用品。

It sells lots of things. Look, they have clothes, stationery, as well as electronics.

张安娜： 我得买一个手机。我很想我爸妈，要给他们打电话。小姐，请问，这个手机多少钱？

I have to buy a cell phone. I miss my parents, and I want togive them a call. Excuse me, Miss, how much is this cell phone?

售货员： 两百九十块九毛九。

$290.99.

张安娜： 太贵了！一百块卖不卖？

That's too expensive! Will you sell it for $100?

售货员： 不好意思，这个手机的价钱是两百九十块九毛九。

I'm sorry; the price of this phone is $290.99.

张安娜： 这样吧，我给你一百五十块，怎么样？

How about this: I'll give you $150. How does that sound?

孙玛丽： 安娜，他们这儿不讲价！小姐，有没有便宜一点儿的？

Anna, they don't bargain here! Miss, is there one that's a bit cheaper?

张安娜： 我不要便宜的！算了，我们还是去别的商店看一下吧。

I don't want a cheap one! Never mind, let's go to another store to take a look.

What Can You Do?

INTERPRETIVE
- I can interpret or identify the price of an object.
- I can differentiate between different denominations.

INTERPERSONAL
- I can talk to classmates about items that are available in a store.
- I can inquire about and barter over prices.

PRESENTATIONAL
- I can present a list of products and their respective costs.
- I can express opinions about an item's expense.

LESSON TEXT 6.2

Cash or Credit Card?　付现金还是刷卡？

Chen Dadong and Li Zhongping are at the jewelry store together because Li Zhongping wants to buy a present for Sun Mali.

陈大东：　中平，你已经送玛丽生日礼物了，为什么还要再给她买东西？

Zhōngpíng, nǐ yǐjīng sòng Mǎlì shēngrì lǐwù le, wèishénme hái yào zài gěi tā mǎi dōngxi?

李中平：　因为她昨天教我做功课，所以我要谢谢她。

Yīnwèi tā zuótiān jiāo wǒ zuò gōngkè, suǒyǐ wǒ yào xièxie tā.

陈大东：　你要给她买这么贵的礼物啊！

Nǐ yào gěi tā mǎi zhème guì de lǐwù a!

李中平：　不用担心，要是太贵的话我就买别的东西。

Bú yòng dānxīn, yàoshi tài guì de huà wǒ jiù mǎi bié de dōngxi.

李中平：　先生，请问这条项链多少钱？

Xiānsheng, qǐngwèn zhèi tiáo xiàngliàn duōshao qián?

———————

售货员：　一百二十八块。

Yìbǎi èrshíbā kuài.

李中平：　好，那我就买这条。

Hǎo, nà wǒ jiù mǎi zhèi tiáo.

售货员：　请问您是付现金还是刷卡？

Qǐngwèn nín shì fù xiànjīn háishì shuā kǎ?

李中平：　付现金。给你一百三十块。

Fù xiànjīn. Gěi nǐ yìbǎi sānshí kuài.

陈大东：　你花了这么多钱，可以吗？

Nǐ huā le zhème duō qián, kě yǐ ma?

李中平：　没问题。哦，玛丽来了，我们走吧！

Méi wèntí. Ò, Mǎlì lái le, wǒmen zǒu ba!

字 词 VOCABULARY

LESSON VOCABULARY 6.2

	SIMPLIFIED	TRADITIONAL	PINYIN	WORD CATEGORY	DEFINITION
1.	已经	已經	yǐjīng	*adv*	already
2.	再		zài	*adv*	again
3.	功课	功課	gōngkè	*n*	homework
4.	所以		suǒyǐ	*cj*	so; therefore
5.	这么	這麼	zhème	*adv*	so (indicates degree)
6	不用		bú yòng	*ie*	no need
7.	担心		dānxīn	*v*	worry
8.	要是⋯⋯(的话)	要是⋯⋯(的話)	yàoshi . . . (de huà)	*cj*	if
9.	项链	項鏈	xiàngliàn	*n*	necklace
10.	付		fù	*v*	to pay
11.	现金	現金	xiànjīn	*n*	cash
12.	刷卡		shuā kǎ	*vo*	to pay with credit card
	卡		kǎ	*n*	card
13.	花		huā	*v*	to spend (money, time, effort)
14.	没问题	沒問題	méi wèntí	*ie*	no problem

REQUIRED VOCABULARY 6.2

	SIMPLIFIED	TRADITIONAL	PINYIN	WORD CATEGORY	DEFINITION
CONJUNCTIONS					
15.	如果		rúguǒ	*cj*	if
RELATED TO TRANSACTIONS					
16.	银行	銀行	yínháng	*n*	bank
17.	收		shōu	*v*	to accept; to receive (money)
18.	找		zhǎo	*v*	to give change
19.	钱包	錢包	qiánbāo	*n*	wallet
20.	信用卡		xìnyòngkǎ	*n*	credit card
OTHER					
21.	下(个)星期	下(個)星期	xià (gè) xīngqī	*n*	next week
	下		xià	*adj*	next
22.	上(个)星期	上(個)星期	shàng (gè) xīngqī	*n*	last week
	上		shàng	*adj*	last

OPTIONAL VOCABULARY 6.2

	SIMPLIFIED	TRADITIONAL	PINYIN	WORD CATEGORY	DEFINITION
MONEY					
23.	货币	貨幣	huòbì	*n*	currency
24.	支票		zhīpiào	*n*	check
25.	发票	發票	fāpiào	*n*	receipt
26.	收据	收據	shōujù	*n*	receipt

Transaction Words

The following key terms and expressions are commonly used when conducting financial transactions:

付 (used by customer to formally state the amount they are paying)

Ex: 付你二十块。 Here is $20. (lit. "I pay you twenty dollars.")

收 (formally acknowledges the receipt of money from a customer)

Ex: 收您十块。 I have received $10 from you.

找 (used by salesperson to state the amount of change they are giving you)

Ex: 找您两块。 Here is $2 change. (lit. "I give you two dollars in change.")

Countries & Currencies

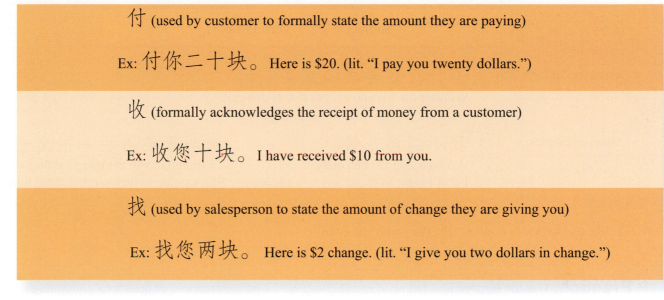

	国家	货币		国家	货币
🇬🇧	英国 Yīngguó U.K.	英镑 Yīngbàng Pound (£)	🇰🇷	韩国 Hánguó S. Korea	韩元 Hányuán Won (₩)
🇺🇸	美国 Měiguó U.S.A.	美金/美元 Měijīn/Měiyuán Dollar ($)	🇯🇵	日本 Rìběn Japan	日元 Rìyuán Yen (¥)
🇨🇳	中国 Zhōngguó China	人民币 Rénmínbì (RMB) (¥)	🇪🇺	欧盟 Ōuméng E.U.	欧元 Ōuyuán Euro (€)

STRUCTURE NOTE 6.7
Use 再 to indicate a repeating action

再 (zài), *meaning "again" or "also," is used after the subject and before a verb phrase to express a recurring event or action.*

Subject + 再 + Verb Phrase

From the Lesson Text:
为什么还要再给她买东西？
Wèishénme hái yào zài gěi tā mǎi dōngxi?
Why are you buying her something else?

Other examples:

我不想再花钱。
Wǒ bù xiǎng zài huā qián.
I don't want to spend any more money.

她明天要再买一张桌子。
Tā míngtiān yào zài mǎi yì zhāng zhuōzi.
She's going to buy another table tomorrow.

NOTE: *Be careful not to confuse* 再 (zài) *with* 在 (zài)!

Practice: Use the information below to create complete Chinese sentences or questions containing 再.

Example: Would you like to buy another book? → 你要再买一本书吗？

1. I don't want to watch any more TV.

   _____

2. Will you go to China again this year?

   _____

3. Does he want to go to Japan again?

   _____

4. Try it again (hint: 一下)

   _____

5. Would you like to buy another cake?

   _____

STRUCTURE NOTE 6.8

Use 因为…所以… *to express causal relationships*

因为 (yīnwèi) *and* 所以 (suǒyǐ) *literally mean "because" and "therefore." In Chinese it is acceptable to include both or just one of these terms to link two phrases.*

> (因为 +) Phrase, + (所以 +) Phrase

From the Lesson Text:

因为她昨天教我做功课，所以我要谢谢她。
Yīnwèi tā zuótiān jiāo wǒ zuò gōngkè, suǒyǐ wǒ yào xièxie tā.
She helped me with my homework yesterday, so I wanted to thank her.

Other examples:

因为他送我一条项链，所以我很高兴。
Yīnwèi tā sòng wǒ yì tiáo xiàngliàn, suǒyǐ wǒ hěn gāoxìng.
I am happy because he gave me a necklace.

因为她妈妈是中国人，她会说中文。
Yīnwèi tā māma shì Zhōngguó rén, tā huì shuō Zhōngwén.
Because her mom is Chinese, she knows how to speak Chinese.

OR

她妈妈是中国人，所以她会说中文。
Tā māma shì Zhōngguó rén, suǒyǐ tā huì shuō Zhōngwén.
Her mom is Chinese, so she knows how to speak Chinese.

Practice: Create complete sentences in Chinese using 因为…所以… and the information provided below.

Example: I don't like to read, so I don't want to go to the library
→ 因为我不喜欢看书，所以不想去图书馆。

1. I went to a party last night, so I didn't do my homework.

    _____

2. Because the television was too expensive, I didn't buy it.

    _____

3. The things I ate at dinner were too salty, so I want to drink water.

    _____

4. He doesn't have money, so he has to work.

    _____

5. She likes to cook, so we went to her house for dinner.

    _____

STRUCTURE NOTE 6.9
Use 不用 to say "need not"

不用 (bú yòng) *means "need not . . . ," "do not have to . . . ," or "do not need to . . . ." In Structure Note 6.2, it was explained that* 得 *cannot be transformed into a negative form to express "do not have to." Instead,* 不用 *is used, followed by the verb phrase describing what is not required.*

Subject + 不用 + Verb Phrase

From the Lesson Text: 不用担心。
Bú yòng dānxīn.
Don't worry.

Other examples: 你今天不用做饭。   他不用去图书馆了。
Nǐ jīntiān bú yòng zuò fàn.   Tā bú yòng qù túshūguǎn le.
You don't need to cook today.   He doesn't need to go to the library anymore.

Practice: Construct sentences using 不用 and the information provided below.

Example: 你 / 给他打电话。 → 你不用给他打电话。
1.   你今天 / 去上课。   _____
2.   她 / 吃早饭。   _____
3.   你 / 买生日礼物。   _____
4.   我们 / 去银行。   _____
5.   他们 / 买这本书。   _____

STRUCTURE NOTE 6.10

Use 这么 *or* 那么 *to intensify adjectives*

The expressions 这么 *(zhème) and* 那么 *(nàme), when applied before an adjective, are used to intensify or indicate a high degree of the referred quality. These terms are akin to the English expressions "so . . ." or "such . . ." when applied in conjunction with an adjective to describe a subject.*

这么 / 那么 + Adjective

From the Lesson Text:

你要给她买这么贵的礼物啊！
Nǐ yào gěi tā mǎi zhème guì de lǐwù a!
You're going to buy her such an expensive present!

Other examples:

你的手机那么便宜啊！
Nǐ de shǒujī nàme piányi a!
Your cell phone is so cheap!

我不想买这么贵的项链。
Wǒ bù xiǎng mǎi zhème guì de xiàngliàn.
I don't want to buy such an expensive necklace.

Practice: Create complete sentences or questions in Chinese using 这么 or 那么 with the details provided below.

Example: 要喝 / 辣的汤 / 吗 → 你要喝这么辣的汤吗？

1. 不喜欢吃 / 咸的菜 _____
2. 宿舍 / 大！ _____
3. 要买 / 小的书桌 / 吗 _____
4. 不想买 / 贵的东西 _____
5. 项链 / 便宜！ _____

STRUCTURE NOTE 6.11

Use Verb + 了 to describe specific completed actions

In Structure Note 5.11, it was shown that the particle 了 is used at the end of a sentence to indicate something that has taken place or an action that has been completed. The use of 了 in this lesson also shows that something happened at some time in the past, but it is placed after the verb instead of at the end of the sentence. While both affect the meaning of an utterance in the same way, they are used under different circumstances. The more specific the situation and the more the object is modified, the more reason one has to use the verb-suffix 了. The sentence-final 了 is applied when the context and/or object is only general. If the object of the sentence is quantified, then it is in fact obligatory to place 了 after the verb.

The verb-suffix 了 is only used with action verbs and it is never paired with habitual actions. Like the sentence-final 了, it is negated by placing (没)有 before the verb.

Subject + Verb + 了 (+ Quantity) + Object

From the Lesson Text:　　你花了这么多钱，可以吗?
Nǐ huā le zhème duō qián, kěyǐ ma?
Is it OK to spend so much money?

Other examples:　　我昨天喝了三杯咖啡。　　　　昨天我买了两本书。
Wǒ zuótiān hē le sān bēi kāfēi.　　　Zuótiān wǒ mǎile liǎng běn shū.
Yesterday I drank three cups of coffee.　I bought two books yesterday.

Practice: Re-write the following sentences using either the sentence-final 了 or the verb-suffix 了, as appropriate. Refer to the Language Notes section on p.109 for time expressions, if necessary.

Example:　我上个月看四本书。 → 我上个月看了四本书。

1.　他去年去中国。

_____

2.　我去年去三个国家：中国、加拿大，还有美国。

_____

3.　她昨天买手机，花三百块钱。

_____

4.　上个星期三我去看足球比赛。

_____

5.　昨天晚上我们吃两盘青菜。

_____

STRUCTURE NOTE 6.12
Use 已经 *to express "already"*

To emphasize that an action has already occurred or has been completed, add 已经 *(yǐjīng) before a verb phrase.* 已经 *is typically coupled with* 了*. Whether the* 了 *follows the verb or comes at the end of the sentence is determined by the rules described in Structure Note 6.11.*

> Subject + 已经 + Verb Phrase (+ 了)

From the Lesson Text:

你已经送玛丽生日礼物了。
Nǐ yǐjīng sòng Mǎlì shēngrì lǐwù le.
You already bought Mali a birthday present.

Other examples:

我今年已经买了一个手机。
Wǒ jīnnián yǐjīng mǎi le yí gè shǒujī.
I have already bought a cell phone this year.

她已经付钱了。
Tā yǐjīng fù qián le.
She has already paid.

Practice: Transform the following phrases into complete sentences by adding 已经.

Example: 她看了三本书 → 她已经看了三本书。

1. 我找到课本了 _____
2. 大东去咖啡店了 _____
3. 哥哥吃了两碗饭 _____
4. 他买电视了 _____
5. 她给爸爸妈妈打电话了 _____

STRUCTURE NOTE 6.13

Use 要是···(的话)···就··· to say "if . . ., then"

One way to make an "if" statement in Chinese is with 要是······的话. 要是 *precedes the clause. For added emphasis,* 的话 *can be added at the end of the clause. The "then" clause is typically marked by the use of* 就, *which is inserted before the verb phrase to indicate a result.*

要是 + Sentence (+ 的话), Subject + 就 + Verb Phrase

From the Lesson Text:

要是太贵的话我就买别的东西。
Yàoshi tài guì dehuà wǒ jiù mǎi bié de dōng xi
If it's too expensive then I'll buy something else.

Other examples:

要是你今晚不去她家的话，就吃不到她做的蛋糕了。
Yàoshi nǐ jīnwǎn bú qù tā jiā dehuà, jiù chī bu dào tā zuò de dàngāo le.
If you do not go to her house tonight, then you will not get to eat the cake she made.

要是你不喜欢足球，我们就不要去看足球比赛了。
Yàoshi nǐ bù xǐhuan zúqiú, wǒmen jiù bú yào qù kàn zúqiú bǐsài le.
If you do not like soccer, then we won't go to the socccer match.

Practice: Create complete if-then statements in Chinese using 要是···(的话),···就··· and the information provided below.

Example: 你不喜欢说英文 → 要是你不喜欢说英文的话，
你就说中文。

1. 他不想去美国

   _____

2. 安娜不想用筷子

   _____

3. 你喜欢那条项链

   _____

4. 你们想吃中国菜

   _____

5. 她还没做功课

   _____

STRUCTURE NOTE 6.14
Use (是)···还是··· *to express either-or questions*

In Structure Note 6.6, 还是 *was introduced as a way to suggest an alternative. In this lesson, the* (是)··· 还是··· *pattern is employed to ask "either-or" questions that offer a choice between two alternatives. When asking such a question,* 是 *is optionally placed before the first choice and* 还是 *before the second.*

> Subject (+ 是) + Verb Phrase/Noun + 还是 + Verb Phrase/Noun

From the Lesson Text:

请问您是付现金还是刷卡？
Qǐngwèn nín shì fù xiànjīn háishì shuā kǎ?
Excuse me, will you be paying with cash or credit card?

Other examples:

你是美国人还是中国人？
Nǐ shì Měiguó rén háishì Zhōngguó rén?
Are you American or Chinese?

你喜欢他还是喜欢他哥哥？
Nǐ xǐhuan tā háishì xǐhuan tā gēge?
Do you like him or his brother?

Practice: Create complete sentences in Chinese using the (是)···还是··· pattern and the information provided below.

Example: 你/喜欢吃/中国菜/美国菜 → 你喜欢吃中国菜还是美国菜？

1. 你/喜欢说/汉语/英语

   _____

2. 我/要付/二十块/三十块

   _____

3. 小美/想/看书/做饭

   _____

4. 你/今天/去/饭馆/商店

   _____

5. 她/下星期/下下星期/买生日礼物

   _____

PRACTICE 6.9

Working with a partner, discuss what birthday present you plan to give to your parent or friend and how much it will cost.

For example,

A: 你要送你爸爸什么礼物?

B: 我想给爸爸买一个手机。

A: 手机要多少钱?

B: 差不多三百块吧。

PRACTICE 6.10

Working with a partner, look at the information below. Ask each other what Zhongping bought, how much it cost, and how he paid for the item.

For example,

A: 中平买了什么东西?

B: 他买了一条项链。

A: 那条项链多少钱?

B: 那条项链一百三十块。

A: 他付现金还是刷卡?

B: 付现金。

1.

$580.00
刷卡

2.

$279.99
现金

3.

$17.99
刷卡

4.

$4.75
现金

5.

$36.90
刷卡

6.

$20.50
现金

✏️ PRACTICE 6.11

	Radical	Stroke Order
问	门 mén door	丶 冂 门 门 问 问
再	冂 jiōng countryside	一 厂 冂 丙 再 再
现	王 wáng king	一 二 千 王 玑 玑 现 现
以	人 rén person	丶 ㄴ 以 以
话	讠(言) yán speech	丶 讠 讠 讵 话 话 话 话
已	已 yǐ already	ㄱ ㄱ 已
经	纟(丝) sī silk	ㄥ 乡 纟 纤 纩 绎 经
刷	刂 dāo knife	ㄱ ㄱ 尸 尸 吊 刷 刷
功	力 lì power	一 丁 工 功 功
所	户 hù door	丶 厂 斤 斤 斤 所 所
金	金 jīn gold	丿 人 人 今 全 全 金 金
收	夂(攴) pū knock	ㄣ ㄐ 乢 収 收
花	⺾(草) cǎo grass	一 十 艹 艹 芢 花 花
题	页 yè page	丶 口 日 日 旦 早 昇 昱 是 是 是 是 题 题 题
行	彳 chì step	丿 彳 彳 彳 行 行

💬 PRACTICE 6.12

🎤 Working with a partner, make an audio recording in which you act out the following scenario:
You are a salesperson. Answer the questions your customer asks. Ask how the customer will pay for his or her purchased items.

When you are finished, send the recording to your teacher.

PRACTICE 6.13

Type the following sentences on your computer.

1. 你不用送我这么贵的项链！
2. 因为电话这么贵，所以我没有买。
3. 收您两百五十块，找您二十块。
4. 我没钱了，所以我明天会去银行。
5. 要是你没有现金的话，你也可以刷卡。

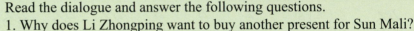

PRACTICE 6.14

王小美：中平已经送玛丽生日礼物了，
为什么还要再买呢？

陈大东：因为玛丽教他做功课。

王小美：可是他没现金。

陈大东：没问题，他可以刷卡。

Read the dialogue and answer the following questions.
1. Why does Li Zhongping want to buy another present for Sun Mali?
2. Which payment method will he use?

PRACTICE 6.15

张安娜：小姐，请问这条项链多少钱？

售货员：两百五十九块。

张安娜：这么贵啊！有便宜一点儿的吗？

售货员：这条怎么样？价钱是一百八十块。

张安娜：这样吧！一百五十块，我付现金。

售货员：对不起！我们这儿不讲价。

Read the dialogue and answer the following questions.
1. How much is the cheaper necklace?
2. How much does Zhang Anna offer for it?

PRACTICE 6.16

我昨天跟小美一起去商店买东西。我
买了一个手机和一条项链。我花了很
多钱，没有现金买咖啡了。小美帮我
刷卡付钱买的咖啡。

Read Zhang Anna's diary and answer the following questions.
1. Why did Zhang Anna have no more cash?
2. How did Wang Xiaomei pay for the coffee?

Trade Along the Silk Road

For thousands of years people have been buying and selling products along the most famous historic trading route in China — the Silk Road (丝绸之路 Sīchóu zhī lù). The Silk Road originally began in Xi'an, the capital of numerous Chinese dynasties, and spread out west across Central Asia, India, and the Middle East, eventually coming to an end in Europe. One of the most popular products bought and sold along the Silk Road was Chinese silk, hence the name the route is known by today. In addition to silk, traders along these routes exchanged all kinds of items. Porcelain was another in-demand export from China, while on the Chinese side, Middle Eastern spices and, for a time, even glassware

from the Roman Empire were highly popular. Goods were not the only things that were exchanged along the Silk Road; in fact, the route was one of the main mediums of cultural exchange across Asia and between East and West. It was via the Silk Road that Buddhism first reached China, and it is also along this road that the monk Xuanzang travels in the epic *Journey to the West*.

While the rise of maritime trade quieted traffic on the Silk Road for a time, the last few decades have seen it begin to make a comeback as China and its neighbors have actively sought to revive the vibrance of the original route. Since 1990, there has been a rail link between China's Xinjiang province and Kazakhstan, and even cities in Europe can now claim railroad trade links with China. Nowadays, China's busy eastern ports send everything from cars and computers to shoes and toys west across the Silk Road, while oil, metals, and chemicals are just some of the commodities going the other way.

Western Chains in China

Western fast food chains were first introduced to China in the 1980s. Compared to their counterparts in the US, fast food restaurants were comparatively expensive and were initially viewed as a form of culinary luxury; eating at a fast food restaurant in China twenty years ago was, in fact, something of a special occasion. Today, this is no longer the case, as these chains are common sights in urban areas throughout China.

In addition to the fare that you are probably familiar with, Western fast food chains in China also offer special menu items aimed at pleasing Chinese tastes. Red bean ice cream, congee (a rice-based porridge), and seafood wraps are just a few of the kinds of Chinese-style snacks that you can find on their locally adapted menus.

There are also a number of large Western supermarket chains now established across China. In most major cities, these retail giants vie to lure Chinese customers away from the more traditional street markets. As with the fast food chains, these stores have adapted their wares to local tastes. Aisles loaded with instant noodles, tanks containing live fish, and spicy sheep's feet at the meat counter are just some examples of how the Chinese incarnations of these retailers differ from their Western equivalents.

陈大东：	中平，你已经送玛丽生日礼物了，为什么还要再给她买东西？	Zhongping, you already bought Mali a birthday present, why are you buying h[er] somthing else?
李中平：	因为她昨天教我做功课，所以我要谢谢她。	She helped me with my homework yesterday, so I wanted to thank her.
陈大东：	你要给她买这么贵的礼物啊！	You're going to buy her such an expensive present!
李中平：	不用担心，要是太贵的话我就买别的东西。	Don't worry, if it's too expensive then buy something else.

李中平：	先生，请问这条项链多少钱？	Mister, may I please ask how much thi[s] necklace is?
售货员：	一百二十八块。	$128.00.
李中平：	好，那我就买这条。	Great, then I'll buy this one.
售货员：	请问您是付现金还是刷卡？	Excuse me, will you be paying with ca[sh] or credit card?
李中平：	付现金。给你一百三十块。	Cash. Here's $130.00.
陈大东：	你花了这么多钱，可以吗？	Is it OK to spend so much money?
李中平：	没问题。哦，玛丽来了，我们走吧！	It's no problem. Oh, here comes Mali; let's go!

What Can You Do?

INTERPRETIVE

- I can understand the appropriate expressions to use in a transaction.

INTERPERSONAL

- I can ask and answer "either-or" questions.
- I can respond to questions about different methods of payment.

PRESENTATIONAL

- I can express the causal relationship between two things.
- I can present a choice of payment methods for a transaction.

ACT IT OUT

Working in groups, compose an original three-minute skit that utilizes the vocabulary and structures introduced in Unit 6. Each of you should assume a role and have a roughly equal number of lines in the skit. Be prepared to perform your skit in class. You can either come up with your own story or choose from one of the following situations:

a) You work at a department store and run into some customers that want to bargain with you.

b) You and your friends are shopping for a mutual friend's birthday present and discuss options.

CHECK WHAT YOU CAN DO

RECOGNIZE

Adjectives
- ☐ 贵
- ☐ 便宜
- ☐ 别的

Adverbs
- ☐ 还是
- ☐ 一共
- ☐ 已经
- ☐ 再
- ☐ 这么

Auxiliary Verb
- ☐ 得

Conjunctions
- ☐ 所以

- ☐ 要是…
- ☐ …(的话)
- ☐ 如果

Idiomatic Expressions
- ☐ 算了
- ☐ 不用
- ☐ 没问题
- ☐ 不好意思
- ☐ 这样吧

Measure Words
- ☐ 元
- ☐ 块
- ☐ 毛
- ☐ 分

Nouns
- ☐ 商店
- ☐ 东西
- ☐ 衣服
- ☐ 文具
- ☐ 电子用品
- ☐ 手机
- ☐ 价钱
- ☐ 人民币
- ☐ 售货员
- ☐ 功课
- ☐ 项链
- ☐ 现金
- ☐ 下(个)星期
- ☐ 上(个)星期

- ☐ 银行
- ☐ 钱包
- ☐ 信用卡

Numbers
- ☐ 百
- ☐ 千
- ☐ 万

Pronoun
- ☐ 别的

Question Word
- ☐ 多少钱

Verbs
- ☐ 卖
- ☐ 买

- ☐ 想
- ☐ 打电话
- ☐ 讲价
- ☐ 担心
- ☐ 写信
- ☐ 付
- ☐ 刷卡
- ☐ 收
- ☐ 找
- ☐ 花

WRITE
- ☐ 写
- ☐ 买
- ☐ 卖
- ☐ 东
- ☐ 西
- ☐ 手
- ☐ 得
- ☐ 少
- ☐ 钱
- ☐ 百
- ☐ 块
- ☐ 意
- ☐ 思
- ☐ 价
- ☐ 信

- ☐ 问
- ☐ 再
- ☐ 现
- ☐ 以
- ☐ 话
- ☐ 已
- ☐ 经
- ☐ 刷
- ☐ 功
- ☐ 所
- ☐ 金
- ☐ 收
- ☐ 花
- ☐ 题
- ☐ 行

USE

- ☐ 有 to express existence rather than possession
- ☐ 得 to express "must"
- ☐ 给 as the preposition "to"
- ☐ 多少 to ask "how many" or "how much"
- ☐ Adjectives with (一)点(儿) to express "a little more"
- ☐ 还是……吧 to express a suggested alternative

- ☐ 再 to indicate a repeating action
- ☐ 因为…所以… to express causal relationships
- ☐ 不用 to say "need not"
- ☐ 这么 or 那么 to intensify adjectives
- ☐ Verb + 了 to describe specific completed actions
- ☐ 已经 to express "already"
- ☐ 要是…(的话)…就… to say "if…, then…"
- ☐ (是)…还是… to express either-or questions

行

Travel & Navigation

第七单元
UNIT 7

Communication Goals

Lesson 1: 放假的计划 **Travel Plans**
- Ask and answer questions about vacation plans
- Give information about one's hometown and family background
- Describe the attractions of China's capital

Lesson 2: 去机场 **To the Airport**
- Express the distance between two places
- Give and receive directions
- Describe different modes of transportation

LESSON TEXT 7.1

Travel Plans 放假的计划

Wang Xiaomei, Chen Dadong, and Sun Mali are discussing their vacation plans for winter break. Wang Xiaomei describes her hometown, Beijing, to Mali. Then, Mali explains where she is from.

陈大东：	小美，你放假的时候有什么计划？	Xiǎoměi, nǐ fàngjià de shíhou yǒu shénme jìhuà?
王小美：	我打算去北京，下个月回来。	Wǒ dǎsuàn qù Běijīng, xià gè yuè huílái.
陈大东：	是吗？你老家在北京吗？	Shì ma? Nǐ lǎojiā zài Běijīng ma?
王小美：	对，我出生在北京，十岁才来美国，是在加州长大的。	Duì, wǒ chūshēng zài Běijīng, shí suì cái lái Měiguó, shì zài Jiāzhōu zhǎng dà de.
孙玛丽：	北京有什么好玩儿的？	Běijīng yǒu shénme hǎowánr de?
王小美：	有长城，有故宫，还可以吃北京烤鸭呢！	Yǒu Chángchéng, yǒu Gùgōng, hái kěyǐ chī Běijīng kǎoyā ne!

孙玛丽：	哇，北京这么好玩儿，我也很想去！	Wā, Běijīng zhème hǎowánr, wǒ yě hěn xiǎng qù!
陈大东：	玛丽，你家在什么地方？	Mǎlì, nǐ jiā zài shénme dìfang?
孙玛丽：	我家在波士顿。我爸是从西班牙来的，我妈是从爱尔兰来的。	Wǒ jiā zài Bōshìdùn. Wǒ bà shì cóng Xībānyá lái de, wǒ mā shì cóng Ài'ěrlán lái de.
陈大东：	是吗？我家在加拿大。今年寒假回家我买了一张火车票。因为飞机票太贵了！	Shì ma? Wǒ jiā zài Jiā'nádà. Jīnnián hánjià huí jiā wǒ mǎile yì zhāng huǒchē piào. Yīnwèi fēijī piào tài guì le!
王小美：	对不起，我得走了。祝你们寒假快乐！	Duìbuqǐ, wǒ děi zǒu le. Zhù nǐmen hánjià kuàilè!

字 词 VOCABULARY

LESSON VOCABULARY 7.1

	Simplified	Traditional	Pinyin	Word Category	Definition
1.	放假		fàngjià	*vo*	to go on vacation
2.	的时候	的時候	de shíhou	*adv*	when, at that time
3.	计划	計劃	jìhuà	*n, v*	plan; to plan
4.	打算		dǎsuàn	*v, n*	to plan; plan
5.	北京		Běijīng	*n*	Beijing
6.	回来	回來	huílái	*v*	to return
7.	老家		lǎojiā	*n*	hometown
8.	出生		chūshēng	*v*	to be born
9.	才		cái	*adv*	not until; (indicates delay of action)
10.	加州		Jiāzhōu	*n*	California
11.	长大	長大	zhǎng dà	*v*	to grow up
12.	好玩（儿）	好玩（兒）	hǎowán(r)	*adj*	fun
13.	长城		Chángchéng	*n*	the Great Wall
14.	故宫		Gùgōng	*n*	the Forbidden City
15.	北京烤鸭	北京烤鴨	Běijīng kǎoyā	*n*	Peking Duck
16.	哇		wā	*interj*	wow
17.	地方		dìfang	*n*	place
18.	波士顿	波士頓	Bōshìdùn	*n*	Boston
19.	从	從	cóng	*prep*	from
20.	西班牙		Xībānyá	*n*	Spain
21.	爱尔兰	愛爾蘭	Ài'ěrlán	*n*	Ireland
22.	今年		jīnnián	*n*	this year
23.	寒假		hánjià	*n*	winter vacation
24.	火车票	火車票	huǒchē piào	*n*	train ticket
	火车	火車	huǒchē	*n*	train
	车	車	chē	*n*	car, vehicle
	票		piào	*n*	ticket

LESSON VOCABULARY 7.1 (continued)

	SIMPLIFIED	TRADITIONAL	PINYIN	WORD CATEGORY	DEFINITION
25.	回家		huí jiā	*vo*	to go home
26.	飞机票	飛機票	fēijī piào	*n*	plane ticket
	飞机	飛機	fēijī	*n*	airplane

REQUIRED VOCABULARY 7.1

CONJUNCTIONS

27.	但是		dànshì	*cj*	but

ORDINAL DIRECTIONS

28.	东	東	dōng	*n*	east
29.	南		nán	*n*	south
30.	西		xī	*n*	west
31.	北		běi	*n*	north

TRAVEL

32.	旅行		lǚxíng	*v, n*	to travel; travel
33.	公共汽车	公共汽車	gōnggòng qìchē	*n*	public bus

TIME

34.	明年		míngnián	*n*	next year

OPTIONAL VOCABULARY 7.1

VACATION

35.	暑假		shǔjià	*n*	summer vacation
36.	故乡	故鄉	gùxiāng	*n*	hometown, birthplace

Meaning of 老家

老家 (lǎojiā) is often translated as "hometown" in English, however, unlike its general English definition, the Chinese term is deeply rooted in history and culture and refers to one's ancestral home. For example, a young person who was born and raised in Beijing, but whose parents were not originally from Beijing, would probably identify their 老家 as being the place where his or her father's family is from.

In a Western context, 老家 usually refers to where one was born, raised, or currently resides, but can also sometimes refer to one's ethnic background (e.g., Italian American). Thus, in the Lesson Text, Mali responds to a question about her 老家 by discussing both her hometown and her parents' backgrounds.

Seasons and Vacations

Here are some useful terms to know for the seasonal breaks during the school year. Notice that the terms for winter and summer vacation do not make use of the most common terms for those particular seasons.

	Season		**Vacation**	
	Chinese	Pinyin	Chinese	Pinyin
Spring	春天	chūntiān	春假	chūnjià
Summer	夏天	xiàtiān	暑假	shǔjià
Fall/Autumn	秋天	qiūtiān	秋假	qiūjià
Winter	冬天	dōngtiān	寒假	hánjià

STRUCTURE NOTE 7.1
Use 的时候 to create "when" expressions

The phrase 的时候 (de shíhou) expresses "when" or "during" and is used to construct sentences such as: "When I was in Beijing, I didn't eat dumplings." Unlike in English, 的时候 appears after the time expression rather than before. The subject of the sentence is generally introduced in the time clause and is not repeated in the second part of the sentence:

> Subject + Verb Phrase or Time Expression + 的时候 + Verb Phrase

From the Lesson Text:

小美，你放假的时候有什么计划？
Xiǎoměi, nǐ fàngjià de shíhou yǒu shénme jìhuà?
Xiaomei, what are your plans for the vacation?

Other examples:

她看书的时候喜欢喝茶。
Tā kàn shū de shíhou xǐhuan hē chá.
She likes to drink tea when she reads.

我在北京的时候没吃饺子。
Wǒ zài Běijīng de shíhou méi chī jiǎozi.
I didn't eat dumplings when I was in Beijing.

Practice: Create sentences using 的时候 and the information given below.

Example: 在咖啡店 → 我在咖啡店的时候喝了三杯咖啡。

1. 吃中国菜 _____
2. 在餐厅 _____
3. 去学校 _____
4. 在商店买 _____
5. 看足球比赛 _____

STRUCTURE NOTE 7.2
Use 才 to indicate an action occurring later than anticipated

才 (cái) is used in sentences with a time expression to indicate the speaker believes the action in the sentence is happening later than expected. It is similar to English expressions such as "only," or "not until," and appears before the verb phrase.

> Subject + Time Expression + 才 + Verb Phrase

From the Lesson Text:

我出生在北京，十岁才来美国。
Wǒ chūshēng zài Běijīng, shí suì cái lái Měiguó.
I was born in Beijing. I didn't come to the US until I was 10 years old.

Other examples:　　　　　我上个星期三才来北京。　　他今天才开始做功课。
Wǒ shàng gè Xīngqīsān cái lái　　Tā jīntiān cái kāishǐ zuò gōngkè.
Běijīng.　　　　　　　　　　He didn't start his homework until
I didn't get to Beijing until last　　today.
Wednesday.

NOTE: 才 *cannot be used to construct sentences with negated verbs. In English "until" is used with negative constructions, as in: "I won't come back until next month," but in Chinese, the same meaning is communicated by combining* 才 *with an affirmative verb, as in:* "我下个月才回来" *(I won't be back until next month).*

The opposite of this usage of 才 *is* 就, *which indicates that an action has been completed promptly or earlier than expected.*

Examples:　　　　　　　他早上七点钟就来了。　　我昨天就开始做功课了。
Tā zǎoshàng qī diǎn zhōng jiù lái le.　Wǒ zuótiān jiù kāishǐ zuò gōngkè le.
He came by 7:00 a.m.　　　　I began to do my homework yesterday.

Practice: Transform the sentences below using 才.

Example:　　　He didn't return home until yesterday. → 他昨天才回家。

1.　He didn't go to the gym until 12 o'clock yesterday.

_____

2.　They won't return to China until this July.

_____

3.　She didn't return to eat dinner until 8 o'clock.

_____

4.　Xiaomei didn't begin doing homework until 9 o'clock last night.

_____

5.　Dadong did not call his parents until last week.

_____

STRUCTURE NOTE 7.3
Use 从 with a place word to indicate origin

从 (cóng) *is a preposition meaning "from," signaling an origin or starting point. In Chinese, prepositional phrases generally appear immediately after time expressions and auxiliary verbs, but before main verb phrases.*

> Subject + 从 + Location + Verb Phrase

From the Lesson Text:　　我爸是从西班牙来的，我妈是从爱尔兰来的。
Wǒ bà shì cóng Xībānyá lái de, wǒ mā shì cóng Ài'ěrlán lái de.
My dad is from Spain, and my mom is from Ireland.

Other examples:
我下星期要从中国去
美国。
Wǒ xià xīngqī yào cóng Zhōngguó
qù Měiguó.
Next week, I will go from China to
America.

我跟同学一起从图书馆
回宿舍。
Wǒ gēn tóngxué yìqǐ cóng túshūguǎn
huí sùshè.
I returned to the dorm from the library
with my classmate.

Practice: Create sentences using the following locations and 从.

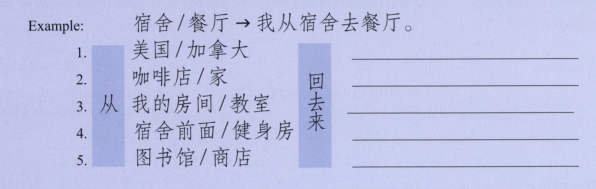

Example: 宿舍 / 餐厅 → 我从宿舍去餐厅。
1.   美国 / 加拿大
2.   咖啡店 / 家
3. 从   我的房间 / 教室
4.   宿舍前面 / 健身房
5.   图书馆 / 商店

回
去
来

_____
_____
_____
_____
_____

STRUCTURE NOTE 7.4

Use 是……的 to emphasize the time, locale, or manner of a completed action

The 是……的 *pattern is another way to talk about the past by highlighting some detail about how something took place such as where, when, or how. In this pattern,* 是 *occurs before the emphasized phrase, while* 的 *occurs either at the end of the sentence or between the main verb and object (object cannot be a pronoun).*

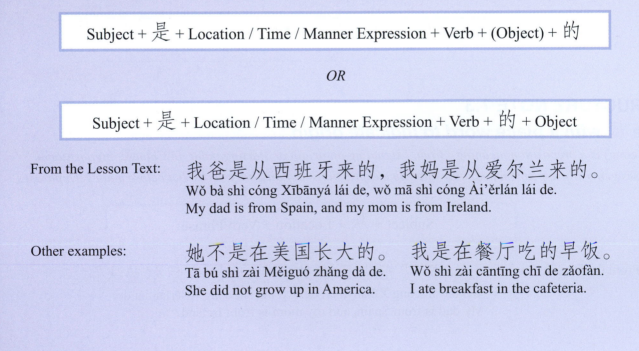

| Subject + 是 + Location / Time / Manner Expression + Verb + (Object) + 的 |

OR

| Subject + 是 + Location / Time / Manner Expression + Verb + 的 + Object |

From the Lesson Text: 我爸是从西班牙来的，我妈是从爱尔兰来的。
Wǒ bà shì cóng Xībānyá lái de, wǒ mā shì cóng Ài'ěrlán lái de.
My dad is from Spain, and my mom is from Ireland.

Other examples:
她不是在美国长大的。
Tā bú shì zài Měiguó zhǎng dà de.
She did not grow up in America.

我是在餐厅吃的早饭。
Wǒ shì zài cāntīng chī de zǎofàn.
I ate breakfast in the cafeteria.

Practice: Answer the following questions using the 是……的 pattern.

Example: 玛丽是在哪儿长大的？ → 玛丽是在美国长大的。

1. 你是在哪儿出生的？

   _____

2. 你爸爸妈妈是在哪儿长大的？

   _____

3. 昨天你是在哪个餐厅吃的晚饭？

   _____

4. 你的中文是在哪儿学的？

   _____

5. 陈大东是在哪儿找到的课本？

   _____

PRACTICE 7.1

Working with a partner, talk about a planned trip to Beijing for the upcoming winter vacation. Who will go with you? What will you do? What attractions will you see?

Example:

A: 你寒假有什么计划？

B: 我和我的家人要去北京。

A: 北京有什么好玩的？

B: 北京有长城，有故宫，还有很多商店。

PRACTICE 7.2

Working with a partner, match a picture from each of the three categories below to create complete sentences. Ask questions based on the information provided about their winter break plans and have your partner answer accordingly.

Example:

A: 玛丽寒假要去哪儿？

B: 她要去西班牙。

A: 玛丽去那儿做什么？

B: 她想去博物馆。

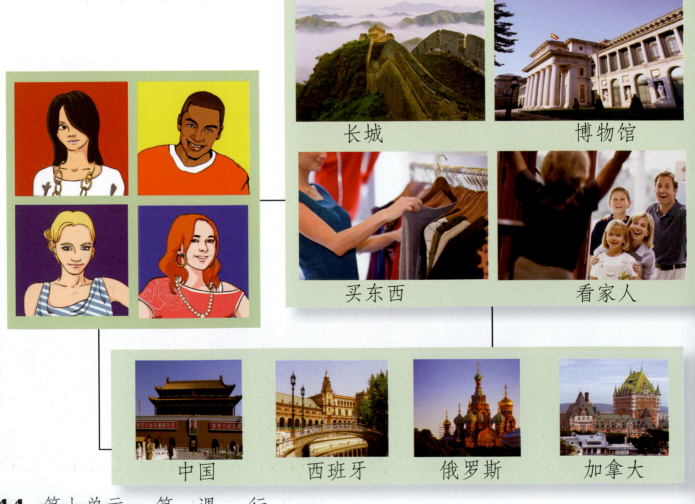

长城　　　　　博物馆

买东西　　　　看家人

中国　　　西班牙　　　俄罗斯　　　加拿大

PRACTICE 7.3

Consult four or five of your classmates in order to fill out the questionnaire below. Share your findings with the class.

名字	你在哪儿出生？	你是哪儿人？	那儿有什么好玩儿的？

PRACTICE 7.4

Take a survey of the class to find out which country students would most like to go to in the next vacation. Record the most popular response below.

Country	Number of Students

5209	17：15	SAPPORO	17：15	札幌
213	17：45	SAN FRANCISCO	17：45	旧金山
4665	17：45	SAN FRANCISCO	17：45	旧金山
866	18：00	GUANGZHOU	18：00	广州
702	18：00	MANILA	18：00	马尼拉
758	18：00	NAGOYA	18：00	名古屋
5219	18：00	NAGOYA	18：00	名古屋
602	18：00	SYDNEY	18：00	悉尼
367	18：00	SYDNEY	18：00	悉尼
103	18：20	TOKYO/NARITA	18：20	东京／成田
6973	18：20	TOKYO/NARITA	18：20	东京／成田
201	18：30	LOS ANGELES	18：30	洛杉矶
4661	18：30	LOS ANGELES	18：30	洛杉矶
818	18：45	MELBOURNE	18：45	墨尔本
133	18：50	FUKUOKA	18：50	福冈
113	19：00	OSAKA/KANSAI	19：00	大阪／关西

国际出发
International Departure

	Radical	Stroke Order
加	力 lì power	フ 力 加 加 加
候	亻(人) rén person	ノ 亻 亻 伫 伫 伫 侯 侯 候
飞	飞 fēi fly	乁 飞 飞
机	木 mù wood	一 十 才 木 札 机
算	𥫗(竹) zhú bamboo	ノ 𠂉 𥫗 𥫗 竺 竺 筲 筲 筲 筲 筧 算 算
计	讠(言) yán speech	丶 讠 计 计
北	匕 bǐ ladle	丨 丬 扌 北 北
京	亠 tóu lid	丶 一 亠 亠 古 宁 宁 京
从	人 rén person	ノ 人 从 从
出	凵 kǎn open box	凵 凵 中 出 出
长	长 cháng/ zhǎng long/grow	ノ 长 长 长
地	土 tǔ earth	一 十 土 圦 圽 地
爱	爫(爪) zhǎo claw	一 爫 爫 爫 爫 爫 爫 爱 爱
车	车 chē cart	一 𰀁 𰀁 车
方	方 fāng square	丶 一 宁 方

💬 PRACTICE 7.6

Make an audio recording and send it to your teacher. In the recording, talk about your summer vacation plans. Where will you go and who will go with you? What attractions are there? What kinds of food will you eat? Refer to the Optional Vocabulary, if necessary.

PRACTICE 7.7

Create complete sentences using the following scenarios.

1. 寒假的时候
2. 在学校的时候
3. 买东西的时候
4. 在北京的时候
5. 在饭馆吃饭的时候

PRACTICE 7.8

Write an e-mail to a friend and share your vacation itinerary. What will you be doing each day? What foods will you eat? Who will be going with you? Answer as many of these questions as you can.

PRACTICE 7.9

王小美今年十八岁，她在北京出生，两岁的时候和爸爸妈妈来到美国，在加州长大。寒假的时候，她想去北京。她要去鸟巢 (Niǎocháo: Bird's Nest)、水立方 (Shuǐ Lìfāng: Water Cube)，还要去吃北京烤鸭。

Read the passage and answer the following questions.
1. Where was Wang Xiaomei born?
2. Which places will she visit during the winter vacation?

PRACTICE 7.10

陈大东：玛丽，你的老家在什么地方？
孙玛丽：我的老家在西班牙。
陈大东：是吗？那你是西班牙人吗？
孙玛丽：不是，我爸爸是。我是在波士顿出生的。

Read the dialogue and answer the following questions.
1. Where was Sun Mali born?
2. Is Sun Mali Spanish?

PRACTICE 7.11

寒假的时候，大家都有计划。大东想回加拿大，可是飞机票太贵了。中平要和朋友去西班牙。安娜打算回俄罗斯看家人。我很想跟安娜一起去，可是我爸爸妈妈要我回家。

Read Huang Xiang'an's diary and answer the following questions.
1. What is Li Zhongping doing for the winter vacation?
2. Will Huang Xiang'an go with Zhang Anna to Russia?

Transportation in China

For much of the 20th century, the traditional image of transport in China was that of hundreds of bicycles crowding city streets. Nowadays, this impression is no longer accurate, as most major cities have upgraded their infrastructure in order to cater to the demands of a modern metropolitan population.

China now has total highway lengths in excess of two million miles, with navigable inland waterways stretching nearly 100,000 miles, and over 1,000 domestic and international airlines. More recent transportation advancements include the implementation of extensive subway systems in metropolitan areas, an elaborate High-Speed Rail system (the longest network in the world), and Shanghai's Maglev Train. In addition, major bridge-building projects, such as the Jiaozhou Bay Bridge and the Hangzhou Bay Bridge, have helped to reduce driving times between built-up areas.

Despite the emergence of cutting-edge technology that has contributed significantly to the world of travel, traditional modes of transportation remain an integral part of Chinese culture. For many, bicycles are still an easy way of getting from place to place, especially in less modernized areas. Similarly, sedan chairs, rickshaws, and bicycle-rickshaws remain popular modes of exploring tourist sites such as the Great Wall and traditional villages.

China's "Golden Weeks"

The busiest travel periods in China are based around two major public holidays: the Spring Festival (Chinese New Year), and China's National Day, which honors the founding of the People's Republic of China on October 1st, 1949. Taking into account the weekend, these holidays generally add up to seven consecutive days away from work and school. During this time, families and individuals take the opportunity to go out and travel around the country, resulting in a huge boom in China's tourism industry. The near certainty of additional business during these weeks has resulted in the development of the term "黄金周" (huángjīn zhōu: "Golden Week").

The Spring Festival Golden Week, which typically occurs around February, is considered the most important holiday in Chinese culture, with millions of migrant workers traveling back home for the holidays. Major cities tend to remain relatively quiet due to the mass exodus of migrant workers, and many restaurants and tourist spots also close down for the holidays. Services and facilities all over China are in huge demand during this period; booking flights, hotel rooms, train tickets, or restaurant tables can be extraordinarily difficult. Although these conditions are not as extreme during the National Day Golden Week, traveling at this time can also be very problematic.

If you are studying or working in China, you may have little choice but to take your travel breaks during the Golden Weeks. In this case, booking in advance and closely following a schedule can help with vacation plans. For a more relaxed and convenient travel experience, though, it is recommended that domestic and international tourists try to visit China's tourist hotspots at a less busy time of year.

陈大东：	小美，你放假的时候有什么计划？	Xiaomei, what are your plans for the vacation?
王小美：	我打算去北京，下个月回来。	I plan to go to Beijing; I'll be back next month.
陈大东：	是吗？你老家在北京吗？	Really? Is Beijing your hometown?
王小美：	对，我出生在北京，十岁才来美国，是在加州长大的。	Yes, I was born in Beijing. I didn't come to the US until I was 10 years old and I grew up in California.
孙玛丽：	北京有什么好玩儿的？	What's fun to do in Beijing?
王小美：	有长城，有故宫，还可以吃北京烤鸭呢！	There's the Great Wall, the Forbidden City, and you can also eat Peking Duck!
孙玛丽：	哇，北京这么好玩儿，我也很想去！	Wow, Beijing sounds like a fun place, I want to go too!

陈大东：	玛丽，你家在什么地方？	Mali, where are you from?
孙玛丽：	我家在波士顿。我爸是从西班牙来的，我妈是从爱尔兰来的。	Boston is my hometown. My dad is from Spain, and my mom is from Ireland.
陈大东：	是吗？我家在加拿大。今年寒假回家我买了一张火车票。因为飞机票太贵了！	Really? I'm from Canada. For winter vacation this year, I bought a train ticket to go home because plane tickets are too expensive!
王小美：	对不起，我得走了。祝你们寒假快乐！	Sorry, I have to go. Have a nice winter vacation!

What Can You Do?

INTERPRETIVE
- I can understand explanations of people's origins.
- I can identify some famous locations in Beijing.

INTERPERSONAL
- I can discuss my vacation plans with others.
- I can ask and answer questions about where people come from.

PRESENTATIONAL
- I can give a basic introduction about my family background.
- I can present a list of the local attractions in Beijing.

mí lù
我们迷路了吗？
bié chǎo
你们别吵了。
xiǎo xīn
小心啊！
前面有
只猫！
āi yā zuò
哎呀，我还是去坐
chū zū chē
出租车吧。

LESSON TEXT 7.2

To the Airport 到机场

Li Zhongping is taking Sun Mali, Zhang Anna, and Wang Xiaomei to the airport. On the way, Li Zhongping, Sun Mali, and Zhang Anna offer different directions on the route from the school to the airport.

孙玛丽:	中平，谢谢你开车送我们去机场！	Zhōngpíng, xièxie nǐ kāi chē sòng wǒmen qù jīchǎng!
李中平:	不用谢！机场离学校不太远。	Bú yòng xiè! Jīchǎng lí xuéxiào bú tài yuǎn.
孙玛丽:	中平，你知道从这儿到机场怎么走吗？	Zhōngpíng, nǐ zhīdào cóng zhèr dào jīchǎng zěnme zǒu ma?
李中平:	当然！我们先一直往前开，到了路口再往左转。	Dāngrán! Wǒmen xiān yìzhí wǎng qián kāi, dào le lùkǒu zài wǎng zuǒ zhuǎn.
张安娜:	不对！我们到路口应该往右转。	Bú duì! Wǒmen dào lùkǒu yīnggāi wǎng yòu zhuǎn.
孙玛丽:	不对！先往左转，再穿过大街，然后往右转。	Bú duì! Xiān wǎng zuǒ zhuǎn, zài chuān guò dàjiē, ránhòu wǎng yòu zhuǎn.

王小美:	我们迷路了吗？	Wǒmen mílù le ma?
李中平:	你们别吵了。	Nǐmen bié chǎo le.
王小美:	小心啊！前面有只猫！	Xiǎoxīn a! Qiánmiàn yǒu zhī māo!
张安娜:	哎呀，我还是去坐出租车吧。	Āiyā, wǒ háishì qù zuò chūzūchē ba.

字 词 VOCABULARY

LESSON VOCABULARY 7.2

	SIMPLIFIED	TRADITIONAL	PINYIN	WORD CATEGORY	DEFINITION
1.	开车	開車	kāi chē	vo	to drive (a car)
2.	(飞)机场	(飛)機場	(fēi)jīchǎng	n	airport
3.	不用谢	不用謝	bú yòng xiè	ie	you're welcome
4.	离	離	lí	prep	distant from; apart from
5.	远	遠	yuǎn	adj	far
6.	知道		zhīdào	v	to know (something)
7.	到		dào	prep; v	to; to arrive
8.	怎么走	怎麼走	zěnme zǒu	qph	how to get to (somewhere)
9	先		xiān	adv	first
10.	一直		yìzhí	adv	straight forward
11.	往		wǎng	prep	toward, in the direction of
12.	路口		lùkǒu	n	intersection
	路		lù	n	road
13.	左		zuǒ	n	left
14.	转	轉	zhuǎn	v	to turn
15.	应该	應該	yīnggāi	av	should
16.	右		yòu	n	right
17.	穿过	穿過	chuān guò	rv	to cross
18.	大街		dàjiē	n	main street; street
	街		jiē	n	street
19.	然后	然後	ránhòu	adv	then
20.	迷路		mílù	vo	to be lost
21.	别	別	bié	adv	don't
22.	吵		chǎo	v, adj	to make noise; to argue; noisy
23.	小心		xiǎoxīn	adj	careful
24.	哎呀		āiyā	interj	oh!
25.	坐		zuò	v	to ride (in a car, etc.); to travel by
26.	出租车	出租車	chūzūchē	n	taxi

	SIMPLIFIED	TRADITIONAL	PINYIN	WORD CATEGORY	DEFINITION
DISTANCE					
27.	近		jìn	*adj*	close
TRANSPORTATION					
28.	走路		zǒu lù	*vo*	to walk
29.	道		dào	*n*	road; path; way

OPTIONAL VOCABULARY 7.2

TRANSPORTATION

	SIMPLIFIED	TRADITIONAL	PINYIN	WORD CATEGORY	DEFINITION
30.	自行车	自行車	zìxíngchē	*n*	bicycle
31	地铁	地鐵	dìtiě	*n*	subway
32.	摩托车	摩托車	mótuōchē	*n*	motorcycle
33.	车站	車站	chēzhàn	*n*	railway or subway station, bus sto
34	停车	停車	tíng chē	*vo*	to stop a car; to park
35.	地图	地圖	dìtú	*n*	map

 **ONLINE RESOURCES**

Visit *http://college.betterchinese.com* for a list of other words related to transportation.

Common Direction Expressions

Whether lost or helping a lost traveler, here are some common phrases used when giving and receiving directions:

到 ___ 怎么走？	Dào____ zěnme zǒu?	How do you get to ____?
从 A 到 B 怎么走？	Cóng A dào B zěnme zǒu?	How do you get from A to B?
一直往前走	Yìzhí wǎng qián zǒu	Keep going straight
往右/左转	Wǎng yòu/zuǒ zhuǎn	Turn right/left
往右/左拐	Wǎng yòu/zuǒ guǎi	Turn right/left (Northern China)
到___	Dào____	When you reach ____
___ 就在右边 / 左边	____ jiù zài yòubian / zuǒbian	You'll find____ there on the right / left (lit.:____ is just on the right / left)

Example:

A: 请问，从这里到图书馆怎么走？

Excuse me, how do I get to the library from here?

B: 往前走，到路口往右转。
图书馆就在左边。

Go straight ahead, then turn right when you get to the intersection. The library will be there on the left.

STRUCTURE NOTE 7.5

Use 送……去 to mean "take"

In Structure Note 3.11, 送 was introduced as to "give a gift." In this lesson, 送 is used to mean to escort or transport a person or an object somewhere. The 送 phrase typically appears after the subject and before the main verb. When a mode of transportation is specified, as in "by car," this information is placed immediately before 送.

Subject (+ Means of Transport) + 送 + Object + 去/到 + Location

From the Lesson Text:　谢谢你开车送我们去机场!
Xièxie nǐ kāi chē sòng wǒmen qù jīchǎng!
Thank you for driving us to the airport!

Other examples:　陈大东送王小美到宿舍。　　我得开车送妹妹去学校。
Chén Dàdōng sòng Wáng Xiǎoměi dào　　Wǒ děi kāi chē sòng mèimei qù xuéxiào.
sùshè.　　　　　　　　　　　　　　I must drive my little sister to school.
Dadong Chen took Xiaomei Wang back to
her dorm.

Practice: Create complete questions and sentences using 送. Include the details provided below and fit the verb where appropriate.

Example:　他 / 开车 / 大东 / 咖啡店 → 他开车送大东去咖啡店。

1. 我 / 他 / 车站

   _____

2. 她 / 开车 / 小美 / 健身房

   _____

3. 玛丽 / 开车 / 弟弟 / 饭馆

   _____

4. 爸爸 / 坐火车 / 我 / 北京

   _____

5. 妈妈 / 我 / 学校

   _____

STRUCTURE NOTE 7.6
Use 离 to express location relative to a reference point

离 (lí) *is used to express the relative location or distance to a reference point. In contrast to English where one would say A is "adjective distance phrase" from B, as in "my house is not far from yours," Chinese uses the pattern, A 离 B, followed by the adjective distance phrase.*

> Location A + 离 + Location B + Adjective Distance Phrase

From the Lesson Text:
机场离学校不太远。
Jīchǎng lí xuéxiào bú tài yuǎn.
The airport is not too far from the school.

Other examples:
图书馆离我们家很近。
Túshūguǎn lí wǒmen jiā hěn jìn.
The library is very close to our house.

那家饭馆离宿舍太远了！
Nèi jiā fànguǎn lí sùshè tài yuǎn le!
That restaurant is too far from the dorm!

NOTE: *Recall from Structure Note 1.1 that adjectives in Chinese should always be preceded by modifiers such as* 很, 太, 不, *etc. in affirmative sentences.*

Practice: Create complete location sentences in Chinese by applying the 离 structure and using the information provided below.

Example: The school campus is not far from here. → 校园离这里不远。

1. The library is very close to the coffee shop.

   _____

2. The restaurant is very far from the store.

   _____

3. The coffee shop is not far from the gym.

   _____

4. You are too close to the TV!

   _____

5. My friend's house is not too far from my house.

   _____

STRUCTURE NOTE 7.7
Use 到 *with place words to indicate destination*

到 *can be used in prepositional phrases to indicate final destinations in the same way* 从 *is used to indicate origin points. In cases where the origin also needs to be specified,* 从 *goes before* 到. *The* 从…到… *structure is akin to the English structure "from A to B." Unlike English, however, the verb phrase appears after the* 从…到… *structure.*

Subject (+ 从 + Location A) (+ 到 + Location B) + Verb Phrase

From the Lesson Text:

你知道从这儿到机场怎么走吗？
Nǐ zhīdào cóng zhèr dào jīchǎng zěnme zǒu ma?
Do you know how to get to the airport from here?

Other examples:

我想跟你一起到餐厅去。
Wǒ xiǎng gēn nǐ yìqǐ dào cāntīng qù.
I want to go to the cafeteria with you.

你到哪儿去？
Nǐ dào nǎr qù?
Where are you going?

NOTE: *Notice that in Chinese, the meaning "go to (destination)" can be expressed using "*去 *(destination)" or "*到 *(destination)* 去*." These two patterns are mostly equivalent, but the* 到 *pattern provides emphasis regarding the arrival or termination at the destination.*

Practice: Create complete questions or sentences in Chinese by applying the 到 or 从…到… structure. Use the information below when constructing your statement.

Example: 饭馆 → 我到饭馆去。

1. 法国／中国

   _____

2. 校园（到）

   _____

3. 他们家／图书馆（从……到）

   _____

4. 商店／对面的餐厅（从……到）

   _____

5. 餐厅／对面的宿舍（从……到）

   _____

STRUCTURE NOTE 7.8
Use 怎么 *to ask how something is done*

In Structure Note 4.7, 怎么样 *was introduced as a way of asking about how something is, as in,* "那本书怎么样？" *("how is that book?"). In this lesson, the question word* 怎么 *precedes the verb phrase and is used to ask about how something is done.*

Subject + 怎么 + Verb Phrase

From the Lesson Text: 你知道从这儿到机场怎么走吗？
Nǐ zhīdào cóng zhèr dào jīchǎng zěnme zǒu ma?
Do you know how to get to the airport from here?

Other examples:

这个菜怎么做？
Zhèige cài zěnme zuò?
How did you cook this dish?

请问，这个汉字怎么写？
Qǐngwèn, zhèige Hànzì zěnme xiě?
Excuse me, how do you write this character?

Practice: Create complete sentences or questions by selecting the appropriate verb and using the information provided below.

Example: 从这儿到饭馆 / 走 → 你知道从这儿到饭馆怎么走吗？

1. 那个字 / 写

   _____

2. 去饭馆 / 走

   _____

3. 今天的功课 / 做

   _____

4. 北京烤鸭 / 吃

   _____

5. 从这儿到宿舍 / 走

   _____

STRUCTURE NOTE 7.9

Use 往 *to indicate directional movement*

In contrast to the 到 *pattern introduced in Structure Note 7.7,* 往 *is a prepositional phrase indicating progression towards a direction or destination, but not necessarily reaching that destination.* 往 *is frequently used to describe turning toward the left or right, or toward one of the cardinal directions (north, south, east, west).* 往 *is generally used with verbs involving motion such as* 走 *or* 开.

Subject + 往 + Direction + Verb

From the Lesson Text:

我们到路口应该往右转。
Wǒmen dào lùkǒu yīnggāi wǎng yòu zhuǎn.
At the intersection, we should make a right.

Other examples:

往前走！
Wǎng qián zǒu!
Go forward!

我们得往东开。
Wǒmen děi wǎng dōng kāi.
We need to drive east.

Practice: Create sentences using the following directions with 往.

Example:　　左　→　请往左转。

1.　东　_____

2.　右　_____

3.　北　_____

4.　校园　_____

5.　他家　_____

STRUCTURE NOTE 7.10

Use 先…，再…，然后… to indicate a sequence of events

再 *was previously introduced to indicate a repeating action.* 再 *can also be used to mean "then," in a sentence meaning "first do A, then do B."* 先 *(xiān) precedes the first verb phrase to mark the first action, and* 再 *and* 然后 *(ránhòu) mark the later actions. If only two actions need to be listed, the second action can be marked by either* 再 *or* 然后 *(or by both at once, "*然后再*").*

Subject + 先 + Verb Phrase, + 再 + Verb Phrase, + 然后 + Verb Phrase

---

From the Lesson Text: 先往左转，再穿过大街，然后往右转。
Xiān wǎng zuǒ zhuǎn, zài chuān guò dàjiē, ránhòu wǎng yòu zhuǎn.
First turn left, then cross the street, and then turn right.

Other examples:

我们先买东西，再吃午饭，然后去看足球比赛。
Wǒmen xiān mǎi dōngxi, zài chī wǔfàn, ránhòu qù kàn zúqiú bǐsài.
Let's first go shopping, then eat lunch, and then go to see the soccer game.

先往前走，再往右转，然后往左转。
Xiān wǎng qián zǒu, zài wǎng yòu zhuǎn, ránhòu wǎng zuǒ zhuǎn.
First go straight ahead, then turn right, and then turn left.

Practice: Create sentences using the following phrases and the 先…，再…，然后… pattern.

Example: 吃北京烤鸭，喝汤，吃蛋糕
→先吃北京烤鸭，再喝汤，然后吃蛋糕。

1. 看书，做功课，回宿舍

   _____

2. 给爸爸打电话，给朋友写信，给妹妹买礼物

   _____

3. 做饭，吃饭，看比赛

   _____

4. 去图书馆，去健身房，去餐厅

   _____

5. 往北开，往右转，往东开

   _____

PRACTICE 7.12

Imagine that you are one of the characters below. Working with a partner, ask for directions to the given locations.

Example:

小美: 请问，从学校到图书馆怎么走？

A: 先到东路和七街的路口，再往左转。

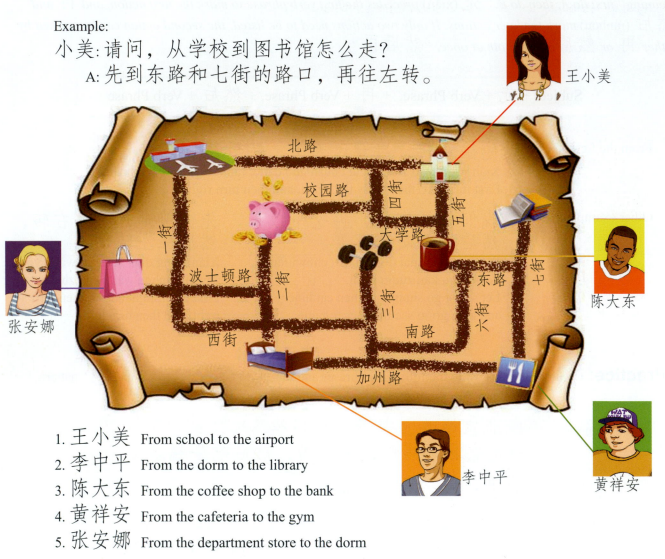

王小美

张安娜

陈大东

李中平

黄祥安

1. 王小美 From school to the airport
2. 李中平 From the dorm to the library
3. 陈大东 From the coffee shop to the bank
4. 黄祥安 From the cafeteria to the gym
5. 张安娜 From the department store to the dorm

PRACTICE 7.13

Working with a partner, role-play the following situation. Use the words in the word bank below in your dialogue.

路口	怎么走	往	左转	右转
应该	穿过	大街	迷路	出租车
机场	到	先	再	然后

Situation: Your friend is giving you a ride to the airport, but he or she does not know the way there. You offer direction but he or she does not follow them. Finally, you decide to take a taxi.

PRACTICE 7.14

Fill in the Chinese words for the modes of transportation in the spaces provided. Then, working with a partner, practice the dialogue pattern using the information below.

Example:
A: 你怎么去加拿大？
B: 我坐飞机去。

_____

_____

_____

_____

PRACTICE 7.15

Take a survey of the class to determine which mode of transportation students use most frequently to get to school. Record the most popular answer below.

Mode of Transportation	Number of Students

PRACTICE 7.16

Make an audio recording and send it to your teacher. In the recording, give directions to a location of your choice that is near to your campus.

	Radical	Stroke Order
谢	讠(言) yán speech	丶 讠 讠 讠 讠 讠 讠 讠 讠 谢 谢
走	走 zǒu walk	一 十 土 キ キ 走 走
场	土 tǔ earth	一 十 土 圹 场 场
离	亠 tóu lid	丶 亠 宀 文 离 卤 离 离 离
远	辶 chuò walk	一 二 亍 元 远 远 远
知	矢 shǐ arrow	丿 𠂉 𠂉 牛 矢 知 知 知
往	彳 chì step	丿 彳 彳 彳 彳 往 往 往
左	工 gōng work	一 ナ 𠂇 左 左
右	口 kǒu mouth	一 ナ 才 右 右
转	车 chē cart	一 𡗗 车 车 车 转 转 转
应	广 guǎng shelter	丶 亠 广 广 应 应 应
该	讠(言) yán speech	丶 讠 讠 讠 讠 该 该
后	口 kǒu mouth	一 厂 厂 斤 后 后
小	小 xiǎo small	亅 小 小
心	心 xīn heart	丶 心 心 心

PRACTICE 7.18

Type the following sentences on your computer.

1. 飞机场离学校不远。
2. 你先开到路口，再往右转。
3. 我们迷路了。
4. 我还是坐出租车去吧。
5. 谢谢你开车送我去图书馆。

孙玛丽：谢谢你开车送我去机场。
李中平：不用谢！从这里到机场只要半个小时。
孙玛丽：这里应该往右转。
李中平：不对，下个路口才要右转。

Read the dialogue and answer the following questions.
1. How long does it take to get to the airport?
2. Where does Zhongping think they should make a right turn?

Read Chen Dadong's diary and answer the following questions.
1. What time did Wang Xiaomei need to go to the airport?
2. Why couldn't Chen Dadong take her to the airport?

小美上个星期五回北京了。她要我开车送她去机场。她坐中午十二点二十五分的飞机，上午九点半要到机场。可是因为我九点钟要上课，所以小美还是坐出租车去了。

孙先生和孙太太开车去北京烤鸭店。
孙太太：你应该先穿过大街，然后左转。
孙先生：不对！穿过大街后要右转。
孙太太：不对！应该是左转才对。
孙先生：是你开车还是我开车？
孙太太：小心啊！前面有人！
孙先生：我们别吵了，还是看地图吧！

Read the dialogue and answer the following questions. Refer to the Optional Vocabulary, if necessary.
1. What directions does Mrs. Sun give to Mr. Sun?
2. What does Mrs. Sun tell Mr. Sun to look out for?

Beijing's Historical Hotspots

Beijing, the capital of China, is a bustling city immersed in China's rich history. In addition to seeking out gastronomic delights such as Peking Duck, visitors typically spend their time admiring Beijing's historic attractions. Below are five of the most popular of the city's tourist sites.

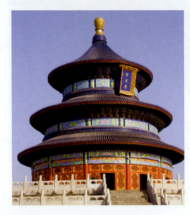

The Temple of Heaven 天坛 (Tiāntán)

A masterpiece of Ming architecture, the Temple of Heaven is one of the most photographed buildings in the world today. Built in 1420, The Temple of Heaven was the place where Ming and Qing emperors prayed to heaven for a good harvest.

Tian'anmen Square 天安门广场 (Tiān'ānmén Guángchǎng)

Tian'anmen Square is the largest public square in the world. Occupying a central location in the capital city, this space has hosted massive public announcements, parades, and rallies throughout modern Chinese history. It was at this site that Chairman Mao proclaimed the establishment of the People's Republic of China in 1949.

The Summer Palace 颐和园 (Yíhéyuán)

Built in 1750, the Palace overlooks tranquil Kunming Lake. Here, one can stroll along corridors where the royal families spent their summers hundreds of years ago. The site is considered the largest and most complete royal garden in China, and spans ten square miles.

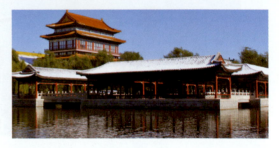

The Forbidden City (the Palace Museum) 故宫博物院 (Gùgōng Bówùyuàn)

Built during the Ming dynasty, the Forbidden City is a vast palace complex including 9,999 rooms and spanning over 250 acres. During the Ming and Qing dynasties, 24 emperors made this site their home. Today, it functions as a public museum and hosts many treasures once owned by the imperial families, though many of the artifacts originally found in the Forbidden City are displayed in the National Palace Museum in Taipei.

The Great Wall of China 万里长城 (Wànlǐ Chángchéng)

The Great Wall is indisputably the largest manmade cultural relic in the world, passing through 156 counties and spanning over 5500 miles (8850 km) in length. The Great Wall was originally built to keep out invaders from the north. Construction of the wall began in the 7th century BC, and additions and rebuilding continued well into the 16th century AD. Today, tourists can appreciate the wall's vast scale firsthand by visiting one of the restored sections that are open to the public (a number of which are located near Beijing).

孙玛丽：	中平，谢谢你开车送我们去机场！	Zhongping, thank you for driving us to the airport!
李中平：	不用谢！机场离学校不太远。	You're welcome! The airport is not too far away from the school.
孙玛丽：	中平，你知道从这儿到机场怎么走吗？	Zhongping, do you know how to get to the airport from here?
李中平：	当然！我们先一直往前开，到了路口再往左转。	Of course! First we keep going straight, and then turn left when we get to the intersection.
张安娜：	不对！我们到路口应该往右转。	That's not right! At the intersection, we should turn right.

孙玛丽：	不对！先往左转，再穿过大街，然后往右转。	That's not right! First turn left, then cross the main street, and then turn right.
王小美：	我们迷路了吗？	Are we lost?
李中平：	你们别吵了。	Stop bickering.
王小美：	小心啊！前面有只猫！	Look out! There's a cat up ahead!
张安娜：	哎呀，我还是去坐出租车吧。	Oh! I'd better take a taxi instead.

What Can You Do?

INTERPRETIVE
- I can understand directions to and from a certain place.

INTERPERSONAL
- I can ask for directions and give them to others.
- I can offer or ask to accompany somebody somewhere.

PRESENTATIONAL
- I can present a selection of different transportation options.
- I can express the distance to a location from a given point.

ACT IT OUT

Working in groups, compose an original three-minute skit that utilizes the vocabulary and structures introduced in Unit 7. Each of you should assume a role and have a roughly equal number of lines in the skit. Be prepared to perform your skit in class. You can either come up with your own story or choose from one of the following situations:

a) A visitor on campus is lost, and you help direct him or her.

b) You and a group of friends are planning a weekend trip together. Discuss your destination, possible activities, and mode(s) of transportation.

c) You and your friends are comparing where you live on or near campus. Describe where you live based on nearby landmarks and buildings.

d) You are taking a prospective student on a tour around campus. Ask your friends about which way to walk in order to efficiently see all of the campus highlights.

CHECK WHAT YOU CAN DO

RECOGNIZE

Adjectives
- 好玩 (儿)
- 远
- 小心
- 近

Adverbs
- 的时候
- 才
- 一直
- 先
- 然后
- 别

Auxiliary Verbs
- 应该

Conjunctions
- 但是

Idiomatic Expressions
- 不用谢

Interjections
- 哇
- 哎呀

Nouns
- 计划
- 北京
- 加州
- 长城
- 故宫
- 北京烤鸭
- 老家

- 地方
- 波士顿
- 西班牙
- 爱尔兰
- 飞机票
- 今年
- 火车票
- 寒假
- 东
- 南
- 西
- 北
- 公共汽车
- (飞)机场
- 路口
- 左
- 右

- 大街
- 出租车
- 道

Prepositions
- 从
- 到
- 往
- 离

Question Word
- 怎么走

Verbs
- 打算
- 回来
- 出生

- 长大
- 知道
- 转
- 穿过
- 吵
- 坐
- 旅行
- 放假
- 回家
- 开车
- 迷路
- 走路

WRITE

- 加
- 候
- 飞
- 机
- 算
- 计
- 北
- 京
- 从
- 出
- 长
- 地
- 爱
- 车
- 方

- 谢
- 走
- 场
- 离
- 远
- 知
- 往
- 左
- 右
- 转
- 应
- 该
- 后
- 小心

USE

- 的时候 to create "when" expressions
- 才 to indicate an action occuring later than anticipated
- 从 with a place word to indicate origin
- 是……的 to emphasize the time, locale, or manner of a completed action

- 送……去 to mean "take"
- 离 to express location relative to a reference point
- 到 with place words to indicate destination
- 怎么 to ask how something is done
- 往 to indicate directional movement
- 先…，再…，然后… to indicate a sequence of events

学

第八单元

UNIT 8

Communication Goals

Lesson 1: 选课 **Taking Classes**
- Discuss classes and school subjects
- Express interest in something
- Indicate levels of difficulty

Lesson 2: 上课的时候 **In Class**
- Discuss exams, homework, and classroom situations
- Ask to borrow something
- Express subjective opinions

LESSON TEXT 8.1

Taking Classes 你选几门课？

Sun Mali encounters Li Zhongping studying in the library. She asks him how many classes he is taking.

孙玛丽：	中平，这么多书，你这个学期选了几门课？	Zhōngpíng, zhème duō shū, nǐ zhèige xuéqī xuǎnle jǐ mén kè?
李中平：	我选了四门课：英国文学、数学、中文，还有美国历史。	Wǒ xuǎnle sì mén kè, Yīngguó wénxué, shùxué, zhōngwén, háiyǒu Měiguó lìshǐ.
孙玛丽：	你比较喜欢哪门课？	Nǐ bǐjiào xǐhuan nǎ mén kè?
李中平：	我觉得中文课很有意思。	Wǒ juéde Zhōngwén kè hěn yǒu yìsi.

孙玛丽：	二年级的中文课很难，对不对？	Èr niánjí de Zhōngwén kè hěn nán, duì bu duì?
李中平：	语法和生词比较容易，可是我的听力太差了，我有时候上课听不懂。	Yǔfǎ hé shēngcí bǐjiào róngyì, kěshì wǒ de tīnglì tài chà le, wǒ yǒu shíhou shàng kè tīng bu dǒng.
孙玛丽：	你应该多听录音！	Nǐ yīnggāi duō tīng lùyīn!
李中平：	是的，如果想进步，我只好周末多练习了。	Shì de, rúguǒ xiǎng jìnbù, wǒ zhǐhǎo zhōumò duō liànxí le.
孙玛丽：	这样的话，这个周末你是不是就没时间来参加我的派对了？	Zhèyàng dehuà, zhèige zhōumò nǐ shì bu shì jiù méi shíjiān lái cānjiā wǒ de pàiduì le?
李中平：	那怎么行，我听完了录音以后马上就去！	Nà zěnme xíng, wǒ tīng wán le lùyīn yǐhòu mǎshàng jiù qù!

LESSON VOCABULARY 8.1

	SIMPLIFIED	TRADITIONAL	PINYIN	WORD CATEGORY	DEFINITION
1.	学期	學期	xuéqī	n	school term; semester
2.	选	選	xuǎn	v	to choose; select
3.	门	門	mén	mw	(used for courses)
4.	课	課	kè	n	course; class
5.	英国	英國	Yīngguó	n	Britain; U.K.; England
6.	文学	文學	wénxué	n	literature
7.	数学	數學	shùxué	n	mathematics
8.	历史	歷史	lìshǐ	n	history
9.	觉得	覺得	juéde	v	to feel; to think
10.	有意思		yǒu yìsi	adj	interesting
	意思		yìsi	n	meaning; interest
11.	年级	年级	niánjí	n	grade or level (in school)
12.	难	難	nán	adj	difficult
13.	语法	語法	yǔfǎ	n	grammar
14.	生词	生詞	shēngcí	n	vocabulary
15.	比较	比較	bǐjiào	adv	relatively; quite
16.	容易		róngyì	adj	easy
17.	听力	聽力	tīnglì	n	listening skills, oral comprehension
18.	差		chà	adj	poor; fall short; not up to standard
19.	有(的)时候	有(的)時候	yǒu (de) shíhou	ie	sometimes
20.	上课	上課	shàng kè	vo	to go to class
21.	听	聽	tīng	v	to listen
22.	懂		dǒng	v, rc	to understand
23.	录音	錄音	lùyīn	n, vo	recording; to record
24.	进步	進步	jìnbù	v, n	to improve; to advance; improvement
25.	只好		zhǐhǎo	adv	have to; be forced to
26.	周末	週末	zhōumò	n	weekend
27.	练习	練習	liànxí	v, n	to practice; practice

Simplified	Traditional	Pinyin	Word Category	Definition
28. 这样的话	這樣的話	zhèyàng dehuà	*ie*	this way; if that's the case; in that case
29. 参加	參加	cānjiā	*v*	to take part in, to participate in
30. 那怎么行 行	那怎麼行 行	nà zěnme xíng	*ie*	That won't do
		xíng	*adj*	OK; all right
31. 完		wán	*v, rc*	to complete; to finish
32. 以后	以後	yǐhòu	*prep*	after, afterwards

REQUIRED VOCABULARY 8.1

STUDYING

33. 专业	專業	zhuānyè	*n, adj*	field of study; major; professional
34. 下课	下課	xià kè	*vo*	to finish class
35. 系		xì	*n*	department
36. 学习	學習	xuéxí	*v, n*	to study; studies
37. 复习	復習	fùxí	*v, n*	to review; revision

OPTIONAL VOCABULARY 8.1

OTHER ACADEMIC SUBJECTS

38. 教育		jiàoyù	*n*	education
39. 科学	科學	kēxué	*n*	science
40. 经济学	經濟學	jīngjìxué	*n*	economics
41. 心理学	心理學	xīnlǐxué	*n*	psychology
42. 哲学	哲學	zhéxué	*n*	philosophy
43. 音乐	音樂	yīnyuè	*n*	music
44. 艺术	藝術	yìshù	*n*	art

ONLINE RESOURCES

Visit *http://college.betterchinese.com* for a list of words related to other academic subjects.

Radicals

By now, it is likely clear that many Chinese characters share some of the same components. In fact, every single character has a base component, or radical, which gives us some clues as to the character's meaning. The following are some examples of common radicals:

Radical	Derivative	Pinyin	Meaning	Examples
言	讠	yán	The "speech" or "language" radical	语 (语法, 语言), 说, 话, 谢谢
食	饣	shí	The "food" radical	饭 (吃饭), 饺子, 饿, 馆 (饭馆),
木		mù	The "wood" radical	椅子, 桌子, 床, 校 (校园), 杯子
水	氵	shuǐ	The "water" radical	海 (海鲜, 上海), 渴, 汁 (果汁), 洗
女		nǚ	The "female" radical	妹妹, 姐姐, 妈妈, 她

Phono-semantic Compounds

Most Chinese characters are formed by combining a radical with an additional component or components. These components can give some indication as to how the character is pronounced. This is referred to as a phono-semantic compound. The following are examples of phono-semantic compounds.

Compound = Radical Significance + Phonetic Component

- 饱 (bǎo: "full") is a combination of the radical 食 and the phonetic component 包 (bāo).

- 请 (qǐng "to ask") is a combination of radical 言 and the phonetic component 青 (qīng).

- In the following characters, the phonetic component 马 (mǎ: "horse") is used to indicate pronunciation: 吗 (ma) 玛 (mǎ) 妈 (mā).

STRUCTURE NOTE 8.1

Use 懂 as a resultative complement to indicate ability to understand

As a main verb, 懂 *(dǒng) means "to understand."* 懂 *can also be used as a resultative complement to indicate some status or action has been achieved to the point of understanding. As a resultative complement,* 懂 *can appear in isolation, with* 得 *to emphasize ability to understand, or with* 不 *to express inability to understand (See Structure Note 5.9).*

Subject + Verb + 懂

Subject + Verb + 得 + 懂

Subject + Verb + 不 + 懂

From the Lesson Text: 我有时候上课听不懂。
Wǒ yǒu shíhou shàng kè tīng bu dǒng.
Sometimes I don't understand what's going on in class.

Other examples: 我没(有)听懂。   你看得懂这个字吗？
Wǒ méi(yǒu) tīng dǒng.   Nǐ kàn de dǒng zhèige zì ma?
I didn't understand.   Can you read this character?

Practice: Create complete affirmative and negative sentences with 得懂 or 不懂 using the information provided below.

Example: 看 / 汉字 → 我看得懂汉字。
1. 听 / 这门课的录音 (affirmative)   _____
2. 看 / 西班牙文书 (affirmative)   _____
3. 看 / 语法课本 (affirmative)   _____
4. 听 / 法语 (negative)   _____
5. 看 / 书上写的字 (negative)   _____

STRUCTURE NOTE 8.2

Use 多 or 少 to express doing an activity more or less often

多 *can be used as an adjective or adverb meaning more or many, and* 少 *as an adjective or adverb meaning few or less frequently. In this pattern,* 多 *or* 少 *directly precede the main verb phrase, to express that the subject wants to or should do something more or less frequently, respectively.*

Subject + 多 / 少 + Verb Phrase

From the Lesson Text:　你应该多听录音！
Nǐ yīnggāi duō tīng lùyīn!
You should listen to the recordings more often!

Other examples:　你得少喝咖啡。
Nǐ děi shǎo hē kāfēi.
You have to drink less coffee.

她想多说中文。
Tā xiǎng duō shuō Zhōngwén.
She would like to speak more Chinese.

Practice: Create complete sentences using either 多 or 少 and the information provided below.

Example:　下个月 / 中文书 → 下个月我得多看中文书。

1. 早上 / 得 / 咖啡 (negative)

　　_____

2. 没钱 / 要 / 东西 (negative)

　　_____

3. 去中国 / 要 / 筷子 (affirmative)

　　_____

4. 晚上 / 得 / 电视 (negative)

　　_____

5. 这个学期 / 想 / 学 (affirmative)

　　_____

STRUCTURE NOTE 8.3
Use 只好 to indicate the the best course of action among limited options

只好 (zhǐhǎo) *expresses the meaning "have to" or "the only thing to do is," and is generally used when advising someone faced by limited and unfavorable options on the best course of action available.*

Subject + 只好 + Verb Phrase

From the Lesson Text:　如果想进步，我只好周末多练习了。
Rúguǒ xiǎng jìn bù, wǒ zhǐhǎo zhōumò duō liànxí le.
If I want to improve, I'll have to practice more on the weekend.

Other examples:

在商店我没有现金，只好刷卡了。
Zài shāngdiàn wǒ méiyǒu xiànjīn, zhǐhǎo shuā kǎ le.
I didn't have cash when I was at the store, so I had to pay with a credit card.

要是你买不到车票的话，你只好开车去了。
Yàoshì nǐ mǎi bu dào chēpiào de huà, nǐ zhǐhǎo kāi chē qù le.
If you're unable to buy a train ticket then you'll just have to drive.

Practice: Give advice about the situations below using 只好.

Example: 我想去机场，可是我不会开车。
→ 那你只好坐出租车吧。

1. 这个手机太贵了！

   _____

2. 我们的中文老师不懂英文。

   _____

3. 我不喜欢这家饭馆的饺子。

   _____

4. 这门课太难了。

   _____

5. 我们还没买书 。

   _____

STRUCTURE NOTE 8.4
Use Verb + 完 to describe completed actions

As shown in Structure Note 5.8, 到 can be used as a resultative complement to indicate the completion of an action, and in Structure Note 8.1 it was observed that 懂 functions in the same way in order to express understanding. 完 (wán) is another resultative complement and is used to indicate the completion of a process. For example: 看完, 做完, 写完, 吃完 *all imply the action was taking place, but has since been completed. Expressions using* 完 *are similar to the English "finished," as in "finished reading" or "finished watching."*

Subject + Verb + 完

From the Lesson Text: 我听完了录音以后马上就去！
Wǒ tīngwánle lùyīn yǐhòu mǎshàng jiù qù!
I'll come after I finish listening to the recordings!

Other examples: 你功课做完了没有？   我还没看完那本书。
Nǐ gōngkè zuòwánle méiyǒu?   Wǒ hái méi kànwán nà běn shū.
Have you finished your homework?   I haven't finished reading that book yet.

Practice: Using the information below, create sentences in Chinese with the appropriate verb and 完.

Example: 我 / 看 / 那本书 → 我已经看完那本书了。

1. 他 / 听 / 这课的录音   _____
2. 我 / 吃 / 早饭   _____
3. 妈妈 / 做 / 晚饭   _____
4. 我 / 做 / 昨天的功课   _____
5. 爸爸/买/东西   _____

STRUCTURE NOTE 8.5

Use 以后 to express "after doing something"

以后 (yǐhòu) *is used to create "after" clauses. Like the expression* 的时候, 以后 *must come at the end of the clause, never the beginning, as would be the case in English. Naturally, a second clause follows, which describes what comes next in the sequence, and is often preceded by* 就.

Subject + Verb Phrase + 以后 + Verb Phrase

From the Lesson Text:

我听完了录音以后马上就去！
Wǒ tīngwánle lùyīn yǐhòu mǎshàng jiù qù!
I'll come after I finish listening to the recordings!

Other examples:

你下课以后就跟我一起去
咖啡店吧。
Nǐ xiàkè yǐhòu jiù gēn wǒ yìqǐ qù
kāfēidiàn ba.
After class, come with me to the coffee
shop.

我吃完早饭以后就去
看足球比赛。
Wǒ chī wán zǎofàn yǐhòu jiù qù
kàn zúqiú bǐsài.
After I finish breakfast, I will go to
watch a soccer game.

Practice: Rewrite the following sentences in Chinese.

Example: After I eat breakfast, I will go to the gym.
→ 我吃完早饭以后就去健身房。

1.   After I review today's vocabulary, I will go home.

   _____

2.   After you cross the street, you should turn right.

   _____

3.   After I have eaten dinner, I will drink some tea.

   _____

4.   After he goes to the Great Wall, he plans to go to the Forbidden City.

   _____

5.   After she goes to the bank, she wants to buy a necklace.

   _____

STRUCTURE NOTE 8.6
Use Verb + 了 *to describe a sequence of events*

In Structure Note 6.11, it was shown that 了 *is placed after the verb when one talks about completed actions that involve a quantified object. In this lesson, verb +* 了 *is used to describe a chain of events. This, too, is a way to indicate completion, as the* 了 *marks one occurrence that is completed before another can take place. As with* 以后 *sentences, the second clause is usually preceded by* 就, 马上, *or* 才 *if one wants to stress "only after" or "only then." Because this usage of verb +* 了 *is similar in meaning to "after," it may appear in conjunction with* 以后, *though it must be noted that this pairing is not required.*

> Subject + Verb Phrase + 了 (+ Object) + Verb Phrase

From the Lesson Text:

我听完了录音以后马上就去!
Wǒ tīngwánle lùyīn yǐhòu mǎshàng jiù qù!
I'll come after I finish listening to the recordings!

Other examples:

他吃了早饭就去上课。
Tā chīle zǎofàn jiù qù shàng kè.
After he finishes breakfast, he will go to class.

她在西班牙住了三年才会说西班牙语。
Tā zài Xībānyá zhùle sān nián cái huì shuō Xībānyáyǔ.
Only after he lived in Spain for three years was he able to speak Spanish.

Practice: Use verb + 了 and the information provided below to create sequential sentences.

Example:　晚饭 / 功课 → 他吃了晚饭就做功课。

1.　中国 / 美国 　　＿＿＿＿＿＿＿＿＿＿＿＿＿＿＿
2.　足球比赛 / 回家 　＿＿＿＿＿＿＿＿＿＿＿＿＿＿＿
3.　票 / 火车 　　　＿＿＿＿＿＿＿＿＿＿＿＿＿＿＿
4.　录音 / 派对 　　＿＿＿＿＿＿＿＿＿＿＿＿＿＿＿
5.　午饭 / 走 　　　＿＿＿＿＿＿＿＿＿＿＿＿＿＿＿

PRACTICE 8.1

Working with a partner, use the character profiles and the lesson timetable below to discuss what classes you think each character would take for each day of the week.

小美 – likes math and history   玛丽 – likes languages and literature
祥安 – likes math and languages   大东 – likes languages and history

Example:

A: 星期一有数学、西班牙文和中国历史。小美会选哪门？
B: 小美星期一会选中国历史。

星期/时间	一	二	三	四	五
上午10:00 到上午11:30		英国文学		英国文学	
上午11:30 到中午12:00			美国文学	美国历史	
下午1:00 到下午2:30	数学	数学	中国历史	数学	中国历史
下午2:30 到下午4:00	西班牙文	中文	法文	中文	西班牙文
下午4:30 到下午6:00	中国历史	英国历史			

PRACTICE 8.2

Working with a partner, talk about the courses you are taking. Are they easy or difficult?

Example:

A: 你选了几门课？
B: 我选了三门课：一年级中文、数学和经济。
A: 中文课很难吗？
B: 语法比较难。我周末要多练习。

PRACTICE 8.3

Take a survey of the class to find out what the most popular course among your classmates is. Record your findings below.

Course	Number of Students

	Radical	Stroke Order
语	讠(言) yán speech	丶 讠 讠 订 评 语 语 语
法	氵(水) shuǐ water	丶 冫 氵 氵 汁 汢 法 法
差	工 gōng work	丶 丷 丷 兰 兰 羊 羊 差 差
选	辶 chuò walk	丿 丿 屮 生 失 先 先 选 选
门	门 mén door	丶 冂 门
历	厂 hǎn cliff	一 厂 厉 历
史	口 kǒu mouth	丶 口 口 史 史
年	丿 piě slash	丿 丿 乍 乍 乍 年
容	宀 mián roof	丶 丷 宀 宀 宀 欠 突 容 容
易	日 rì sun	丨 口 日 日 月 昜 昜 易
听	口 kǒu mouth	丨 口 口 叮 听 听 听
力	力 lì power	乛 力
觉	见 jiàn see	丶 丷 丷 爫 兴 兴 觉 觉
步	止 zhǐ stop	丨 卜 止 步 步 步 步
完	宀 mián roof	丶 丷 宀 宀 宀 宇 完

💻 PRACTICE 8.5

Type the following sentences on your computer and provide answers to the questions.

1. 你学什么专业？

2. 中文课很有意思。

3. 你这个学期选了几门课？

4. 我的听力太差了，我有时候听不懂。

5. 如果你想进步，就要多听录音。

PRACTICE 8.6

Make an audio recording and send it to your teacher. In the recording, state what your favorite course is, the name of the teacher, the reason why you like the course, and whether it is easy or hard.

PRACTICE 8.7

我这个学期选了四门课：数学、中文、英国文学，还有美国历史。上中文课的时候，我有的时候听不懂。老师要我多听录音，才会进步。

Read Chen Dadong's diary and answer the following questions.
1. What courses has Chen Dadong chosen?
2. What does the teacher want Chen Dadong to do to improve his Chinese?

PRACTICE 8.8

Sender	玛丽
Subject	选课

大东：
这个学期我想选比较有意思的课，可是我不知道应该选哪门课。你学什么专业？这个学期你选了什么课？哪门课比较容易？哪门课比较难？

Sender	大东
Subject	Re: 选课

玛丽：
我的专业是英国文学。因为我喜欢学不同的语言，所以也选了中文课。一年级中文课的语法和生词比较容易，听力和说话比较难。我也想学习中国历史，可是小美说这门课很难。

Read the e-mails and answer the following questions.
1. What does Chen Dadong think about the Chinese class?
2. Which course does Wang Xiaomei think is hard?

PRACTICE 8.9

孙玛丽：喂？我是玛丽，请问安娜在吗？
张安娜：我就是，你找我有事吗？
孙玛丽：这个周末我家有个派对，你能来吗？
张安娜：我得先做完功课，再去买点东西，然后才能去。
孙玛丽：你几点可以来？
张安娜：六点半吧！
孙玛丽：没问题。

Read the dialogue and answer the following questions.
1. What does Zhang Anna need to do before going to the party?
2. What time can Zhang Anna go to the party?

The Four Great Inventions

Chinese civilization has contributed immeasurably to the world's cultural heritage, but the 四大发明 (sì dà fāmíng: "four great inventions") are especially revered for helping advance China and the rest of the globe to its modern form. The four great inventions are the compass, gunpowder, paper, and printing:

Compass

The first generation compass was heavy and bulky, comprising of a bronze board and a natural magnet that would orient individuals by pointing in one of 24 possible directions. The device was later modified and suspended in water, enabling easy navigation at sea and eventually leading to the development of a more portable device, what we know as the modern day compass.

Gunpowder

Gunpowder was supposedly discovered by accident when Taoist alchemists were experimenting with various concoctions. The refinement of this explosive powder proved useful for things such as firecrackers, dynamite, and weapons.

Paper

Prior to the invention of paper, Chinese characters could only be recorded by carving them on pottery, animal bones, tortoise shells, and stones, or by writing them on bamboo slips, wood, and silk fabric. The literate world required a simpler, cheaper, and more versatile material, and so the world's first paper was duly invented in the 2nd century AD.

Printing

Carved woodblock printing was invented in China circa 600 AD, but it had obvious shortcomings as the single-use blocks were time-consuming to engrave, troublesome to store, and errors were difficult to revise. These challenges were overcome about four hundred years later with the advent of a movable-type printing method. This system used individual characters carved on squares of sticky clay which were then baked to make clay type pieces, thereby making the print making process much more cost effective and efficient.

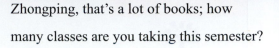
孙玛丽：	中平，这么多书，你这个学期选了几门课？

Zhongping, that's a lot of books; how many classes are you taking this semester?

李中平：	我选了四门课：英国文学、数学、中文，还有美国历史。

I'm taking four classes: British Literature, Mathematics, Chinese, and US. History.

孙玛丽：	你比较喜欢哪门课？

Which classes do you like better?

李中平：	我觉得中文课很有意思。

I think Chinese is very interesting.

孙玛丽：	二年级的中文课很难，对不对？

Second year Chinese class is really difficult, right?

李中平：	语法和生词比较容易，可是我的听力太差了，我有时候上课听不懂。

Grammar and vocabulary are quite easy, but my listening comprehension skills are really poor. Sometimes I don't understand what's going on in class.

孙玛丽：	你应该多听录音！

You should listen to the recordings more often!

李中平：	是的，如果想进步，我只好周末多练习了。

Yes, you're right. If I want to improve, I'll have to practice more on the weekend.

孙玛丽：	这样的话，这个周末你是不是就没时间来参加我的派对了？

If that's the case, will you not have time to come to my party this weekend?

李中平：	那怎么行，我听完录音以后马上就去！

That won't do! I'll come after I finish listening to the recordings!

What Can You Do?

INTERPRETIVE
- I can differentiate between the different aspects of a language course.
- I can identify places where I have difficulty in class.

INTERPERSONAL
- I can ask people about which classes they attend.
- I can ask someone what their college major is and tell them what mine is.

PRESENTATIONAL
- I can list and talk about school subjects and classes I am taking.
- I can express which aspects of a language I find easy and which I find difficult.

LESSON TEXT 8.2

In Class 上课的时候

Chen Dadong wakes up Huang Xiang'an who was sleeping before class and asks why he's so tired.

刘老师： 好，我先把昨天的作业发还给你们。

Hǎo, wǒ xiān bǎ zuótiān de zuòyè fā huán gěi nǐmen.

陈大东： 喂，上课了！你今天怎么这么累？你昨天晚上几点才睡觉？

Wèi, shàngkè le! Nǐ jīntiān zěnme zhème lèi? Nǐ zuótiān wǎnshàng jǐ diǎn cái shuì jiào?

黄祥安： 我去听音乐会了，昨天晚上12点才睡觉！

Wǒ qù tīng yīnyuèhuì le, zuótiān wǎn shàng shíèr diǎn cái shuìjiào!

陈大东： 我们明天要考试，你准备了吗？

Wǒmen míngtiān yào kǎoshì, nǐ zhǔnbèi le ma?

黄祥安： 我一起床就来上课了，还没有时间准备呢！

Wǒ yì qǐchuáng jiù lái shàngkè le, hái méiyǒu shíjiān zhǔnbèi ne!

陈大东： 你觉得考试重要还是听音乐会重要？

Nǐ juéde kǎoshì zhòngyào háishì tīng yīnyuèhuì zhòngyào?

黄祥安： 好了，好了！糟糕！我忘了带我的笔记本了，怎么办？

Hǎo le, hǎo le! Zāogāo! Wǒ wàngle dài wǒ de bǐjìběn le, zěnme bàn?

陈大东： 我给你一张纸吧。

Wǒ gěi nǐ yì zhāng zhǐ ba.

黄祥安： 谢谢。我们昨天学到哪儿了？

Xièxie. Wǒmen zuótiān xué dào nǎr le?

陈大东： 我们已经把第三课的课文念完了。今天学语法。老师正在白板上写语法点呢！

Wǒmen yǐjīng bǎ dì-sān kè de kèwén niàn wán le. Jīntiān xué yǔfǎ. Lǎoshī zhèngzài báibǎn shàng xiě yǔfǎ diǎn ne!

黄祥安： 我找不到我的笔了，可以借你的吗？

Wǒ zhǎo bu dào wǒ de bǐ le, kěyǐ jiè nǐ de ma?

刘老师： 上课了！大东，祥安，你们还有什么问题吗？

Shàng kè le! Dàdōng, Xiáng'ān, nǐmen háiyǒu shénme wèntí ma?

黄祥安： 没有问题。对不起！   Méiyǒu wèntí. Duìbuqǐ!

LESSON VOCABULARY 8.2

	SIMPLIFIED	TRADITIONAL	PINYIN	WORD CATEGORY	DEFINITION
1.	把		bǎ	prep	(introduces the object of a verb)
2.	作业	作業	zuòyè	n	homework; assignment
3	发还	發還	fā huán	v	to give back
	发	發	fā	v	to give out, to deliver, to issue
	还	還	huán	v	to return; to give back
4.	怎么这么	怎麼這麼	zěnme zhème	qph	how come (it's) so
	怎么	怎麼	zěnme	qw	how; how come
5.	累		lèi	adj	tired
6.	睡觉	睡覺	shuìjiào	vo	to sleep
7.	音乐会	音樂會	yīnyuèhuì	n	concert
8.	考试	考試	kǎoshì	n, vo	test; to give or take a test
9.	准备	準備	zhǔnbèi	v	to prepare; to plan
10.	起床		qǐchuáng	vo	to get up (from bed)
11.	重要		zhòngyào	adj	important
12.	好了, 好了		hǎole hǎole	ie	alright, alright
13.	糟糕		zāogāo	interj, adj	oh no; what bad luck; terrible
14.	忘		wàng	v	to forget
15.	带	帶	dài	v	to bring
16.	笔记本	筆記本	bǐjìběn	n	notebook
17.	怎么办	怎麼辦	zěnme bàn	qph	what to do; what can be done; what shall I do
18.	张	張	zhāng	mw	(used for flat objects like paper)
19.	纸	紙	zhǐ	n	paper
20.	第		dì	mw	(a prefix for ordinal numbers)
21.	课文	課文	kèwén	n	lesson text
22.	念		niàn	v	to read aloud

LESSON VOCABULARY 8.2 (continued)

	SIMPLIFIED	TRADITIONAL	PINYIN	WORD CATEGORY	DEFINITION
23.	正在		zhèngzài	*adv*	right now
24.	白板		báibǎn	*n*	whiteboard
25.	笔	筆	bǐ	*n*	pen
26.	借		jiè	*v*	to lend or borrow

REQUIRED VOCABULARY 8.2

RELATED TO STUDYING

27.	注意		zhùyì	*v*	to be careful; to pay attention to
28.	读	讀	dú	*v*	to read; to study
29.	小考		xiǎokǎo	*n*	quiz

OTHER

30.	安静	安靜	ānjìng	*v, adj*	to be quiet; quiet; peaceful

OPTIONAL VOCABULARY 8.2

STATIONERY

31.	铅笔	鉛筆	qiānbǐ	*n*	pencil
32.	橡皮		xiàngpí	*n*	eraser
33.	黑板		hēibǎn	*n*	blackboard, chalkboard
34.	圆珠笔	圓珠筆	yuánzhūbǐ	*n*	ball-point pen

DAILY ROUTINE

35.	洗澡		xǐzǎo	*vo*	to take a shower or bath
36.	刷牙		shuā yá	*vo*	to brush one's teeth

ONLINE RESOURCES
Visit *http://college.betterchinese.com* for a list of words related to classroom equipment and stationery.

Homographs

In Chinese, a 多音字 (duōyīnzì: "multiple-sound character"), or homograph, is a character which can be pronounced in more than one way and has more than one meaning. One such example which appears in this lesson is the character 觉. When used in the verb "to sleep," the character 觉 is pronounced jiào – 睡觉 (shuì jiào). However, in the verb "to feel," it is pronounced júe – 觉得 (júede).

There are various examples of this phenomenon in Chinese. Here are a few of them:

Character		Example		Meaning
还	hái	还是	háishì	had better; should
	huán	还	huán	to return
行	xíng	旅行	lǚxíng	travel; to travel
	háng	银行	yínháng	bank
乐	lè	快乐	kuàilè	happy
	yuè	音乐	yīnyuè	music
只	zhī	只	zhī	measure word for animals, etc
	zhǐ	只	zhǐ	only
好	hǎo	你好	nǐ hǎo	hello
	hào	好奇	hàoqí	curious
教	jiāo	教书	jiāoshū	teach
	jiào	教师	jiàoshī	teacher

Interjection Review

Using Chinese interjections, or exclamatory phrases, can help make one's Chinese conversation sound more natural. Sometimes the pinyin used to transcribe interjections does not exactly match their pronunciation in real speech, so be sure to ask a native speaker to demonstrate. Here are the interjections introduced thus far:

Chinese	Pinyin	Meaning
喂	wèi, wéi	Hey, Hello (used to answer the phone or to get someone's attention)
哎呀	āiyā	Oh no! (expresses dismay)
哦	ò	Oh (expresses realization)
哇	wā	Wow! (expresses surprise, amazement)
啊	ā	Ah . . . (thought up something unexpected)

Online Resources

Visit *http://college.betterchinese.com* for a list of other homographs and interjections.

STRUCTURE NOTE 8.7
Use 把 *to indicate an action performed on a specific object*

The 把 *(bǎ) construction is a pattern in which the verb is moved to the end of a sentence. It is used when describing a situation where a subject takes an object and does something with it. For example,* 我做晚饭了 *would become* 我把晚饭做好了. *The latter pattern places more emphasis on the object rather than the action.* 把 *sentences involve an action that depicts a change of state or has been completed. For this reason,* 把 *constructions must be followed by a supplemental phrase indicating such, as with a* 了 *particle to indicate a change of state, a resultative complement (e.g.* 完*), or a* 给 *expression with a recipient. Note that the object of* 把 *must always be definite ("the"), it cannot be "a" or "some." It would be incorrect, for example, to say* *我把一本书还给他 *(I returned a book to him).*

> Subject + 把 + Object + Verb + 了 / Resultative Complement / 给 Expression

From the Lesson Text:

我先把昨天的作业发还给你们。
Wǒ xiān bǎ zuótiān de zuòyè fā huán gěi nǐmen.
I will first return yesterday's assignments to everyone.

Other examples:

你把书看完了吗？
Nǐ bǎ shū kànwánle ma?
Did you finish reading the book?

他今天把课都选好了。
Tā jīntiān bǎ kè dōu xuǎnhǎo le.
He finished picking his classes today.

Practice: Change the following sentences into 把 sentences.

Example: 我已经听完录音了。 → 我已经把录音听完了。
1. 他念完第七课了。　　＿＿＿＿＿＿＿＿＿＿＿＿
2. 他借我车了。　　＿＿＿＿＿＿＿＿＿＿＿＿
3. 她送玛丽生日礼物了。　　＿＿＿＿＿＿＿＿＿＿＿＿
4. 你做完晚饭了吗？　　＿＿＿＿＿＿＿＿＿＿＿＿
5. 我看完那本书了。　　＿＿＿＿＿＿＿＿＿＿＿＿

STRUCTURE NOTE 8.8
Use 怎么 *to ask "how come" questions*

In Structure Note 7.8, 怎么 *was introduced as a question word meaning "how." In this lesson, it is used to mean "how come." This usage is similar to* 为什么, *but carries a tone of surprise or incredulity.*

> Subject + 怎么 + Verb Phrase

From the Lesson Text:

你今天怎么这么累？
Nǐ jīntiān zěnme zhème lèi?
How come you're so tired today?

Other examples:

你怎么来这儿了？
Nǐ zěnme lái zhèr le?
What are you doing here?

你怎么没给她买生日礼物？
Nǐ zěnme méi gěi tā mǎi shēngrì lǐwù?
How come you didn't buy her a birthday present?

Practice: Change the following questions into Chinese using 怎么.

Example: How come he can speak French? → 他怎么会说法语呢？

1. How come there's no test today?

   _____

2. How come she can't use chopsticks?

   _____

3. How come he's sleeping in the library?

   _____

4. How come you don't like to go to the gym?

   _____

5. How come your roommate still hasn't arrived?

   _____

STRUCTURE NOTE 8.9

Use 怎么这么 / 那么 to express incredulity or amazement regarding a situation

这么 *and* 那么 *can follow* 怎么 *to express surprise about a particular situation, meaning "why is something so (adjective)?"*

> Subject + 怎么 + 这么 / 那么 + Adjective?

From the Lesson Text:

你今天怎么这么累？
Nǐ jīntiān zěnme zhème lèi?
How come you're so tired today?

Other examples:

他怎么那么高兴？
Tā zěnme nàme gāoxìng?
How come he is so happy?

你的房间怎么这么大？
Nǐ de fángjiān zěnme zhème dà?
How come your room is so big?

Practice: Rewrite the following statements using the 怎么这么 / 那么 construction.

Example: 他买的项链很贵。→ 他买的项链怎么这么贵？

1. 这盘青菜很咸。 _____

2. 他写的字很小。 _____

3. 第八课太难了。 _____

4. 他今天很饿。 _____

5. 这个手机很便宜。 _____

STRUCTURE NOTE 8.10

Use 一⋯就⋯ to express "as soon as A, B"

一 and 就 are used jointly to denote a sequence of events, where the second event immediately follows the initial event, as with the pattern "as soon as (A), then (B)." If the subsequent action pertains to the same subject, the subject may be omitted in the second clause. Otherwise, it must be explicitly stated before the second 就.

> Subject + 一 + Verb Phrase (+ Subject 2) + 就 + Verb Phrase

From the Lesson Text:

我一起床就来上课了。
Wǒ yì qǐchuáng jiù lái shàngkè le.
As soon as I got up, I came straight to class.

Other examples:

我一来，她就走了。
Wǒ yì lái, tā jiù zǒu le.
As soon as I came, she left.

他一到图书馆就开始做作业。
Tā yí dào túshūguǎn jiù kāishǐ zuò zuòyè.
He started doing his homework as soon as he arrived at the library.

Practice: Create complete sentences in Chinese using 一⋯就⋯ and the information provided below.

Example: 吃完饭／回家 → 我一吃完饭，就回家了。

1. 上课／睡觉 _____
2. 到北京／去长城 _____
3. 去完银行／去买东西 _____
4. 服务员来／点菜 _____
5. 到咖啡店／大东来了 _____

STRUCTURE NOTE 8.11

Use 觉得 to express subjective opinions

觉得 (juéde) means "to feel" or "to think." It typically prefaces a subjective opinion, rather than a statement of a possible fact.

> Subject + 觉得 + Sentence

From the Lesson Text:

你觉得考试重要还是听音乐会重要？
Nǐ juéde kǎoshì zhòngyào háishì tīng yīnyuèhuì zhòngyào?
Which do you feel is more important, studying for a test or going to a concert?

Other examples:

我觉得饺子很好吃。
Wǒ juéde jiǎozi hěn hǎo chī.
I think dumplings are very tasty.

我觉得生日派对应该有蛋糕。
Wǒ juéde shēngrì pàiduì yīnggāi yǒu dàngāo.
I think there should be cake at a birthday party.

Practice: Transform the following sentences into Chinese using the verb 觉得.

Example: I think that Chinese characters are difficult to write.
→ 我觉得汉字很难写。

1. I think the vocabulary in lesson five is very easy.

_____

2. He thinks that the Hot and Sour Soup in that restaurant is too spicy.

_____

3. I feel that we shouldn't have so many tests.

_____

4. I think bargaining is really fun.

_____

5. I think the stationery in this shop is really expensive.

_____

STRUCTURE NOTE 8.12
Use 还是 with adjectives to compare qualities

In Structure Note 6.6 and 6.14, 还是 was used to ask about alternatives. In this lesson, 还是 is used to compare a particular characteristic of a couple of objects or activities. In this instance, 还是 is used to ask, "A or B, which is more (adjective)?"

A + Adjective + 还是 + B + Adjective?

From the Lesson Text: 你觉得考试重要还是听音乐会重要？
Nǐ juéde kǎoshì zhòngyào háishì tīng yīnyuèhuì zhòngyào?
Which do you feel is more important, studying for a test or going to a concert?

Other examples: 中国菜好吃还是西班牙菜好吃？
Zhōngguó cài hǎo chī háishì Xībānyá cài hǎo chī?
Which do you think is tastier: Chinese food or Spanish food?

大东觉得中国的东西贵还是英国的东西贵？
Dàdōng juéde Zhōngguó de dōngxi guì háishì Yīngguó de dōngxi guì?
Does Dadong feel things are more expensive in China or the U.K.?

NOTE: In this pattern, the adjective appears without 很 or any other modifiers. When adjectives are used in their basic form without any modifiers, some type of comparison is generally involved.

Practice: Write complete sentences in Chinese using 还是 and the information given below.

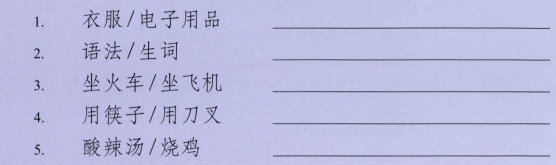

Example: 中文 / 西班牙语 → 你觉得中文难还是西班牙语难？

1. 衣服 / 电子用品 _____
2. 语法 / 生词 _____
3. 坐火车 / 坐飞机 _____
4. 用筷子 / 用刀叉 _____
5. 酸辣汤 / 烧鸡 _____

STRUCTURE NOTE 8.13

Use 第 to express ordinal numbers

Ordinal numbers in English, such as "first", "second," "third," etc., are expressed in Chinese by adding 第 (dì) *before the number. This addition helps to delineate quantities versus ordinal numbering. For example, while* 一课 *means "one lesson,"* 第一课 *refers to "Lesson One," or literally, "the first lesson." In certain cases where it is clear that something is a noun (e.g.* 三月*, "March") or part of a distinct ordinal sequence, as with dates,* 第 *need not be applied.*

第 + Number

From the Lesson Text:

我们已经把第三课的课文念完了。
Wǒmen yǐjīng bǎ dì-sān kè de kèwén niànwán le.
We already finished reading Lesson Three of the lesson text.

Other examples:

第一个到餐厅的人是大东，
第二个是祥安。
Dì-yī gè dào cāntīng de rén shì Dàdōng,
dì-èr gè shì Xiáng'ān.
The first to arrive at the restaurant was
Dadong, and the second was Xiang'an.

我觉得第五本书很有意思。
Wǒ juéde dì-wǔ běn shū hěn yǒu yìsi.
I think the fifth book is very interesting.

Practice: Read the following phrases and decide whether or not they can be modified with 第. If so, write the modified phrase in the space provided.

Example: 三个人 → 第三个人

1. 星期一 _____
2. 三月五号 _____
3. 五课 _____
4. 七点钟 _____
5. 八个月 _____

STRUCTURE NOTE 8.14
Use (正)在……(呢) to indicate ongoing actions

In English, the suffix "-ing" is used to indicate an ongoing action at a particular point of reference. Ongoing actions are expressed in Chinese by applying 在 *before the verb phrase and* 呢 *after it, or simply* 在 *on its own.* 在 *can also be combined with* 正 *(zhèng) to create* 正在, *which makes for a stronger emphasis akin to "just in the middle of" or "right in the middle of (doing something)." In both cases, the* 呢 *at the end of the phrase is optional.*

Note that the pattern for ongoing actions is negated by 没(有), *not* 不.

Subject + (正)在 + Verb Phrase + (呢)

From the Lesson Text:
老师正在白板上写语法点呢！
Lǎoshī zhèngzài báibǎn shàng xiě yǔfǎ diǎn ne!
The teacher is writing the grammar points on the whiteboard!

Other examples:

他来的时候，我正在看书。
Tā lái de shíhou, wǒ zhèngzài kàn shū.
When he arrived, I was in the middle of reading a book.

小孩子没在睡觉。
Xiǎoháizi méi zài shuì jiào.
The kids are not sleeping.

Practice: Transform the following sentences into Chinese using (正)在……(呢)

Example:　　　　Dadong is watching the soccer match.
→ 大东在看足球比赛。

1.　　He don't want to go to the library now because I'm eating.
_____

2.　　When I arrived at the party everyone was eating cake.
_____

3.　　He's exercising right now.
_____

4.　　She's watching television now because she already finished her homework.
_____

5.　　They are in the coffee shop reading.
_____

PRACTICE 8.10

Working with a partner, create conversations based on the objects you have around you.

Example:

A: 你的笔记本在哪儿？

B: 我的笔记本在桌上。/
哎呀！我找不到我的笔记本了，可
以借你的吗？

PRACTICE 8.11

Help Wang Xiaomei to create her schedule for the day using the following vocabulary. Present the schedule to a classmate.

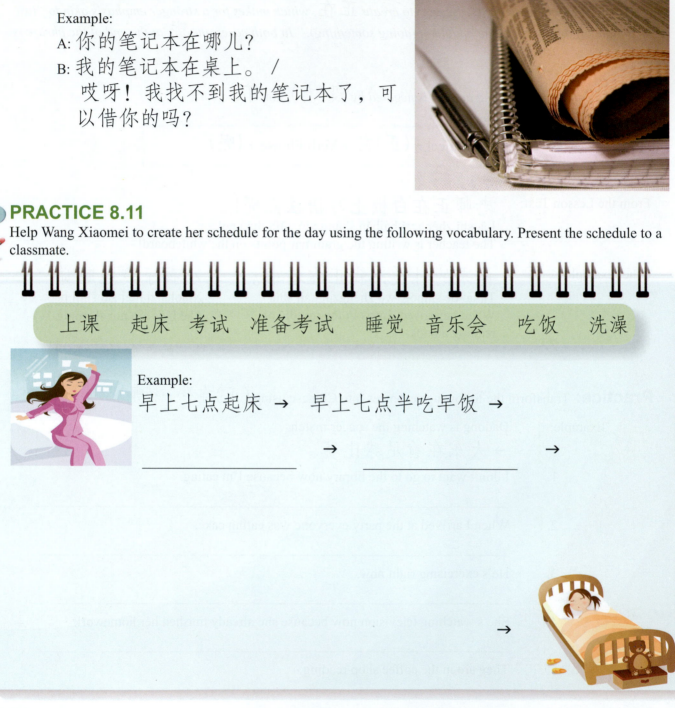

上课　起床　考试　准备考试　睡觉　音乐会　吃饭　洗澡

Example:

早上七点起床 → 早上七点半吃早饭 →

_____ → _____ →

→

PRACTICE 8.12

Do a survey to determine which aspects of learning Chinese your classmates find the easiest and which they find the most difficult. Record your findings below.

	Aspect of Chinese	Number of Students
Easiest		
Most Difficult		

	Radical	Stroke Order
考	耂 lǎo old	一 十 土 耂 耂 考
试	讠(言) yán speech	丶 讠 讠 讠 讠 试 试 试
业	业 yè industry	丨 丨丨 业 业 业
把	扌(手) shǒu hand	一 扌 扌 扣 扣 扣 把
音	音 yīn sound	丶 二 六 立 产 音 音 音
准	冫(冰) bīng ice	丶 冫 冫 冫 冫 冫 准 准 准
备	夂 zhǐ walk slowly	丿 夂 夂 冬 各 各 备 备
重	里 lǐ village	丿 一 二 亡 盲 盲 审 重 重
办	力 lì power	刀 力 办 办
张	弓 gōng bow	一 コ 弓 弘 张 张
念	心 xīn heart	丿 人 今 今 今 念 念 念
第	竹(竹) zhú bamboo	丿 卜 大 竺 竹 竹 笃 笃 第 第
正	止 zhǐ stop	一 丁 下 正 正
白	白 bái white	丿 亻 白 白 白
笔	竹(竹) zhú bamboo	丿 卜 大 竺 竹 竹 笁 笁 笔 笔

💬 **PRACTICE 8.14**

🎤 Make an audio recording and send it to your teacher. In the recording, talk about your Chinese class. What kinds of activities do you do in class? When do you have an exam? What materials do you bring with you to class?

PRACTICE 8.15

Type the following sentences on your computer and provide answers to the questions.

1. 你今天怎么这么累？
2. 你准备了吗？
3. 我找不到我的笔了，可以借你的吗？
4. 老师已经把第三课念完了。
5. 请大家把笔记本还给我。

PRACTICE 8.16

今天我很累，又忘了带笔记本去上课。因为昨晚我在准备今天的语法考试，所以晚上十一点半才睡觉。可是今天回到学校以后，玛丽说今天要考的是生词，下星期才考语法。

Read Huang Xiang'an's diary and answer the following questions.
1. What time did Huang Xiang'an go to sleep last night?
2. What test is he taking today?

PRACTICE 8.17

Sender	祥安
Subject	音乐会

安娜：
今天晚上的音乐会，大东和小美都会去，你去吗？我们听完音乐会以后会去吃饭。我知道你后天有英国文学的考试，可是你可以明天准备。

Sender	安娜
Subject	Re: 音乐会

祥安：
不行，明天我要去朋友的生日派对。如果我今天去听音乐会，我就没有时间准备考试了。这次英国文学考的生词很难，我要多一点的时间准备。我觉得考试很重要。

Read the e-mails and answer the following questions.
1. What exam does Zhang Anna need to prepare for?
2. Why can't she prepare for the exam tomorrow?

PRACTICE 8.18

黄祥安：刘老师，对不起，我忘了带我的作业。
刘老师：今天下午给我也可以。
黄祥安：谢谢老师！我下午一点半把作业给您。
刘老师：好的。别再忘了。写在你的笔记本上吧。
黄祥安：对不起，我也忘了带我的笔记本。
刘老师：我给你一张纸吧。
黄祥安：哎呀！我找不到我的笔。

Read the dialogue and answer the following questions.
1. When does Teacher Liu tell Huang Xiang'an he can give her his homework?
2. What things does Huang Xiang'an forget to bring?

Examinations in China

For centuries, national civil service examinations occupied a critical role in Chinese society. By the Tang Dynasty, the practice of announcing the names of high-scoring exam participants in a process known as 放榜 (fàngbǎng: "releasing the roll") had become an established tradition, as had the public announcement of the 状元 (zhuàngyuan, "the best"), a title granted to the individual who received the highest score. Because they would be assigned ranks and political posts based on their score, men from all social standings were inspired to study hard in hopes of acquiring recognition for their family.

Today, many Chinese students face a level of exam-related pressure that their forebearers would no doubt empathize with. The National Higher Education Entrance Examination, or 高考 (gāokǎo), is considered the primary admissions criteria for tertiary education, and so the pressure from this one exam can be enormous. Students will spend endless nights studying for the three-day exam, as a solid performance is viewed as a means to secure honor for one's family and access to a promising future with a university degree.

The Four Treasures of the Study

笔、墨、纸、砚, (bǐ, mò, zhǐ, yàn: "brush, ink, paper, inkstone") are the four essential elements found in classical Chinese painting and calligraphy. Chinese scholars considered these items to be indispensable treasures, as it was these tools that enabled a scholar to demonstrate his mastery of Chinese painting and calligraphy to his peers.

Brush 毛笔 (máobǐ)

Brushes for were made of various animal hairs and varied in thickness and in length.

Ink 墨 (mò)

Ink was typically made from a mixture of soot and resin. The best inksticks were fine-grained, with an even and smooth texture.

Paper 纸 (zhǐ)

First invented during the Han dynasty, paper was originally made from a wide range of fibrous materials that were mixed, pounded, then dried.

Inkstone 砚 (yàn)

Inkstones supplied a surface that allowed the grinding of the inkstick into powder, which was then mixed with water to produce ink.

刘老师： 好，我先把昨天的作业发还给你们。

Ok, I will first return yesterday's assignments to everyone.

陈大东： 喂，上课了！你今天怎么这么累？昨天晚上几点睡觉的？

Hey, class has started! How come you're so tired today? What time did you sleep last night?

黄祥安： 我去听音乐会了，昨天晚上12点才睡觉！

I went to a concert and didn't sleep until 12 a.m. last night!

陈大东： 我们明天要考试，你准备了吗？

We're having a test tomorrow. Did you prepare for it?

黄祥安： 我一起床就来上课了，还没有时间准备呢！

As soon as I got up, I came straight to class. I haven't had time to prepare yet!

陈大东： 你觉得考试重要还是听音乐会重要？

Which do you feel is more important, studying for a test or going to a concert?

黄祥安： 好了，好了！糟糕！我忘了带我的笔记本了，怎么办？

OK, OK! Oh no! I forgot my notebook, what should I do?

陈大东： 我给你一张纸吧。

I'll give you a sheet of paper.

黄祥安： 谢谢。我们昨天学到哪儿了？

Thank you. Where did we last leave off yesterday?

陈大东： 我们已经把第三课的课文念完了。今天学语法。老师正在白板上写语法点呢！

We already finished reading Lesson Three of the lesson text. Today, we're studying grammar. The teacher is writing the grammar points on the whiteboard!

黄祥安： 我找不到我的笔了，可以借你的吗？

I can't find my pen. May I borrow yours?

刘老师： 上课了！大东，祥安，你们还有什么问题吗？

Class has started! Dadong, Xiang'an, do you guys still have any questions?

黄祥安： 没有问题！对不起。

No questions! Sorry.

What Can You Do?

INTERPRETIVE
- I can understand a rhetorical question.
- I can understand ordinal numbers.

INTERPERSONAL
- I can discuss test preparation and lesson progress with classmates.
- I can ask to borrow an item.

PRESENTATIONAL
- I can offer a subjective opinion on something.

ACT IT OUT

Working in groups, compose an original three-minute skit that utilizes the vocabulary and structures introduced in Unit 8. Each of you should assume a role and have a roughly equal number of lines in the skit. Be prepared to perform your skit in class. You can either come up with your own story or choose from one of the following situations:

a) You are the teacher of a class and none of your students has done the homework.

b) It's the end of summer vacation and you and your friends need to decide what school supplies to buy for college.

CHECK WHAT YOU CAN DO

Recognize						Write	
Adjectives	*Idiomatic Expressions*	□ 专业	□ 考试	□ 完	□ 语	□ 考
□ 有意思	□ 有(的)时候	□ 英国	□ 录音	□ 学习	□ 法	□ 试
□ 难	□ 这样的话	□ 年级	*Prepositions*	□ 复习	□ 差	□ 业
□ 容易	□ 那怎么行	□ 语法	□ 把	□ 发还	□ 选	□ 把
□ 差	□ 好了，好了	□ 生词	□ 以后	□ 准备	□ 门	□ 音
□ 累		□ 听力		□ 忘	□ 历	□ 准
□ 重要	*Measure Words*	□ 周末	*Question Words*	□ 带	□ 史	□ 备
□ 安静	□ 门	□ 系	□ 怎么这么	□ 念	□ 年	□ 重
	□ 张	□ 作业	□ 怎么办	□ 借	□ 容	□ 办
Adverbs	□ 第	□ 音乐会		□ 注意	□ 易	□ 张
□ 比较		□ 笔记本	*Verbs*	□ 读	□ 听	□ 念
□ 只好	*Nouns*	□ 纸	□ 选	□ 上课	□ 力	□ 第
□ 正在	□ 学期	□ 白板	□ 觉得	□ 下课	□ 觉	□ 正
	□ 课	□ 课文	□ 听	□ 睡觉	□ 步	□ 白
Interjection	□ 文学	□ 笔	□ 懂	□ 进步	□ 完	□ 笔
□ 糟糕	□ 数学	□ 小考	□ 练习	□ 起床		
	□ 历史		□ 参加			

Use

□ 懂 as a resultative verb to indicate ability to understand

□ 多 or 少 to express doing an activity more or less often

□ 只好 to indicate the best course of action among limited options

□ Verb + 完 to describe completed actions

□ 以后 to express "after doing something"

□ Verb + 了 to describe a sequence of events

□ 把 to indicate an action performed on a specific object

□ 怎么 to ask "how come" questions

□ 怎么这么 / 那么 to express incredulity or amazement regarding a situation

□ 一······就······ to express "as soon as A, B"

□ 觉得 to express subjective opinions

□ 还是 with adjectives to compare qualities

□ 第 to express ordinal numbers

□ (正)在······(呢) to indicate ongoing actions

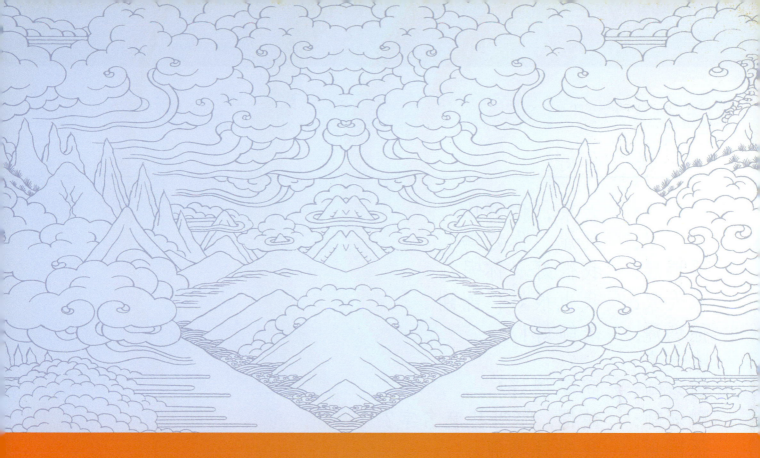

附录
APPENDIX

第一單元

第一課　你好！

孫瑪麗：	大東，你好！
陳大東：	瑪麗，你好嗎？
孫瑪麗：	我很好。你呢？
陳大東：	我也很好，謝謝。
孫瑪麗，	老師好！
陳大東：	
劉老師：	同學們好！
劉老師：	請問，你叫甚麼名字？
孫瑪麗：	我叫孫瑪麗。
劉老師：	他叫甚麼名字？
孫瑪麗：	他叫陳大東。
劉老師：	瑪麗，大東，再見！
孫瑪麗，	老師，再見！
陳大東：	

第二課　你多大？你是哪國人？

劉老師：	瑪麗，你多大？
孫瑪麗：	我十九歲。
劉老師：	陳大東呢？
孫瑪麗：	他二十歲。
劉老師：	你是哪國人？
孫瑪麗：	我是美國人。
劉老師：	陳大東是不是美國人？
孫瑪麗：	不是，他不是美國人。他是加拿大人。

第二單元

第一課　　家人和寵物

李中平：　小美，你好。這是我爸爸、媽媽和哥哥。你家有幾個人？

王小美：　我家有五個人：爸爸、媽媽、姐姐、妹妹和我。

李中平：　這是我家的狗。你家有什麼寵物？有沒有狗？

王小美：　没有。我家有两只猫。我很喜欢狗，可是我妈妈喜欢猫。

第二課　　工作和语言

王小美：　這個男孩是誰？

李中平：　他是我的朋友陳大東。那個女孩是他妹妹。

王小美：　他做甚麼工作？

李中平：　他是學生，也是咖啡店的服務員。

王小美：　他會說甚麼語言？

李中平：　他會说英語、法語，還會说一點兒漢語。

王小美：　他會不會寫漢字？

李中平：　他只會一點兒。

第三單元

第一課　星期幾？幾點？

黃祥安：　這個星期有足球比賽，你會去看嗎？
陳大東：　星期幾？什麼時候？
黃祥安：　星期三晚上六點半。
陳大東：　好，我去。瑪麗，你呢？
孫瑪麗：　我也會去。我們六點見吧。
黃祥安：　現在幾點？瑪麗還沒有來！
陳大東：　現在差不多六點一刻。
孫瑪麗：　對不起！
陳大東：　没关系，比赛还没开始呢！
黃祥安：　我們走吧。

第二課　生日快樂！

李中平：　瑪麗的生日是幾月幾號？是今天還是明天？
王小美：　是明天。她的生日是十月三號。
李中平：　是嗎？有生日派對嗎？
王小美：　有！明天下午瑪麗家有派對。
　大家：　瑪麗，生日快樂！
孫瑪麗：　你們都來了！我真高興！
王小美：　大家吃蛋糕吧！
李中平：　這是我送你的生日禮物，祝你生日快樂！
孫瑪麗：　謝謝你！

第四單元

第一課　點菜

服務員：　歡迎光臨！請問，幾位？

陳大東：　三位。

服務員：　請坐。請問想喝什麼？

孫瑪麗：　請給我們三杯茶。

服務員：　好。這是我們的菜單。

孫瑪麗：　那是不是安娜？她是個新同學。

李中平：　安娜！——安娜，你喜歡不喜歡吃中國菜？

張安娜：　我只喜歡吃餃子。

陳大東：　那，我們點一盤餃子，一衹燒雞，一份青菜和一碗酸辣湯。好不好？

孫瑪麗：　好。這家飯館的燒雞很好吃。我餓了，我們點菜吧！

第二課　味道怎麼樣？

陳大東：　酸辣湯真好喝！我喜歡酸辣的味道。

孫瑪麗：　燒雞也不錯。中平，青菜的味道怎麼樣？

李中平：　太鹹了。我要叫一碗米飯。

陳大東：　中平，你爲甚麼不吃肉？

李中平：　因爲我吃素。

孫瑪麗：　安娜，你不會用筷子嗎？

張安娜：　不會。我衹會用刀子，叉子……

李中平：　試一下吧！我教你。

張安娜：　哦，用筷子很簡單啊！

陳大東：　大家吃飽了嗎？今天晚飯我請客！

第五單元

第一課　校園生活

李中平：　小美，我來介紹一下。這是陳大東，祥安的室友。
陳大東：　你好，很高興認識你。
王小美：　你好，大東。你住在哪兒？
陳大東：　我住在校內。我的公寓在餐廳對面。
王小美：　你們現在去哪兒？
李中平：　我去健身房運動，大東去圖書館。
王小美：　可以不可以跟你一起去？
陳大東：　當然可以。中平，回頭見！

第二課　在哪裏？

黃祥安：　喂？你好。
陳大東：　祥安，我是大東。你在哪兒？
黃祥安：　我在宿捨看電視。有事嗎？
陳大東：　我找不到我的課本了。幫我找一下，好嗎？
黃祥安：　好吧。你的課本在臥室裏面嗎？
陳大東：　可能在我的床上。
黃祥安：　不在那兒，也不在書桌上。
陳大東：　……那會在哪兒呢？
黃祥安：　哦，我找到了！課本就在客廳的沙發下面！
陳大東：　太好了！我現在馬上回去拿。

第六單元

第一課　　買東西

張安娜：　這家商店賣甚麼東西？

孫瑪麗：　這兒賣的東西很多。你看，有衣服，有文具，還有電子用品。

張安娜：　我得買一個手機。我很想我爸媽，要給他們打電話。小姐，請問，這個手機多少錢？

售貨員：　兩百九十塊九毛九。

張安娜：　太貴了！一百塊賣不賣？

售貨員：　不好意思，這個手機的價錢是兩百九十塊九毛九。

張安娜：　這樣吧，我給你一百五十塊，怎麼樣？

孫瑪麗：　安娜，他們這兒不講價！小姐，有沒有便宜一點兒的？

張安娜：　我不要便宜的！算了，我們還是去別的商店看一下吧。

第二課　　付現金還是刷卡？

陳大東：　中平，你已經送瑪麗生日禮物了，為什麼還要再給她買東西？

李中平：　因為她昨天教我做功課，所以我要謝謝她。

陳大東：　你要給她買這麼貴的禮物啊！

李中平：　不用擔心，要是太貴的話我就買別的東西。

售貨員：　一百二十八塊。

李中平：　好，那我就買這條。

售貨員：　請問您是付現金還是刷卡？

李中平：　付現金。給你一百三十塊。

陳大東：　你花了这么多钱，可以吗？

李中平：　没问题。哦，瑪麗來了，我們走吧！

第七單元

第一課　放假的計劃

陳大東：　小美，你放假的時候有甚麼計劃？
王小美：　我打算去北京，下個月回來。
陳大東：　是嗎？你老家在北京嗎？
王小美：　對，我出生在北京，十歲才來美國，是在加州長大的。
孫瑪麗：　北京有甚麼好玩兒的？
王小美：　有長城，有故宮，還可以吃北京烤鴨呢！
孫瑪麗：　哇，北京這麼好玩兒，我也很想去！
陳大東：　瑪麗，你家在什麼地方？
孫瑪麗：　我家在波士頓。我爸是從西班牙來的，我媽是從愛爾蘭來的。
陳大東：　是嗎？我家在加拿大。今年寒假回家我買了一張火車票。因為飛機票太貴了！
王小美：　對不起，我得走了。祝你們寒假快樂！

第二課　到機場

孫瑪麗：　中平，謝謝你開車送我們去機場！
李中平：　不用謝！機場離學校不太遠。
孫瑪麗：　中平，你知道從這兒到機場怎麼走嗎？
李中平：　當然！我們先一直往前開，到了路口再往左轉。
張安娜：　不對！我們到路口應該往右轉。
孫瑪麗：　不對！先往左轉，再穿過大街，然後往右轉。
王小美：　我們迷路了嗎？
李中平：　你們別吵了。
王小美：　小心啊！前面有隻貓！
張安娜：　哎呀，我還是去坐出租車吧。

第八單元

第一課　你選幾門課？

孫瑪麗：　中平，這麼多書，你這個學期選了幾門課？

李中平：　我選了四門課：英國文學、數學、中文，還有美國歷史。

孫瑪麗：　你比較喜歡哪門課？

李中平：　我覺得中文課很有意思。

孫瑪麗：　二年級的中文課很難，對不對？

李中平：　語法和生詞比較容易，可是我的聽力太差了，我有時候上課聽不懂。

孫瑪麗：　你應該多聽錄音

李中平：　對啊，如果我想進步，我只好週末多練習了。

孫瑪麗：　這樣的話，這個週末你就沒時間來我的派對了。

李中平：　那怎麼行，我聽完了錄音以後馬上去找你！

第二課　上課的時候

劉老師：　好，我先把昨天的作業發還給你們。

陳大東：　喂，上課了！你今天怎麼這麼累，昨天晚上幾點睡覺的？

黃祥安：　我去聽音樂會了，昨天晚上12點才睡覺！

陳大東：　我們明天要考試，你準備了嗎？

黃祥安：　我一起床就來上課了，還沒有時間準備呢！

陳大東：　祥安，你覺得考試重要還是音樂會重要？

黃祥安：　好了，好了！糟糕！我忘了帶我的筆記本了，怎麼辦？

陳大東：　我給你一張紙吧。

黃祥安：　謝謝。我們昨天學到哪兒了？

陳大東：　我们已经把第三课的课文念完了。今天学语法。老师正在白板上写语法点呢！

黃祥安：　我找不到我的筆了，可以借你的嗎？

劉老師：　上課了！大東，祥安，你們還有什麼問題嗎？

黃祥安：　沒有問題！對不起。

Vocabulary Index (Chinese-English)

The Chinese-English index is alphabetized according to pinyin. Required Vocabulary is shown in purple. Optional Vocabulary is shown in green.

Characters	Pinyin	Word Category	Definition	Lesson
A				
啊	a	p	(used to make a question less abrupt)	4.2
哎呀	āiyā	interj	oh!	7.2
爱尔兰	Ài'ěrlán	n	Ireland	7.1
安静	ānjìng	v, adj	to be quiet; quiet; peaceful	8.2
安娜	ānnà	given name	Anna	4.1
澳大利亚	Àodàlìyà	n	Australia	1.2
B				
八	bā	nu	eight	1.2
八月	Bāyuè	n	August	3.2
巴西	Bāxī	n	Brazil	1.2
吧	ba	p	(indicates suggestion)	3.1
把	bǎ	prep	(introduces the object of a verb)	8.2
爸爸	bàba	n	father (informal)	2.1
白板	báibǎn	n	whiteboard	8.2
白饭	báifàn	n	white rice (alternate term for 米饭)	4.2
百	bǎi	nu	hundred	6.1
百货公司	bǎihuò gōngsī	n	department store	6.1
办公室	bàngōngshì	n	office	5.1
棒球	bàngqiú	n	baseball	3.1
半	bàn	n	half	3.1
帮	bāng	v	to help	5.2
杯	bēi	n, mw	cup; (used for liquid)	4.1
北	běi	n	north	7.1
北京	Běijīng	n	Beijing	7.1
北京烤鸭	Běijīng kǎoyā	n	Peking Duck	7.1
本	běn	mw	(used for books and bound volumes)	5.1
比较	bǐjiào	adv	relatively; quite	8.1

Characters	Pinyin	Word Category	Definition	Lesson
比赛	bǐsài	n	match; competition	3.1
笔	bǐ	n	pen	8.2
笔记本	bǐjìběn	n	notebook	8.2
边	biān	n	side	5.1
别	bié	adv	don't	7.2
别的	bié de	adj	other	6.1
波士顿	Bōshìdùn	n	Boston	7.1
博物馆	bówùguǎn	n	museum	5.1
不	bù	adv	not; no	1.2
不错	bú cuò	adj	not bad, pretty good	4.2
不好意思	bù hǎoyìsi	ie	sorry for the inconvenience	6.1
不客气	bú kèqi	ie	you're welcome	3.1
不用	bú yòng	ie	no need	6.2
不用谢	bú yòng xiè	ie	you're welcome	7.2

C

Characters	Pinyin	Word Category	Definition	Lesson
才	cái	adv	not until; (indicates delay of action)	7.1
菜	cài	n	dish, food	4.1
菜单	càidān	n	menu	4.1
参加	cānjiā	v	to take part in, to participate in	8.1
餐厅	cāntīng	n	dining hall	5.1
厕所	cèsuǒ	n	toilet; bathroom	5.2
叉子	chāzi	n	fork	4.2
茶	chá	n	tea	4.1
差	chà	adj	poor; fall short; not up to standard	8.1
差不多	chàbuduō	adv, adj	almost; about; around	3.1
长城	Chángchéng	n	the Great Wall	7.1
吵	chǎo	v, adj	to make noise; to argue; noisy	7.2
车	chē	n	car, vehicle	7.1
车站	chēzhàn	n	railway or subway station, bus stop	7.2
陈	Chén	surname	Chen	1.1
陈大东	Chén Dàdōng	name	Chen Dadong	1.1
吃	chī	v	to eat	3.2
吃饱	chī bǎo	rv	to be full	4.2
吃饭	chī fàn	vo	to eat	4.1
吃素	chī sù	vo	to be vegetarian	4.2

Characters	Pinyin	Word Category	Definition	Lesson
宠物	chǒngwù	n	pet	2.1
出生	chūshēng	v	to be born	7.1
出租车	chūzū chē	n	taxi	7.2
厨房	chúfáng	n	kitchen	5.2
穿过	chuān guò	rv	to cross	7.2
窗户	chuānghu	n	window	5.2
床	chuáng	n	bed	5.2
从	cóng	prep	from	7.1
错	cuò	adj	wrong	4.2

D

Characters	Pinyin	Word Category	Definition	Lesson
打	dǎ	v	to hit; strike	6.1
打电话	dǎ diànhuà	vo	to make a phone call	6.1
打算	dǎsuan	v, n	to plan; plan	7.1
大	dà	adj	big; old	1.2
大东	Dàdōng	given name	Dadong	1.1
大家	dàjiā	n	everyone	3.2
大街	dàjiē	n	main street; street	7.2
大学	dàxué	n	college, university	2.2
大学生	dàxuéshēng	n	college student	2.2
担心	dān xīn	v	worry	6.2
但是	dànshì	cj	but	7.1
蛋糕	dàngāo	n	cake	3.2
当然	dāngrán	adv	of course	5.1
刀子	dāozi	n	knife	4.2
带	dài	v	to bring	8.2
到	dào	rc	(indicates completion or arrival at a goal)	5.2
到	dào	prep; v	to; to arrive	7.2
道	dào	n	road; path; way	7.2
得	de	p	(indicates the potential to achieve an action or goal)	5.2
得	děi	av	must	6.1
德国	Déguó	n	Germany	1.2
德语	Déyǔ	n	German language (spoken)	2.2
的	de	p	(particle indicating possession)	2.1
的时候	de shíhou	adv	when, at that time	7.1

Characters	Pinyin	Word Category	Definition	Lesson
地方	dìfang	n	place	7.1
地铁	dìtiě	n	subway	7.2
地图	dìtú	n	map	7.2
弟弟	dìdi	n	younger brother	2.1
第	dì	mw	(a prefix for ordinal numbers)	8.2
点（菜）	diǎn (cài)	v	to order (food)	4.1
点（钟）	diǎn (zhōng)	n	o'clock (hour unit of time)	3.1
电话	diànhuà	n	telephone	6.1
电视	diànshì	n	television	5.2
电子用品	diànzǐ yòngpǐn	n	electronic device	6.1
店	diàn	n	shop, store	2.2
东	dōng	n	east	7.1
东西	dōngxi	n	thing	6.1
懂	dǒng	v, rc	to understand	8.1
都	dōu	adv	both; all	3.2
读	dú	v	to read; to study	8.2
对	duì	adj	correct; right	5.1
对不起	duìbuqǐ	ie	sorry	3.1
对面	duìmian	adj	across; facing	5.1
多	duō	adj, qw	many; how many	1.2
多少	duōshao	qw	how much; how many	6.1
多少钱	duōshao qián	qw	how much is it	6.1

E

Characters	Pinyin	Word Category	Definition	Lesson
俄罗斯	Eluósī	n	Russia	1.2
儿子	érzi	n	son	2.1
饿	è	adj	hungry	4.1
二	èr	nu	two	1.2
二十	èr shí	nu	twenty	1.2
二月	Èryuè	n	February	3.2

F

Characters	Pinyin	Word Category	Definition	Lesson
发	fā	v	to give out, to deliver, to issue	8.2
发还	fā huán	v	to give back	8.2
发票	fāpiào	n	receipt	6.2
法国	Fǎguó	n	France	1.2

Characters	Pinyin	Word Category	Definition	Lesson
法文	Fǎwén	n	French language (written)	2.2
法语	Fǎyǔ	n	French language (spoken)	2.2
饭	fàn	n	meal; rice	4.1
饭馆	fànguǎn	n	restaurant	4.1
房间	fángjiān	n	room	5.2
放假	fàng jià	vo	to go on vacation	7.1
飞机	fēijī	n	airplane	7.1
飞机票	fēijī piào	n	plane ticket	7.1
非洲	Fēizhōu	n	Africa	1.2
分	fēn	n	minute	3.1
分	fēn	mw	1/100 of a kuai	6.1
份	fèn	mw	(used for portions of food and for gifts)	4.1
服务员	fúwùyuán	n	waiter, server	2.2
父亲	fùqin	n	father (formal)	2.1
付	fù	v	to pay	6.2
付钱	fù qián	vo	to pay (money)	6.1
复习	fùxí	v, n	to review; revision	8.1

G

Characters	Pinyin	Word Category	Definition	Lesson
橄榄球	gǎnlǎn qiú	n	rugby; football (American)	3.1
高兴	gāoxìng	adj	pleased; happy	3.2
哥哥	gēge	n	elder brother	2.1
个	gè	mw	(used for most nouns)	2.1
给	gěi	v	to give	4.1
跟	gēn	cj	with	5.1
工作	gōngzuò	n, v	work, job; to work	2.2
公共汽车	gōnggòng qìchē	n	public bus	7.1
功课	gōngkè	n	homework	6.2
公寓	gōngyù	n	apartment	5.1
狗	gǒu	n	dog	2.1
购物中心	gòuwù zhōngxīn	n	shopping center	6.1
故宫	Gùgōng	n	the Forbidden City	7.1
故乡	gùxiāng	n	hometown, birthplace	7.1
广东话	Guǎngdōng huà	n	Cantonese	2.2
贵	guì	adj	expensive	6.1
国	guó	n	country	1.2

Characters	Pinyin	Word Category	Definition	Lesson
国家	guójiā	n	country	1.2
果汁	guǒzhī	n	fruit juice	4.1

H

Characters	Pinyin	Word Category	Definition	Lesson
还	hái	adv	also	2.2
还	hái	adv	still	3.1
还没（有）	hái méi (yǒu)	adv	not yet, still have not	3.1
还是	háishì	cj	or	3.2
还是	háishì	adv	had better; should	6.1
孩子	háizi	n	child; children	2.1
海鲜	hǎixiān	n	seafood	4.2
寒假	hánjià	n	winter vacation	7.1
韩国	Hánguó	n	Korea	1.2
汉语	Hànyǔ	n	Chinese language (spoken)	2.2
汉字	Hànzì	n	Chinese characters	2.2
好	hǎo	adj	good, well, fine	1.1
好吃	hǎo chī	adj	tasty (of solid food)	4.1
好喝	hǎo hē	adj	tasty (of liquids)	4.2
好了，好了	hǎole hǎole	ie	all right, all right	8.2
好玩（儿）	hǎowán(r)	adj	fun	7.1
号	hào	n	day; number	3.2
喝	hē	v	to drink; to eat (soup)	4.1
和	hé	cj	and, as well as	2.1
黑板	hēibǎn	n	blackboard, chalkboard	8.2
很	hěn	adv	very	1.1
很高兴认识你	hěn gāoxìng rènshi nǐ	ie	pleased to meet you	5.1
后面	hòumian	adj, n	behind	5.1
花	huā	v	to spend (money, time, effort)	6.2
欢迎	huānyíng	v	to welcome	4.1
欢迎光临	huānyíng guānglín	ie	welcome (to a store/restaurant)	4.1
还	huán	v	to return; to give back	8.2
黄	Huáng	surname	Huang	3.1
黄祥安	Huáng Xiáng'ān	name	Huang Xiang'an	3.1
回	huí	v	to return	5.2
回家	huí jiā	vo	to go home	7.1
回来	huílai	v	to return	7.1

Characters	Pinyin	Word Category	Definition	Lesson
回头	huítóu	adv	in a moment; later	5.1
回头见	huítóu jiàn	ie	see you later	5.1
会	huì	av	to know how; can	2.2
活动中心	huódòng zhōngxīn	n	activity center	5.1
火车	huǒchē	n	train	7.1
火车票	huǒchē piào	n	train ticket	7.1
货币	huòbì	n	currency	6.2

J

Characters	Pinyin	Word Category	Definition	Lesson
(飞)机场	(fēi)jīchǎng	n	airport	7.2
鸡肉	jī ròu	n	chicken	4.2
几	jǐ	qw	how many	2.1
几位	jǐ wèi	qph	how many (people)	4.1
计划	jìhuà	n, v	plan; to plan	7.1
加拿大	Jiā'nádà	n	Canada	1.2
加拿大人	Jiā'nádà rén	n	Canadian	1.2
加州	Jiāzhōu	n	California	7.1
家	jiā	n	family, home	2.1
家	jiā	mw	(used for restaurants and companies)	4.1
家人	jiārén	n	family members	2.1
价钱	jiàqián	n	price	6.1
间	jiān	mw	(used for rooms)	5.2
简单	jiǎndān	adj	simple	2.2
见	jiàn	v	to meet, to see	3.1
健身	jiànshēn	v	to work out, to exercise	5.1
健身房	jiànshēnfáng	n	fitness room	5.1
讲	jiǎng	v	to speak, to say	6.1
讲价	jiǎng jià	vo	to haggle; to bargain	6.1
饺子	jiǎozi	n	dumplings	4.1
叫	jiào	v	to call; to be called	1.1
叫	jiào	v	to order	4.2
教	jiāo	v	to teach	4.2
教室	jiàoshì	n	classroom	5.1
教授	jiàoshòu	n	professor	2.2
教育	jiàoyù	n	education	8.1
街	jiē	n	street	7.2

Characters	Pinyin	Word Category	Definition	Lesson
结帐	jié zhàng	vo	to pay the bill	4.2
姐姐	jiějie	n	elder sister	2.1
介绍	jièshào	v, n	to introduce; introduction	5.1
借	jiè	v	to lend or borrow	8.2
今	jīn	n	today; now	3.2
今年	jīnnián	n	this year	7.1
今天	jīntiān	n	today	3.2
近	jìn	adj	close	7.2
进步	jìn bù	vo, n	to improve; to advance; improvement	8.1
经济学	jīngjìxué	n	economics	8.1
九	jiǔ	nu	nine	1.2
九月	Jiǔyuè	n	September	3.2
就	jiù	adv	(indicates precision or earliness of action)	5.2
觉得	juéde	v	to feel; to think	8.1

K

Characters	Pinyin	Word Category	Definition	Lesson
咖啡	kāfēi	n	coffee	2.2
咖啡店	kāfēi diàn	n	coffee shop	2.2
卡	kǎ	n	card	6.2
开车	kāi chē	vo	to drive (a car)	7.2
开始	kāishǐ	v, n	to begin; beginning	3.1
看	kàn	v	to look at; to see; to read	3.1
看书	kàn shū	vo	to read (books)	5.1
考试	kǎoshì	n, vo	test; to give or take a test	8.2
科学	kēxué	n	science	8.1
可能	kěnéng	adv, adj	maybe, possibly; possible	5.2
可是	kěshì	cj	but	2.1
可以	kěyǐ	av	can; may	5.1
渴	kě	adj	thirsty	4.1
刻	kè	n	quarter of an hour	3.1
客厅	kètīng	n	living room	5.2
课	kè	n	course; class	8.1
课本	kèběn	n	textbook	5.2
课文	kèwén	n	lesson text	8.2
口	kǒu	n, mw	mouth; (measure word for people)	2.1
苦	kǔ	adj	bitter	4.2

Characters	Pinyin	Word Category	Definition	Lesson
块	kuài	mw	Chinese dollar (colloquial)	6.1
快乐	kuàilè	adj, n	happy; happiness	3.2
筷子	kuàizi	n	chopsticks	4.2

L

Characters	Pinyin	Word Category	Definition	Lesson
辣	là	adj	spicy	4.2
来	lái	v	to come	3.1
篮球	lánqiú	n	basketball	3.1
老家	lǎojiā	n	hometown	7.1
老师	lǎoshī	n	teacher	1.1
累	lèi	adj	tired	8.2
离	lí	prep	distant from; apart from	7.2
礼堂	lǐtáng	n	auditorium	5.1
礼物	lǐwù	n	present	3.2
李	Lǐ	surname	Li	2.1
李中平	Lǐ Zhōngpíng	name	Li Zhongping	2.1
里	lǐ	prep	in	5.2
里面	lǐmian	prep	inside, within	5.2
历史	lìshǐ	n	history	8.1
练习	liànxí	v, n	to practice; practice	8.1
两	liǎng	nu	two (used before measure words)	2.1
了	le	p	(indicates change of state or action completion)	3.2
零	líng	nu	zero	3.1
刘	Liú	surname	Liu	1.1
六	liù	nu	six	1.2
六月	Liùyuè	n	June	3.2
录音	lùyīn	n, vo	recording; to record	8.1
路	lù	n	road	7.2
路口	lùkǒu	n	intersection	7.2
旅行	lǚxíng	v, n	to travel; travel	7.1
律师	lùshī	n	lawyer	2.2

M

Characters	Pinyin	Word Category	Definition	Lesson
妈妈	māma	n	mother (informal)	2.1
麻婆豆腐	Mápó Dòufu	n	Mapo Tofu	4.1

Characters	Pinyin	Word Category	Definition	Lesson
马上	mǎshàng	adv	immediately, right away	5.2
玛丽	Mǎlì	given name	Mali	1.1
吗	ma	p	(indicates a question)	1.1
买	mǎi	v	to buy	6.1
买单	mǎidān	n, vo	check; to pay the bill; "check, please."	4.2
卖	mài	v	to sell	6.1
猫	māo	n	cat	2.1
毛	máo	mw	1/10 of a kuai	6.1
没	méi	adv	not	2.1
没(有)问题	méi (yǒu) wèntí	ie	no problem	3.1
没关系	méi guānxi	ie	it's ok; it doesn't matter	3.1
没事	méi shì	ie	no problem; not a bother	3.1
没问题	méi wèntí	ie	no problem	6.2
美国	Měiguó	n	United States	1.2
美国人	Měiguó rén	n	American	1.2
美元	Měiyuán	n	the American dollar	6.1
妹妹	mèimei	n	younger sister	2.1
门	mén	mw	(used for courses)	8.1
们	men	p	(used after a pronoun or noun, referring to people, to indicate plural form)	1.1
迷路	mí lù	vo	to be lost	7.2
米饭	mǐfàn	n	rice	4.2
面	miàn	n	surface; face	5.1
秒	miǎo	n	second	3.1
名字	míngzi	n	name	1.1
明天	míngtiān	n	tomorrow	3.2
摩托车	mótuōchē	n	motorcycle	7.2
墨西哥	Mòxīgē	n	Mexico	1.2
母亲	mǔqīn	n	mother (formal)	2.1

N

Characters	Pinyin	Word Category	Definition	Lesson
拿	ná	v	to hold; to get; to take	5.2
哪	nǎ, něi	qw	which	1.2
哪儿 / 哪里	nǎr / nǎli	pr	where (regional usage in Northern China) / where	5.1
那	nà, nèi	pr	that	2.2

Characters	Pinyin	Word Category	Definition	Lesson
那（么）	nà (me)	cj	then; in that case	4.1
那儿 / 那里	nàr / nàli	pr	there (regional usage in Northern China) / there	5.2
那怎么行	nà zěnme xíng	ie	That won't do	8.1
男	nán	n	male	2.2
男孩（子）	nánhái(zi)	n	boy	2.2
南	nán	n	south	7.1
南非	Nánfēi	n	South Africa	1.2
难	nán	adj	difficult	8.1
呢	ne	p	(indicates "What about . . .?")	1.1
你	nǐ	pr	you	1.1
你好	nǐ hǎo	ie	hello	1.1
年	nián	n	year	3.2
年级	niánjí	n	grade or level (in school)	8.1
念	niàn	v	to read aloud	8.2
鸟	niǎo	n	bird	2.1
您	nín	pr	you (polite form)	1.1
牛肉	niú ròu	n	beef	4.2
女	nǚ	n	female	2.2
女儿	nǚér	n	daughter	2.1
女孩（子）	nǚhái(zi)	n	girl	2.2
女士	nǚshì	n	Ms.; lady	1.1

O

Characters	Pinyin	Word Category	Definition	Lesson
哦	ò	p	oh! (interjection)	4.2

P

Characters	Pinyin	Word Category	Definition	Lesson
派对	pàiduì	n	party	3.2
盘	pán	n, mw	plate; (used for plates of food)	4.1
旁	páng	prep	side	5.1
旁边	pángbian	adj	(by) the side of; next to	5.1
朋友	péngyou	n	friend	2.2
票	piào	n	ticket	7.1
瓶	píng	n, mw	bottle; (used for bottles)	4.1
普通话	Pǔtōnghuà	n	Mandarin	2.2

Characters	Pinyin	Word Category	Definition	Lesson
Q				
七	qī	nu	seven	1.2
七月	Qīyuè	n	July	3.2
起床	qǐ chuáng	vo	to get up (from bed)	8.2
汽水	qìshuǐ	n	soft drink	4.1
千	qiān	nu	thousand	6.1
铅笔	qiānbǐ	n	pencil	8.2
前面	qiánmian	adj	in front of	5.1
钱	qián	n	money	6.1
钱包	qiánbāo	n	wallet	6.2
青菜	qīngcài	n	green vegetables	4.1
请	qǐng	v	to request; to treat; please	1.1
请客	qǐng kè	vo	to treat one's guests (i.e. to pay for others)	4.2
请问	qǐngwèn	ie	excuse me; may I please ask	1.1
去	qù	v	to go	3.1
R				
然后	ránhòu	adv	then	7.2
人	rén	n	person	1.2
人民币	Rénmínbì	n	RMB (currency of the PRC)	6.1
认识	rènshi	v, n	to know (someone); knowledge	5.1
日	rì	n	day	3.2
日本	Rìběn	n	Japan	1.2
日语	Rìyǔ	n	Japanese language (spoken)	2.2
容易	róngyì	adj	easy	8.1
肉	ròu	n	meat	4.2
如果	rúguǒ	cj	if	6.2
S				
三	sān	nu	three	1.2
三月	Sānyuè	n	March	3.2
沙发	shāfā	n	sofa	5.2
商店	shāngdiàn	n	store; shop	6.1
商人	shāngrén	n	businessman	2.2
上	shàng	prep	up; on	5.2

Characters	Pinyin	Word Category	Definition	Lesson
上海话	Shànghǎi huà	n	Shanghainese	2.2
上课	shàng kè	vo	to go to class	8.1
上午	shàngwǔ	n	morning	3.1
烧鸡	shāojī	n	roasted chicken	4.1
生词	shēngcí	n	vocabulary	8.1
生日	shēngrì	n	birthday	3.2
生日快乐	shēngrì kuàilè	ie	happy birthday	3.2
生日派对	shēngrì pàiduì	n	birthday party	3.2
十	shí	nu	ten	1.2
十二月	Shí'èryuè	n	December	3.2
十九	shí jiǔ	nu	nineteen	1.2
十一月	Shíyīyuè	n	November	3.2
十月	Shíyuè	n	October	3.2
什么	shénme	qw	what	1.1
什么时候	shénme shíhou	qph	when?	3.1
时候	shíhou	n	time	3.1
时间	shíjiān	n	time	3.1
事	shì	n	thing; matter	5.2
试	shì	v	to try	4.2
室友	shìyǒu	n	roommate	5.1
是	shì	v	to be	1.2
收	shōu	v	to accept; to receive (money)	6.2
收据	shōujù	n	receipt	6.2
手机	shǒujī	n	cellular phone	6.1
售货员	shòuhuòyuán	n	salesperson	6.1
书	shū	n	book	5.1
书架	shūjià	n	bookshelf	5.2
书桌	shūzhuō	n	desk	5.2
暑假	shǔjià	n	summer vacation	7.1
数学	shùxué	n	mathematics	8.1
刷卡	shuā kǎ	vo	to pay with credit card	6.2
刷牙	shuā yá	vo	to brush one's teeth	8.2
谁	shéi	qw	who	2.2
水	shuǐ	n	water	4.1
水果	shuǐguǒ	n	fruit	4.2
睡觉	shuì jiào	vo	to sleep	8.2

Characters	Pinyin	Word Category	Definition	Lesson
说	shuō	v	to speak	2.2
四	sì	nu	four	1.2
四月	Sìyuè	n	April	3.2
送	sòng	v	to give (as a gift)	3.2
宿舍	sùshè	n	dormitory	5.2
酸	suān	adj	sour	4.2
酸辣汤	Suānlàtāng	n	Hot and Sour Soup	4.1
算了	suàn le	ie	forget it	6.1
岁	suì	mw, n	age; years old	1.2
孙	Sūn	surname	Sun	1.1
孙玛丽	Sūn Mǎlì	name	Sun Mali	1.1
所以	suǒyǐ	cj	so; therefore	6.2

T

Characters	Pinyin	Word Category	Definition	Lesson
她	tā	pr	she	1.1
他	tā	pr	he	1.1
它	tā	pr	it	1.1
台湾话	Táiwān huà	n	Taiwanese	2.2
太	tài	adv	too, excessively, extremely	4.2
太太	tàitai	n	Mrs.; wife	1.1
体育馆	tǐyùguǎn	n	gymnasium	5.1
天	tiān	n	day; sky; heaven	3.2
甜	tián	adj	sweet	4.2
条	tiáo	mw	(used for fish, roads, and other long, thin animals and objects)	2.1
听	tīng	v	to listen	8.1
听力	tīnglì	n	listening skills, oral comprehension	8.1
停车	tíng chē	vo	to stop a car; to park	7.2
同屋	tóngwū	n	roommate	5.1
同学	tóngxué	n	classmate	1.1
同学们	tóngxuémen	n	classmates	1.1
图书馆	túshūguǎn	n	library	5.1

W

Characters	Pinyin	Word Category	Definition	Lesson
哇	wā	interj	wow	7.1
完	wán	v, rc	to complete; to finish	8.1

Characters	Pinyin	Word Category	Definition	Lesson
晚	wǎn	adj	late	3.1
晚饭	wǎnfàn	n	dinner	4.2
晚上	wǎnshang	n	night; PM	3.1
碗	wǎn	n, mw	bowl; (used for bowls of food)	4.1
万	wàn	nu	ten thousand	6.1
王	Wáng	surname	Wang	2.1
王小美	Wáng Xiǎoměi	name	Wang Xiaomei	2.1
往	wǎng	prep	toward, in the direction of	7.2
忘	wàng	v	to forget	8.2
为什么	wèishénme	qw	why	4.2
位	wèi	mw	(used formally for people)	2.1
味道	wèidào	n	taste, flavor	4.2
喂	wéi, wèi	interj	hello? (for answering telephis only)	5.2
文	wén	n	written language; culture	2.2
文具	wénjù	n	stationary	6.1
文学	wénxué	n	literature	8.1
问	wèn	v	to ask	1.1
我	wǒ	pr	I	1.1
卧室	wòshì	n	bedroom	5.2
五	wǔ	nu	five	1.2
五月	Wǔyuè	n	May	3.2
午饭	wǔfàn	n	lunch	4.2

X

Characters	Pinyin	Word Category	Definition	Lesson
西	xī	n	west	7.1
西班牙	Xībānyá	n	Spain	7.1
西班牙语	Xībānyáyǔ	n	Spanish language (spoken)	2.2
洗手间	xǐshǒujiān	n	restroom	5.2
洗澡	xǐ zǎo	vo	to take a shower or bath	8.2
喜欢	xǐhuan	av	to like	2.1
系	xì	n	department	8.1
下	xià	prep	under; below; down	5.2
下(个)星期	xià (ge) xīngqī	n	next week	6.2
下课	xià kè	vo	to finish class	8.1
下面	xiàmian	prep	under; below	5.2
下午	xiàwǔ	n	afternoon; PM	3.1

Characters	Pinyin	Word Category	Definition	Lesson
先	xiān	adv	first	7.2
先生	xiānsheng	n	Mr.; husband; gentleman	1.1
咸	xián	adj	salty	4.2
现金	xiànjīn	n	cash	6.2
现在	xiànzài	n	now	3.1
祥安	Xiáng'ān	given name	Xiang'an	3.1
想	xiǎng	av	would like to (do something)	4.1
想	xiǎng	v	to miss (someone or something)	6.1
项链	xiàngliàn	n	necklace	6.2
橡皮	xiàngpí	n	eraser	8.2
小姐	xiǎojie	n	Miss; young lady	1.1
小考	xiǎokǎo	n	quiz	8.2
小美	Xiǎoměi	given name	Xiaomei	2.1
小时	xiǎoshí	n	hour	3.1
小心	xiǎoxīn	adj	careful	7.2
校内	xiàonèi	n	on-campus	5.1
校外	xiàowài	n	off-campus	5.1
校园	xiàoyuán	n	campus	5.1
写	xiě	v	write	2.2
写信	xiě xìn	vo	to write a letter	6.1
谢谢	xièxie	ie	thank you	1.1
心理学	xīnlǐxué	n	psychology	8.1
新	xīn	adj	new	4.1
信用卡	xìnyòngkǎ	n	credit card	6.2
星期	xīngqī	n	week	3.1
星期几	xīngqī jǐ	qph	what day is it?	3.1
星期三	Xīngqī sān	n	Wednesday	3.1
行	xíng	adj	OK; all right	8.1
姓	xìng	v	to be surnamed	1.1
兄弟姐妹	xiōngdì jiěmèi	n	siblings	2.1
选	xuǎn	v	to choose; select	8.1
学	xué	v	to learn	1.1
学期	xuéqī	n	school term; semester	8.1
学生	xuéshēng	n	student	2.2
学习	xuéxí	v, n	to study; studies	8.1
学校	xuéxiào	n	school	1.1

Characters	Pinyin	Word Category	Definition	Lesson
Y				
要	yào	av	to want; must; will; should	4.2
要是……(的话)	yàoshì . . . (de huà)	cj	if	6.2
也	yě	adv	also	1.1
一	yī	nu	one	1.2
一点(儿)	yì diǎn(r)	n	a little, some (see Pronunciation Notes)	2.2
一共	yígòng	adv	altogether	6.1
一起	yìqǐ	adv	together	5.1
一下	yí xià	mw	a bit	4.2
一月	Yīyuè	n	January	3.2
一直	yìzhí	adv	straight forward	7.2
衣服	yīfu	n	clothing	6.1
衣柜	yīguì	n	wardrobe	5.2
已经	yǐjīng	adv	already	6.2
以后	yǐhòu	prep	after, afterwards	8.1
椅子	yǐzi	n	chair	5.2
艺术	yìshù	n	art	8.1
意大利	Yìdàlì	n	Italy	1.2
意思	yìsi	n	meaning; interest	8.1
因为	yīnwèi	cj	because	4.2
音乐	yīnyuè	n	music	8.1
音乐会	yīnyuèhuì	n	concert	8.2
银行	yínháng	n	bank	6.2
饮料	yǐnliào	n	beverage	4.1
印度	Yìndù	n	India	1.2
应该	yīnggāi	av	should	7.2
英国	Yīngguó	n	Britain; U.K.; England	8.1
英文	Yīngwén	n	English language (written)	2.2
英语	Yīngyǔ	n	English language (spoken)	2.2
用	yòng	v	to use	4.2
用品	yòngpǐn	n	product; goods	6.1
有	yǒu	v	to have	2.1
有(的)时候	yǒu de shíhou	ie	sometimes	8.1
有事吗?	yǒu shì ma?	ie	what's up?	5.2
有意思	yǒu yìsi	adj	interesting	8.1

Characters	Pinyin	Word Category	Definition	Lesson
右	yòu	n	right	7.2
鱼	yú	n	fish	2.1
语法	yǔfǎ	n	grammar	8.1
语言	yǔyán	n	language	2.2
元	yuán	mw	the Chinese dollar (formal)	6.1
圆珠笔	yuánzhūbǐ	n	ball-point pen	8.2
远	yuǎn	adj	far	7.2
月	yuè	n	month	3.2
越南	Yuènán	n	Vietnam	1.2
运动	yùn dòng	v	to work out, to exercise	5.1

Z

Characters	Pinyin	Word Category	Definition	Lesson
再	zài	adv	again	6.2
再见	zàijiàn	ie	goodbye	1.1
在	zài	prep	at, in, on	5.1
糟糕	zāogāo	interj, adj	oh no; what bad luck; terrible	8.2
早	zǎo	adj	early	3.1
早饭	zǎofàn	n	breakfast	4.2
早上	zǎoshang	n	early morning; AM	3.1
怎么	zěnme	qw	how; how come	8.2
怎么办	zěnme bàn	qph	what to do; what can be done; what shall I do	8.2
怎么卖	zěnme mài	ie	how much does it cost? (colloquial)	6.1
怎么样	zěnmeyàng	qw	how is it	4.2
怎么这么	zěnme zhème	qph	how come (it's) so	8.2
怎么走	zěnme zǒu	qph	how to get to (somewhere)	7.2
张	Zhāng	surname	Zhang	4.1
张	zhāng	mw	(used for tables, desks, and other flat surfaces)	5.2
张	zhāng	mw	(used for flat objects like paper)	8.2
张安娜	Zhāng ānnà	name	Zhang Anna	4.1
长大	zhǎngdà	v	to grow up	7.1
找	zhǎo	v	to look for	5.2
找	zhǎo	v	to give change	6.2
找到	zhǎo dào	rv	to find	5.2
哲学	zhéxué	n	philosophy	8.1

Characters	Pinyin	Word Category	Definition	Lesson
这	zhè, zhèi	pr	this	2.1
这么	zhème	adv	so (indicates degree)	6.2
这儿 /	zhèr /	pr	here (regional usage in Northern China) /	5.2
这里	zhèli		here	
这样吧	zhèyàng ba	ie	how about this	6.1
这样的话	zhè yàng de huà	ie	this way; if that's the case; in that case	8.1
真	zhēn	adv	really, truly	3.2
正在	zhèngzài	adv	right now	8.2
支票	zhīpiào	n	check	6.2
知道	zhīdào	v	to know (something)	7.2
只	zhī	mw	(used for most mammals and birds)	2.1
只	zhǐ	adv	only, just	2.2
只好	zhǐhǎo	adv	have to; be forced to	8.1
纸	zhǐ	n	paper	8.2
中国	Zhōngguó	n	China	1.2
中国	Zhōngguó	n	China	4.1
中国菜	Zhōngguó cài	n	Chinese food	4.1
中平	Zhōngpíng	given name	Zhongping	2.1
中文	Zhōngwén	n	Chinese language	2.2
中午	zhōngwǔ	n	noon, midday	3.1
钟头	zhōngtóu	n	hour (colloquial)	3.1
重要	zhòngyào	adj	important	8.2
周末	zhōumò	n	weekend	8.1
猪肉	zhū ròu	n	pork	4.2
住	zhù	v	to live (somewhere)	5.1
注意	zhùyì	v	to be careful; to pay attention to	8.2
祝	zhù	v	to wish	3.2
专业	zhuānyè	n, adj	field of study; major; professional	8.1
转	zhuǎn	v	to turn	7.2
准备	zhǔnbèi	v	to prepare; to plan	8.2
桌子	zhuōzi	n	table	5.2
自行车	zìxíngchē	n	bicycle	7.2
走	zǒu	v	to go; to leave	3.1
走路	zǒu lù	vo	to walk	7.2
足球	zúqiú	n	soccer	3.1
昨天	zuótiān	n	yesterday	3.2

Characters	Pinyin	Word Category	Definition	Lesson
左	zuǒ	n	left	7.2
作业	zuòyè	n	homework; assignment	8.2
坐	zuò	v	to sit	4.1
坐	zuò	v	to ride (in a car, etc.); to travel by	7.2
做	zuò	v	to do	2.2
做饭	zuò fàn	vo	to cook	4.1

Vocabulary Index (English-Chinese)

The measure words and particles index is arranged according to the lesson. The Chinese-English index is alphabetized according to English. Required Vocabulary is shown in purple. Optional Vocabulary is shown in green.

Definition	Characters	Pinyin	Word Category	Lesson
Measure Words				
years old	岁	suì	mw	1.2
(used for most nouns)	个	gè	mw	2.1
(used for most mammals and birds)	只	zhī	mw	2.1
(used formally for people)	位	wèi	mw	2.1
(used for fish, roads, and other long, thin animals and objects)	条	tiáo	mw	2.1
(measure word for people)	口	kǒu	mw	2.1
(used for liquid)	杯	bēi	mw	4.1
(used for plates of food)	盘	pán	mw	4.1
(used for portions of food and for gifts)	份	fèn	mw	4.1
(used for bowls of food)	碗	wǎn	mw	4.1
(used for restaurants and companies)	家	jiā	mw	4.1
(used for bottles)	瓶	píng	mw	4.1
a bit	一下	yí xià	mw	4.2
(used for books and bound volumes)	本	běn	mw	5.1
(used for tables, desks, and other flat surfaces)	张	zhāng	mw	5.2
(used for rooms)	间	jiān	mw	5.2
Chinese dollar (colloquial)	块	kuài	mw	6.1
1/10 of a kuai	毛	máo	mw	6.1
the Chinese dollar (formal)	元	yuán	mw	6.1
1/100 of a kuai	分	fēn	mw	6.1
(used for courses)	门	mén	mw	8.1
(used for flat objects like paper)	张	zhāng	mw	8.2
(a prefix for ordinal numbers)	第	dì	mw	8.2

Definition	Characters	Pinyin	Word Category	Lesson
Particles				
(indicates a question)	吗	ma	p	1.1
(indicates "What about . . .?")	呢	ne	p	1.1
(used after a pronoun or noun, referring to people, to indicate plural form)	们	men	p	1.1
(particle indicating possession)	的	de	p	2.1
(indicates suggestion)	吧	ba	p	3.1
(indicates change of state or action completion)	了	le	p	3.2
oh! (interjection)	哦	ò	p	4.2
(used to make a question less abrupt)	啊	a	p	4.2
hello? (for answering telephones only)	喂	wéi, wèi	interj	5.2
(indicates the potential to achieve an action or goal)	得	de	p	5.2
wow	哇	wā	interj	7.1
oh!	哎呀	āiyā	interj	7.2
oh no; what bad luck; terrible	糟糕	zāogāo	interj	8.2
A				
a little, some	一点(儿)	yì diǎn(r)	n	2.2
to accept; to receive (money)	收	shōu	v	6.2
across; facing	对面	duìmiàn	adj	5.1
activity center	活动中心	huódòng zhōngxīn	n	5.1
Africa	非洲	Fēizhōu	n	1.2
after, afterwards	以后	yǐhòu	prep	8.1
afternoon; PM	下午	xiàwǔ	n	3.1
again	再	zài	adv	6.2
age; years old	岁	suì	n, mw	1.2
airplane	飞机	fēijī	n	7.1
airport	(飞)机场	(fēi)jīchǎng	n	7.2
all right, all right	好了,好了	hǎole hǎole	ie	8.2
almost; about; around	差不多	chàbuduō	adv, adj	3.1
already	已经	yǐjīng	adv	6.2
also	也	yě	adv	1.1
also	还	hái	adv	2.2
altogether	一共	yígòng	adv	6.1

Definition 英中索引	Characters	Pinyin	Word Category	Lesson
American	美国人	Měiguó rén	n	1.2
and, as well as	和	hé	cj	2.1
apartment	公寓	gōngyù	n	5.1
April	四月	Sìyuè	n	3.2
art	艺术	yìshù	n	8.1
to ask	问	wèn	v	1.1
at, in, on	在	zài	prep	5.1
auditorium	礼堂	lǐtáng	n	5.1
August	八月	Bāyuè	n	3.2
Australia	澳大利亚	Àodàlìyà	n	1.2

B

ball-point pen	圆珠笔	yuánzhūbǐ	n	8.2
bank	银行	yínháng	n	6.2
baseball	棒球	bàngqiú	n	3.1
basketball	篮球	lánqiú	n	3.1
to be	是	shì	v	1.2
to be born	出生	chūshēng	v	7.1
to be careful; to pay attention to	注意	zhùyì	v	8.2
to be full	吃饱	chī bǎo	rv	4.2
to be lost	迷路	mí lù	vo	7.2
to be quiet; quiet; peaceful	安静	ānjìng	v, adj	8.2
to be surnamed	姓	xìng	v	1.1
to be vegetarian	吃素	chī sù	vo	4.2
because	因为	yīnwèi	cj	4.2
bed	床	chuáng	n	5.2
bedroom	卧室	wòshì	n	5.2
beef	牛肉	niú ròu	n	4.2
to begin; beginning	开始	kāishǐ	v, n	3.1
behind	后面	hòumian	adj, n	5.1
Beijing	北京	Běijīng	n	7.1
beverage	饮料	yǐnliào	n	4.1
bicycle	自行车	zìxíngchē	n	7.2
big; old	大	dà	adj	1.2
bird	鸟	niǎo	n	2.1
birthday	生日	shēngrì	n	3.2

Definition	Characters	Pinyin	Word Category	Lesson
birthday party	生日派对	shēngrì pàiduì	n	3.2
bitter	苦	kǔ	adj	4.2
blackboard, chalkboard	黑板	hēibǎn	n	8.2
book	书	shū	n	5.1
bookshelf	书架	shūjià	n	5.2
Boston	波士顿	Bōshìdùn	n	7.1
both; all	都	dōu	adv	3.2
bottle; (used for bottles)	瓶	píng	n, mw	4.1
bowl; (used for bowls of food)	碗	wǎn	n, mw	4.1
boy	男孩（子）	nánhái(zi)	n	2.2
Brazil	巴西	Bāxī	n	1.2
breakfast	早饭	zǎofàn	n	4.2
to bring	带	dài	v	8.2
Britain; U.K.; England	英国	Yīngguó	n	8.1
to brush one's teeth	刷牙	shuā yá	vo	8.2
businessman	商人	shāngrén	n	2.2
but	可是	kěshì	cj	2.1
but	但是	dànshì	cj	7.1
to buy	买	mǎi	v	6.1
(by) the side of; next to	旁边	pángbian	adj	5.1

C

Definition	Characters	Pinyin	Word Category	Lesson
cake	蛋糕	dàngāo	n	3.2
California	加州	Jiāzhōu	n	7.1
to call; to be called	叫	jiào	v	1.1
campus	校园	xiàoyuán	n	5.1
can; may	可以	kěyǐ	av	5.1
Canada	加拿大	Jiā'nádà	n	1.2
Canadian	加拿大人	Jiā'nádà rén	n	1.2
Cantonese	广东话	Guǎngdōng huà	n	2.2
car, vehicle	车	chē	n	7.1
card	卡	kǎ	n	6.2
careful	小心	xiǎoxīn	adj	7.2
cash	现金	xiànjīn	n	6.2
cat	猫	māo	n	2.1
cellular phone	手机	shǒujī	n	6.1

Definition	Characters	Pinyin	Word Category	Lesson
chair	椅子	yǐzi	n	5.2
cheap	便宜	piányi	adj	6.1
check	支票	zhīpiào	n	6.2
check; to pay the bill; "check, please."	买单	mǎidān	n, vo	4.2
chicken	鸡肉	jī ròu	n	4.2
child; children	孩子	háizi	n	2.1
China	中国	Zhōngguó	n	4.1
Chinese characters	汉字	Hànzì	n	2.2
Chinese food	中国菜	Zhōngguó cài	n	4.1
Chinese language	中文	Zhōngwén	n	2.2
Chinese language (spoken)	汉语	Hànyǔ	n	2.2
to choose; select	选	xuǎn	v	8.1
chopsticks	筷子	kuàizi	n	4.2
classmate	同学	tóngxué	n	1.1
classmates	同学们	tóngxuémen	n	1.1
classroom	教室	jiàoshì	n	5.1
close	近	jìn	adj	7.2
clothing	衣服	yīfu	n	6.1
coffee	咖啡	kāfēi	n	2.2
coffee shop	咖啡店	kāfēi diàn	n	2.2
college student	大学生	dàxuéshēng	n	2.2
college, university	大学	dàxué	n	2.2
to come	来	lái	v	3.1
to complete; to finish	完	wán	v, rc	8.1
concert	音乐会	yīnyuèhuì	n	8.2
to cook	做饭	zuò fàn	vo	4.1
correct; right	对	duì	adj	5.1
country	国	guó	n	1.2
country	国家	guójiā	n	1.2
course; class	课	kè	n	8.1
credit card	信用卡	xìnyòngkǎ	n	6.2
to cross	穿过	chuān guò	rv	7.2
cup; (used for liquid)	杯	bēi	n, mw	4.1
currency	货币	huòbì	n	6.2

Definition	Characters	Pinyin	Word Category	Lesson
D				
daughter	女儿	nǚér	n	2.1
day	日	rì	n	3.2
day; number	号	hào	n	3.2
day; sky; heaven	天	tiān	n	3.2
December	十二月	Shí'èryuè	n	3.2
department	系	xì	n	8.1
department store	百货公司	bǎihuò gōngsī	n	6.1
desk	书桌	shūzhuō	n	5.2
difficult	难	nán	adj	8.1
dining hall	餐厅	cāntīng	n	5.1
dinner	晚饭	wǎnfàn	n	4.2
dish, food	菜	cài	n	4.1
distant from; apart from	离	lí	prep	7.2
to do	做	zuò	v	2.2
dog	狗	gǒu	n	2.1
don't	别	bié	adv	7.2
dormitory	宿舍	sùshè	n	5.2
to drink; to eat (soup)	喝	hē	v	4.1
to drive (a car)	开车	kāi chē	vo	7.2
dumplings	饺子	jiǎozi	n	4.1
E				
early	早	zǎo	adj	3.1
early morning; AM	早上	zǎoshang	n	3.1
east	东	dōng	n	7.1
easy	容易	róngyì	adj	8.1
to eat	吃	chī	v	3.2
to eat	吃饭	chī fàn	vo	4.1
economics	经济学	jīngjìxué	n	8.1
education	教育	jiàoyù	n	8.1
eight	八	bā	nu	1.2
elder brother	哥哥	gēge	n	2.1
elder sister	姐姐	jiějie	n	2.1

Definition	Characters	Pinyin	Word Category	Lesson
electronic device	电子用品	diànzǐ yòngpǐn	n	6.1
English language (spoken)	英语	Yīngyǔ	n	2.2
English language (written)	英文	Yīngwén	n	2.2
eraser	橡皮	xiàngpí	n	8.2
everyone	大家	dàjiā	n	3.2
excuse me; may I please ask	请问	qǐngwèn	ie	1.1
expensive	贵	guì	adj	6.1

F

Definition	Characters	Pinyin	Word Category	Lesson
family members	家人	jiārén	n	2.1
family, home	家	jiā	n	2.1
far	远	yuǎn	adj	7.2
father (formal)	父亲	fùqin	n	2.1
father (informal)	爸爸	bàba	n	2.1
February	二月	Èryuè	n	3.2
to feel; to think	觉得	juéde	v	8.1
female	女	nǚ	n	2.2
field of study; major; professional	专业	zhuānyè	n, adj	8.1
to find	找到	zhǎo dào	rv	5.2
to finish class	下课	xià kè	vo	8.1
first	先	xiān	adv	7.2
fish	鱼	yú	n	2.1
fitness room	健身房	jiànshēnfáng	n	5.1
five	五	wǔ	nu	1.2
to forget	忘	wàng	v	8.2
forget it	算了	suàn le	ie	6.1
fork	叉子	chāzi	n	4.2
four	四	sì	nu	1.2
France	法国	Fǎguó	n	1.2
French language (spoken)	法语	Fǎyǔ	n	2.2
French language (written)	法文	Fǎwén	n	2.2
friend	朋友	péngyou	n	2.2
from	从	cóng	prep	7.1
fruit	水果	shuǐguǒ	n	4.2
fruit juice	果汁	guǒzhī	n	4.1
fun	好玩（儿）	hǎowán(r)	adj	7.1

Definition	Characters	Pinyin	Word Category	Lesson
G				
German language (spoken)	德语	Déyǔ	n	2.2
Germany	德国	Déguó	n	1.2
to get up (from bed)	起床	qǐ chuáng	vo	8.2
girl	女孩（子）	nǚhái(zi)	n	2.2
to give	给	gěi	v	4.1
to give (as a gift)	送	sòng	v	3.2
to give back	发还	fā huán	v	8.2
to give change	找	zhǎo	v	6.2
to go	去	qù	v	3.1
to go home	回家	huí jiā	vo	7.1
to go on vacation	放假	fàng jià	vo	7.1
to go to class	上课	shàng kè	vo	8.1
to go; to leave	走	zǒu	v	3.1
good, well, fine	好	hǎo	adj	1.1
goodbye	再见	zàijiàn	ie	1.1
grade or level (in school)	年级	niánjí	n	8.1
grammar	语法	yǔfǎ	n	8.1
green vegetables	青菜	qīngcài	n	4.1
to grow up	长大	zhǎngdà	v	7.1
gymnasium	体育馆	tǐyùguǎn	n	5.1
H				
had better; should	还是	háishì	adv	6.1
to haggle; to bargain	讲价	jiǎng jià	vo	6.1
half	半	bàn	n	3.1
happy birthday	生日快乐	shēngrì kuàilè	ie	3.2
happy; happiness	快乐	kuàilè	adj, n	3.2
to have	有	yǒu	v	2.1
have to; be forced to	只好	zhǐhǎo	adv	8.1
he	他	tā	pr	1.1
hello	你好	nǐ hǎo	ie	1.1
to help	帮	bāng	v	5.2
here (regional usage in Northern China) /	这儿 /	zhèr /	pr	5.2

Definition	Characters	Pinyin	Word Category	Lesson
here	这里	zhèli		
history	历史	lìshǐ	n	8.1
to hit; strike	打	dǎ	v	6.1
to hold; to get; to take	拿	ná	v	5.2
hometown	老家	lǎojiā	n	7.1
hometown, birthplace	故乡	gùxiāng	n	7.1
homework	功课	gōngkè	n	6.2
homework; assignment	作业	zuòyè	n	8.2
Hot and Sour Soup	酸辣汤	Suānlàtāng	n	4.1
hour	小时	xiǎoshí	n	3.1
hour (colloquial)	钟头	zhōngtóu	n	3.1
how about this	这样吧	zhèyàng ba	ie	6.1
how come (it's) so	怎么这么	zěnme zhème	qph	8.2
how is it	怎么样	zěnmeyàng	qw	4.2
how many	几	jǐ	qw	2.1
how many (people)	几位	jǐ wèi	qph	4.1
how much does it cost? (colloquial)	怎么卖	zěnme mài	ie	6.1
how much is it	多少钱	duōshao qián	qw	6.1
how much; how many	多少	duōshao	qw	6.1
how to get to (somewhere)	怎么走	zěnme zǒu	qph	7.2
how; how come	怎么	zěnme	qw	8.2
hundred	百	bǎi	nu	6.1
hungry	饿	è	adj	4.1

I

Definition	Characters	Pinyin	Word Category	Lesson
I	我	wǒ	pr	1.1
if	要是……（的话）	yàoshì . . . (de huà)	cj	6.2
if	如果	rúguǒ	cj	6.2
immediately, right away	马上	mǎshàng	adv	5.2
important	重要	zhòngyào	adj	8.2
to improve; to advance; improvement	进步	jìn bù	vo, n	8.1
in	里	lǐ	prep	5.2
in a moment; later	回头	huítóu	adv	5.1
in front of	前面	qiánmian	adj	5.1
India	印度	Yìndù	n	1.2

Definition	Characters	Pinyin	Word Category	Lesson
(indicates completion or arrival at a goal)	到	dào	rc	5.2
(indicates precision or earliness of action)	就	jiù	adv	5.2
inside, within	里面	lǐmian	prep	5.2
interesting	有意思	yǒu yìsi	adj	8.1
intersection	路口	lùkǒu	n	7.2
(introduces the object of a verb)	把	bǎ	prep	8.2
to introduce; introduction	介绍	jièshào	v, n	5.1
Ireland	爱尔兰	Aì'ěrlán	n	7.1
it	它	tā	pr	1.1
Italy	意大利	Yìdàlì	n	1.2
it's ok; it doesn't matter	没关系	méi guānxi	ie	3.1

J

Definition	Characters	Pinyin	Word Category	Lesson
January	一月	Yīyuè	n	3.2
Japan	日本	Rìběn	n	1.2
Japanese language (spoken)	日语	Rìyǔ	n	2.2
July	七月	Qīyuè	n	3.2
June	六月	Liùyuè	n	3.2

K

Definition	Characters	Pinyin	Word Category	Lesson
kitchen	厨房	chúfáng	n	5.2
knife	刀子	dāozi	n	4.2
to know (someone); knowledge	认识	rènshi	v, n	5.1
to know (something)	知道	zhīdào	v	7.2
to know how; can	会	huì	av	2.2
Korea	韩国	Hánguó	n	1.2

L

Definition	Characters	Pinyin	Word Category	Lesson
language	语言	yǔyán	n	2.2
late	晚	wǎn	adj	3.1
lawyer	律师	lǜshī	n	2.2
to learn	学	xué	v	1.1
left	左	zuǒ	n	7.2
to lend or borrow	借	jiè	v	8.2
lesson text	课文	kèwén	n	8.2

Definition	Characters	Pinyin	Word Category	Lesson
library	图书馆	túshūguǎn	n	5.1
to like	喜欢	xǐhuan	av	2.1
to listen	听	tīng	v	8.1
listening skills, oral comprehension	听力	tīnglì	n	8.1
literature	文学	wénxué	n	8.1
to live (somewhere)	住	zhù	v	5.1
living room	客厅	kètīng	n	5.2
to look at; to see; to read	看	kàn	v	3.1
to look for	找	zhǎo	v	5.2
lunch	午饭	wǔfàn	n	4.2

M

Definition	Characters	Pinyin	Word Category	Lesson
main street; street	大街	dàjiē	n	7.2
to make a phone call	打电话	dǎ diànhuà	vo	6.1
to make noise; to argue; noisy	吵	chǎo	v, adj	7.2
male	男	nán	n	2.2
Mandarin	普通话	Pǔtōnghuà	n	2.2
many; how many	多	duō	adj, qw	1.2
map	地图	dìtú	n	7.2
Mapo Tofu	麻婆豆腐	Mápó Dòufu	n	4.1
March	三月	Sānyuè	n	3.2
match; competition	比赛	bǐsài	n	3.1
mathematics	数学	shùxué	n	8.1
May	五月	Wǔyuè	n	3.2
maybe, possibly; possible	可能	kěnéng	adv, adj	5.2
meal; rice	饭	fàn	n	4.1
meaning; interest	意思	yìsi	n	8.1
meat	肉	ròu	n	4.2
to meet, to see	见	jiàn	v	3.1
menu	菜单	càidān	n	4.1
Mexico	墨西哥	Mòxīgē	n	1.2
minute	分	fēn	n	3.1
to miss (someone or something)	想	xiǎng	v	6.1
Miss; young lady	小姐	xiǎojie	n	1.1
money	钱	qián	n	6.1
month	月	yuè	n	3.2

Definition	Characters	Pinyin	Word Category	Lesson
morning	上午	shàngwǔ	n	3.1
mother (formal)	母亲	mǔqin	n	2.1
mother (informal)	妈妈	māma	n	2.1
motorcycle	摩托车	mótuōchē	n	7.2
mouth; (measure word for people)	口	kǒu	n, mw	2.1
Mr.; husband; gentleman	先生	xiānsheng	n	1.1
Mrs.; wife	太太	tàitai	n	1.1
Ms.; lady	女士	nǚshì	n	1.1
museum	博物馆	bówùguǎn	n	5.1
music	音乐	yīnyuè	n	8.1
must	得	děi	av	6.1

N

Definition	Characters	Pinyin	Word Category	Lesson
name	名字	míngzi	n	1.1
necklace	项链	xiàngliàn	n	6.2
new	新	xīn	adj	4.1
next week	下(个)星期	xià (ge) xīngqī	n	6.2
night; PM	晚上	wǎnshang	n	3.1
nine	九	jiǔ	nu	1.2
nineteen	十九	shí jiǔ	nu	1.2
no need	不用	bú yòng	ie	6.2
no problem	没(有)问题	méi (yǒu) wèntí	ie	3.1
no problem	没问题	méi wèntí	ie	6.2
no problem; not a bother	没事	méi shì	ie	3.1
noon, midday	中午	zhōngwǔ	n	3.1
north	北	běi	n	7.1
not	没	méi	adv	2.1
not bad, pretty good	不错	bú cuò	adj	4.2
not until; (indicates delay of action)	才	cái	adv	7.1
not yet, still have not	还没（有）	hái méi (yǒu)	adv	3.1
not; no	不	bù	adv	1.2
notebook	笔记本	bǐjìběn	n	8.2
November	十一月	Shíyīyuè	n	3.2
now	现在	xiànzài	n	3.1

Definition	Characters	Pinyin	Word Category	Lesson
O				
o'clock (hour unit of time)	点（钟）	diǎn (zhōng)	n	3.1
October	十月	Shíyuè	n	3.2
of course	当然	dāngrán	adv	5.1
off-campus	校外	xiàowài	n	5.1
office	办公室	bàngōngshì	n	5.1
OK; all right	行	xíng	adj	8.1
on-campus	校内	xiàonèi	n	5.1
one	一	yī	nu	1.2
only, just	只	zhǐ	adv	2.2
or	还是	háishì	cj	3.2
to order	叫	jiào	v	4.2
to order (food)	点（菜）	diǎn (cài)	v	4.1
other	别的	bié de	adj	6.1
P				
paper	纸	zhǐ	n	8.2
party	派对	pàiduì	n	3.2
to pay	付	fù	v	6.2
to pay (money)	付钱	fù qián	vo	6.1
to pay the bill	结帐	jié zhàng	vo	4.2
to pay with credit card	刷卡	shuā kǎ	vo	6.2
Peking Duck	北京烤鸭	Běijīng kǎoyā	n	7.1
pen	笔	bǐ	n	8.2
pencil	铅笔	qiānbǐ	n	8.2
person	人	rén	n	1.2
pet	宠物	chǒngwù	n	2.1
philosophy	哲学	zhéxué	n	8.1
place	地方	dìfang	n	7.1
to plan; plan	打算	dǎsuan	v, n	7.1
plan; to plan	计划	jìhuà	n, v	7.1
plane ticket	飞机票	fēijī piào	n	7.1
plate; (used for plates of food)	盘	pán	n, mw	4.1
pleased to meet you	很高兴认识你	hěn gāoxìng rènshi nǐ	ie	5.1

Definition	Characters	Pinyin	Word Category	Lesson
pleased; happy	高兴	gāoxìng	adj	3.2
poor; fall short; not up to standard	差	chà	adj	8.1
pork	猪肉	zhū ròu	n	4.2
to practice; practice	练习	liànxí	v, n	8.1
to prepare; to plan	准备	zhǔnbèi	v	8.2
present	礼物	lǐwù	n	3.2
price	价钱	jiàqián	n	6.1
product; goods	用品	yòngpǐn	n	6.1
professor	教授	jiàoshòu	n	2.2
psychology	心理学	xīnlǐxué	n	8.1
public bus	公共汽车	gōnggòng qìchē	n	7.1

Q

quarter of an hour	刻	kè	n	3.1
quiz	小考	xiǎokǎo	n	8.2

R

railway or subway station, bus stop	车站	chēzhàn	n	7.2
to read (books)	看书	kàn shū	vo	5.1
to read aloud	念	niàn	v	8.2
to read; to study	读	dú	v	8.2
really, truly	真	zhēn	adv	3.2
receipt	发票	fāpiào	n	6.2
receipt	收据	shōujù	n	6.2
recording; to record	录音	lùyīn	n, vo	8.1
relatively; quite	比较	bǐjiào	adv	8.1
to request; to treat; please	请	qǐng	v	1.1
restaurant	饭馆	fànguǎn	n	4.1
restroom	洗手间	xǐshǒujiān	n	5.2
to return	回	huí	v	5.2
to return	回来	huílai	v	7.1
to return; to give back	还	huán	v	8.2
to review; revision	复习	fùxí	v, n	8.1
rice	米饭	mǐfàn	n	4.2
to ride (in a car, etc.); to travel by	坐	zuò	v	7.2
right	右	yòu	n	7.2

Definition	Characters	Pinyin	Word Category	Lesson
right now	正在	zhèngzài	adv	8.2
RMB (currency of the PRC)	人民币	Rénmínbì	n	6.1
road	路	lù	n	7.2
road; path; way	道	dào	n	7.2
roasted chicken	烧鸡	shāojī	n	4.1
room	房间	fángjiān	n	5.2
roommate	室友	shìyǒu	n	5.1
roommate	同屋	tóngwū	n	5.1
rugby; football (American)	橄榄球	gǎnlǎnqiú	n	3.1
Russia	俄罗斯	Éluósī	n	1.2

S

Definition	Characters	Pinyin	Word Category	Lesson
salesperson	售货员	shòuhuòyuán	n	6.1
salty	咸	xián	adj	4.2
school	学校	xuéxiào	n	1.1
school term; semester	学期	xuéqī	n	8.1
science	科学	kēxué	n	8.1
seafood	海鲜	hǎixiān	n	4.2
second	秒	miǎo	n	3.1
see you later	回头见	huítóu jiàn	ie	5.1
to sell	卖	mài	v	6.1
to send (email, text message)	发	fā	v	8.2
September	九月	Jiǔyuè	n	3.2
seven	七	qī	nu	1.2
Shanghainese	上海话	Shànghǎi huà	n	2.2
she	她	tā	pr	1.1
shop, store	店	diàn	n	2.2
shopping center	购物中心	gòuwù zhōngxīn	n	6.1
should	应该	yīnggāi	av	7.2
siblings	兄弟姐妹	xiōngdì jiěmèi	n	2.1
side	边	biān	n	5.1
side	旁	páng	prep	5.1
simple	简单	jiǎndān	adj	2.2
to sit	坐	zuò	v	4.1
six	六	liù	nu	1.2
to sleep	睡觉	shuì jiào	vo	8.2

Definition	Characters	Pinyin	Word Category	Lesson
so (indicates degree)	这么	zhème	adv	6.2
so; therefore	所以	suǒyǐ	cj	6.2
soccer	足球	zúqiú	n	3.1
sofa	沙发	shāfā	n	5.2
soft drink	汽水	qìshuǐ	n	4.1
sometimes	有(的)时候	yǒu de shíhou	ie	8.1
son	儿子	érzi	n	2.1
sorry	对不起	duìbuqǐ	ie	3.1
sorry for the inconvenience	不好意思	bù hǎoyìsi	ie	6.1
sour	酸	suān	adj	4.2
south	南	nán	n	7.1
South Africa	南非	Nánfēi	n	1.2
Spain	西班牙	Xībānyá	n	7.1
Spanish language (spoken)	西班牙语	Xībānyáyǔ	n	2.2
to speak	说	shuō	v	2.2
to speak, to say	讲	jiǎng	v	6.1
to spend (money, time, effort)	花	huā	v	6.2
spicy	辣	là	adj	4.2
stationary	文具	wénjù	n	6.1
still	还	hái	adv	3.1
to stop a car; to park	停车	tíng chē	vo	7.2
store; shop	商店	shāngdiàn	n	6.1
straight forward	一直	yìzhí	adv	7.2
street	街	jiē	n	7.2
student	学生	xuéshēng	n	2.2
to study; studies	学习	xuéxí	v, n	8.1
subway	地铁	dìtiě	n	7.2
summer vacation	暑假	shǔjià	n	7.1
surface; face	面	miàn	n	5.1
sweet	甜	tián	adj	4.2

T

table	桌子	zhuōzi	n	5.2
Taiwanese	台湾话	Táiwān huà	n	2.2
to take a shower or bath	洗澡	xǐ zǎo	vo	8.2
to take part in, to participate in	参加	cānjiā	v	8.1

Definition	Characters	Pinyin	Word Category	Lesson
taste, flavor	味道	wèidào	n	4.2
tasty (of liquids)	好喝	hǎo hē	adj	4.2
tasty (of solid food)	好吃	hǎo chī	adj	4.1
taxi	出租车	chūzū chē	n	7.2
tea	茶	chá	n	4.1
to teach	教	jiāo	v	4.2
teacher	老师	lǎoshī	n	1.1
telephone	电话	diànhuà	n	6.1
television	电视	diànshì	n	5.2
ten	十	shí	nu	1.2
ten thousand	万	wàn	nu	6.1
test; to give or take a test	考试	kǎoshì	n, vo	8.2
textbook	课本	kèběn	n	5.2
thank you	谢谢	xièxie	ie	1.1
that	那	nà, nèi	pr	2.2
That won't do	那怎么行	nà zěnme xíng	ie	8.1
the American dollar	美元	Měiyuán	n	6.1
the Forbidden City	故宫	Gùgōng	n	7.1
the Great Wall	长城	Chángchéng	n	7.1
then	然后	ránhòu	adv	7.2
then; in that case	那（么）	nà (me)	cj	4.1
there (regional usage in Northern China) /	那儿 /	nàr /	pr	5.2
there	那里	nàli		
thing	东西	dōngxi	n	6.1
thing; matter	事	shì	n	5.2
thirsty	渴	kě	adj	4.1
this	这	zhè, zhèi	pr	2.1
this way; if that's the case; in that case	这样的话	zhè yàng de huà	ie	8.1
this year	今年	jīnnián	n	7.1
thousand	千	qiān	nu	6.1
three	三	sān	nu	1.2
ticket	票	piào	n	7.1
time	时候	shíhou	n	3.1
time	时间	shíjiān	n	3.1
tired	累	lèi	adj	8.2
to; to arrive	到	dào	prep; v	7.2

Definition	Characters	Pinyin	Word Category	Lesson
today	今天	jīntiān	n	3.2
today; now	今	jīn	n	3.2
together	一起	yìqǐ	adv	5.1
toilet; bathroom	厕所	cèsuǒ	n	5.2
tomorrow	明天	míngtiān	n	3.2
too, excessively, extremely	太	tài	adv	4.2
toward, in the direction of	往	wǎng	prep	7.2
train	火车	huǒchē	n	7.1
train ticket	火车票	huǒchē piào	n	7.1
to travel; travel	旅行	lǚxíng	v, n	7.1
to treat one's guests (i.e. to pay for others)	请客	qǐng kè	vo	4.2
to try	试	shì	v	4.2
to turn	转	zhuǎn	v	7.2
twenty	二十	èr shí	nu	1.2
two	二	èr	nu	1.2
two (used before measure words)	两	liǎng	nu	2.1

U

under; below	下面	xiàmian	prep	5.2
under; below; down	下	xià	prep	5.2
to understand	懂	dǒng	v, rc	8.1
United States	美国	Měiguó	n	1.2
up; on	上	shàng	prep	5.2
to use	用	yòng	v	4.2

V

very	很	hěn	adv	1.1
Vietnam	越南	Yuènán	n	1.2
vocabulary	生词	shēngcí	n	8.1

W

waiter, server	服务员	fúwùyuán	n	2.2
to walk	走路	zǒu lù	vo	7.2
wallet	钱包	qiánbāo	n	6.2
to want; must; will; should	要	yào	av	4.2

Definition	Characters	Pinyin	Word Category	Lesson
wardrobe	衣柜	yīguì	n	5.2
water	水	shuǐ	n	4.1
Wednesday	星期三	Xīngqī sān	n	3.1
week	星期	xīngqī	n	3.1
weekend	周末	zhōumò	n	8.1
to welcome	欢迎	huānyíng	v	4.1
welcome (to a store/restaurant)	欢迎光临	huānyíng guānglín	ie	4.1
west	西	xī	n	7.1
what	什么	shénme	qw	1.1
what day is it?	星期几	xīngqī jǐ	qph	3.1
what to do; what can be done; what shall I do	怎么办	zěnme bàn	qph	8.2
what's up?	有事吗?	yǒu shì ma?	ie	5.2
when, at that time	的时候	de shíhou	adv	7.1
when?	什么时候	shénme shíhou	qph	3.1
where (regional usage in Northern China) /	哪儿 /	nǎr /	pr	5.1
where	哪里	nǎli		
which	哪	nǎ, něi	qw	1.2
white rice (alternate term for 米饭)	白饭	báifàn	n	4.2
whiteboard	白板	báibǎn	n	8.2
who	谁	shéi	qw	2.2
why	为什么	wèishénme	qw	4.2
window	窗户	chuānghu	n	5.2
winter vacation	寒假	hánjià	n	7.1
to wish	祝	zhù	v	3.2
with	跟	gēn	cj	5.1
to work out, to exercise	健身	jiànshēn	v	5.1
to work out, to exercise	运动	yùn dòng	v	5.1
work, job; to work	工作	gōngzuò	n, v	2.2
worry	担心	dān xīn	v	6.2
would like to (do something)	想	xiǎng	av	4.1
write	写	xiě	v	2.2
to write a letter	写信	xiě xìn	vo	6.1
written language; culture	文	wén	n	2.2
wrong	错	cuò	adj	4.2

Definition	Characters	Pinyin	Word Category	Lesson
Y				
year	年	nián	n	3.2
yesterday	昨天	zuótiān	n	3.2
you	你	nǐ	pr	1.1
you (polite form)	您	nín	pr	1.1
you're welcome	不客气	bú kèqi	ie	3.1
you're welcome	不用谢	bú yòng xiè	ie	7.2
younger brother	弟弟	dìdi	n	2.1
younger sister	妹妹	mèimei	n	2.1
Z				
zero	零	líng	nu	3.1